FRANCO
SILENT ALLY IN WORLD WAR II

Willard L. Beaulac

Southern Illinois University Press

Carbondale and Edwardsville

Library of Congress Cataloging-in-Publication Data
Beaulac, Willard Leon, 1899–
  Franco: silent ally in World War II.
  Bibliography: p.
  Includes index.
  1. World War, 1939–1945—Diplomatic history.
2. Spain—Foreign relations—Germany. 3. Germany—
Foreign relations—Spain. 4. United States—Foreign
relations—Spain. 5. Spain—Foreign relations—United
States. 6. Great Britain—Foreign relations—Spain.
7. Spain—Foreign relations—Great Britain. 8. Beaulac,
Willard Leon, 1899–   . 9. World War, 1939–1945—
Personal narratives, American. 10. Franco, Francisco,
1892–1975. I. Title.
D754.S7B43 1986   940.53′2   85-27896
ISBN 0-8093-1254-9

89 88 87 86   4 3 2 1

CONTENTS

Preface

"In February 1945, with his totalitarian dream a nightmare, Allied soldiers pressing in from three points of the continental compass, and defeat a certainty, Adolf Hitler spent precious moments in retrospective analysis. His concern was to find a satisfactory explanation for the total destruction of his empire. . . . Throughout these deliberations a single theme returned again and again— Spain! Here was the key to German defeat! Hitler observed, 'Taking advantage of the enthusiasm we had aroused in Spain and the shock to which we had subjected Britain, we ought to have attacked Gibraltar in the summer of 1940, immediately after the defeat of France.' As he contemplated the premature end of his Thousand-Year Reich the Fuehrer found the Spanish stalemate sufficient rationalization for his failure."

What follows is a story of British-American diplomatic victory in Spain during World War II, a victory that is seldom hailed and never celebrated. It is also a story of seven Madrid actors in that victory: of Generalissimo Francisco Franco y Bahamonde, Chief of the Spanish State and Caudillo of Spain; of his foreign ministers, Colonel Juan Beigbeder Atienza, don Ramón Serrano Suñer, General Count Francisco Gómez Jordana y Sousa; of the British ambassador to Spain, Sir Samuel Hoare, and the American ambassadors, Alexander W. Weddell and Carlton J. H. Hayes.

Two other persons contributed to this Allied diplomatic victory even though they were far from intending to. They are Adolf Hitler and Joseph Stalin. Hitler made an enormous contribution when he decided, very reluctantly, not to send an army through Spain to Gibraltar and North Africa in 1941, as had been his intention, but to attack Russia first. And Stalin made a comparable contribution by resisting Hitler and helping to defeat him.

Hitler's and Stalin's involvement in Spain antedated World War II of course. During Spain's prolonged and destructive Civil War, which had barely ended when World War II began, Stalin had supported the defending Republican forces. Hitler, on his part, by timely and effective aid, had made Franco's victory over the Republic possible, and by doing that he had placed Franco in his debt. At least he thought he had.

The actors in our story differed greatly among themselves in character and ideology. Three of them, Serrano, Hoare, and Hayes, wrote books in which they recounted in considerable detail what they had done and tried to do in Spain. They revealed a great deal about one another and also about themselves, including some things they did not intend to reveal. A reading of those books and of other material that has become available, and principally of course my own experience and observations as counselor of embassy and chargé d'affaires ad interim in Madrid, have confirmed the opinion I had in Spain—that the United States and Great Britain, together, won a diplomatic victory that strongly influenced the course of the war. Indeed, if our Spanish policy had failed World War II might have lasted much longer than it did and cost great numbers of additional lives. Or it might have been a much shorter war. In either case it might not have ended in Allied triumph.

At the same time it must be recognized that the primary victory in Spain was not ours, although its results were dramatically in our favor. It was Spain's. It would be fatuous to suggest that, if Spain had had any policy other than one of trying to keep out of active participation in the war, anything we could have done would have brought about the victory the Spaniards and we, the British and Americans, in fact gained.

Madariaga tells us that the two constant features of Spanish public life may be symbolized in the words: *dictatorship and separatism.* Today Spain is engaged in the latest of many efforts to achieve lasting free institutions and national unity.

Perhaps the present small volume about Spain in World War II will help in some slight measure to shed light on that new and laudable effort.

FRANCO

1 SPANISH FOREIGN POLICY

On June 27, 1940, German tank units, cutting through a defeated France, reached Spain's northwestern border on their way, many thought, to Gibraltar, Britain's last tiny foothold on the European continent and a natural target for Hitler's arms. Britain and its scattered empire were now fighting alone, while antiwar sentiment in the United States continued strong. It would be three months before President Franklin D. Roosevelt would be able to get a draft bill through a reluctant Congress, and then many of the draftees would have to train with broomsticks for rifles and wooden sawhorses for machine guns. It would be a year and a half before the United States entered the conflict, and that would come only after Japan, without a prior declaration of war, had bombed Pearl Harbor.

What was Spain's attitude toward Germany in that grave emergency? It was essentially a reaction to Germany's policy toward Spain. The aims of that policy were chiefly: to draw

Spain into the war on the Axis side; to march through Spain, seize Gibraltar, close the western entry into the Mediterranean, and spill over into Morocco and adjacent areas; to induce Spain to cede to Germany one of the Canary Islands to serve as a U-boat base and to protect Africa against British (or Allied) invasion; to reward Spain (or at least to give Spain the impression that she would be rewarded) by handing her parts of French Morocco for which a compliant France would be compensated by being given other African territories; and to achieve a degree of political and economic suzerainty over Spain as well as over North and Middle Africa.

Those were Germany's objectives. How did Spain respond? What was her policy in the frightening emergency she found herself in? It was: to keep out of the war if possible; if she were forced into the war, or if Spanish interests should make entry compelling, to enter the war only at the last possible moment, with the smallest possible risk, and with the greatest possible gain to Spain; and meanwhile to survive, to recover from the effects of her own Civil War which had barely ended when World War II began, and to build enough strength to have some option as to what attitude she would finally take toward the warring powers.

Spain's policy was aimed, in practice, at frustrating German designs. In effect therefore it was a pro-Allied policy. But to be successful it had to be based on an overt attitude of friendship toward the Axis powers, toward those who were to be our enemies that is, and an attitude of overt enmity toward a Communist Russia which was to be our powerful ally.

Franco had no good alternative to those attitudes. During the Civil War Russia had given massive aid to the Republican government. Germany and Italy, on the other hand, had come to Franco's aid and provided the margin of power his Nationalists needed for victory. And, most important of all, until well after Hitler's invasion of Russia, Franco had no defense against German invasion except the friendship with Germany that he, his principal aides, and the controlled Spanish media continued to profess until the end of the war. Where were the tanks, the planes, the ships, the munitions and the men to prevent a German thrust through Spain or to protect Spanish vessels carrying food and materials that Spain needed for survival from being torpedoed by German or Italian submarines? They did not exist. That was the awesome truth. Nor did the Spanish people want any more of war. Weak as they were they might have turned in fury upon any regime that threatened to bring war to Spain unless, perhaps, it should be evident to them that victory for the side Franco chose to support was imminent, that the fighting would be done by others, and that war would make living easier and better rather than more difficult for Spaniards. The Germans promised some of those things but the Spanish government did not believe them, nor did it have any confidence that the Spanish people would believe them.

Spain did not announce its policy to the world. To announce it would have meant to defeat it. It was not spelled out in documents that were available to us at the time. It had to be deduced, and it was correctly deduced by the British government and, eventually, by the United States government, too, although not always by persons in the Department of State, or the Treasury Department, or the Board of Economic Warfare, or the Iberian Peninsula Operating Committee. The war in Europe was over before any important segment of the American press evinced an understanding of Spain's policy toward the Axis and of British-American policy toward Spain, and even then understanding was arrived at grudgingly.

Those of us who were in the British and American embassies in Madrid, and our predecessors, deduced the substance of Spanish policy principally through the application of common sense. Why did common sense tell us what Spain's policy was? Because in the perilous position Spain found herself in, and that the Spanish government found itself in within Spain, there was no reasonable alternative to that policy. In the context of that policy all Spain's acts could be rationally explained.

Spain's Civil War had probably cost that small nation more than a half-million lives. The country was prostrate economically and emotionally. Its agriculture was grossly inadequate to feed its people; its transportation system was antiquated and disrupted. Factories had been destroyed or damaged, and those that were intact lacked many of the materials they required for their operation. Spaniards were divided politically and spiritually. They were close to starvation and filled with a great weariness after the savage bloodletting that had taken place and that had aroused intense partisan feeling in many countries of the world.

So what was British-American policy in those circumstances? It was: to help Spain stay out of the war principally through the device of trading with her, of supplying her with commodities she needed for survival and that would limit her dependence upon Germany; to deprive the Axis, to the extent possible, of benefits it might try to obtain from Spain; and to obtain for ourselves as many benefits as we could from a nonbelligerent or neutral Spain.

Trade might not be an effective weapon to accomplish our purposes but until Allied military strength could be built up in Europe it was almost our only weapon. Germany, of course, had the same weapon, but ours was by far the stronger.

Not only was our policy rational; like Spain's policy there was no rational alternative to it. But it was not easy to carry out. During the Civil War American opinion had favored the Republic. The fact that even before the war broke out Republicans had burned more than a hundred Catholic churches, assassinated scores of churchmen, and committed other atrocities against their political opponents and assumed opponents did not detract from their political purity. Nor did their association with the Soviet dictatorship. The Nationalists, on the other hand, were "fascists," and fascism was a harsher word than communism. And they had the support of Nazi Germany and Fascist Italy. Partisan feeling against Nationalist Spain continued in the United States even after we had entered World War II. Many of our citizens, and perhaps a majority of our press, gave the impression that they had rather continue to fight the Spanish Civil War that was already over than, through adequate action in Spain, help to win the new and vastly larger war that threatened to destroy freedom everywhere. Spain's overt friendship toward Germany and her overt enmity toward Soviet Russia made it difficult for our government to follow a policy of cooperation with her. They created a problem for the British, too, but less of a problem because the British had their backs to the wall and they were better prepared than Americans to look beyond words and gestures to facts.

Ramón Serrano Suñer, who was Spain's foreign minister for some two years, has described his country's wartime policy in these words: "If Germany did not cross the Pyrenees . . . it is only because there was, on this side of the border, a state with which it had friendly relations, and which did not arouse its distrust. . . . Spain, despite her sympathy and debt of gratitude, her traditional sense of decency, and her great fear of communism, could abstain from joining the Axis in an offensive alliance, and that is what occurred, although it was not easy. But what she could not do was to go to war against the Axis, or place herself in a position in which the Axis would make war on her. . . . Thus, and thanks to the maintenance of our friendship, we performed the miracle of nonintervention; we obtained delays and postponements which we required in order to maneuver in conformity with our own interest, and not the interest of others."

When Serrano speaks of Spain's sympathy for Germany and her debt of gratitude to that country, he reflects the public attitude of the Spanish government, an attitude that was shared by only a minority of Spaniards. And he is neither accurate nor candid when he says that Spain did not incur Germany's distrust. Germany became not only distrustful of Spain but completely disillusioned with her. The reference to delays and postponements which led to disillusionment, however, is accurate. And while Serrano states, correctly, that Spain operated in her own interest, as indeed every state tries to do, the effects of her maneuvering were dramatically favorable to the Allies. But, as he says, it was not easy, and he should know because, after Franco himself, it was he who did most of the maneuvering.

On March 26, 1939, while the Civil War was still going on, Franco's Nationalists, under heavy German pressure, signed the Anti-Comintern Pact. Four days later, again under pressure, they signed a Pact of Friendship with Germany. It provided that in case one of the parties found itself at war the other would avoid everything in the political, military, and economic spheres that could accrue to the disadvantage of the treaty partner or to the advantage of the partner's opponent. When World War II broke out, Franco found himself bound by those commitments as well as by a number of secret agreements with Germany.

On September 3, 1939, two days after Hitler's tanks had crossed into Poland, a surprised and deeply troubled Spain declared her neutrality, but in June, 1940, after French resistance had crumbled and Italy had entered the war on Germany's side, she declared her nonbelligerency and informed Germany that she was ready, under certain conditions, to follow Italy's example. The conditions were: at war's end Spain would obtain Gibraltar, French Morocco, Oran, and an enlargement of Rio de Oro and Spanish colonies in the Gulf of Guinea; and meanwhile Germany would give Spain military and economic assistance.

Franco was convinced at that point that total German victory was imminent, and he wanted Spain to be on the German side when that occurred. He sent General Juan Vigón, chief of the Army's general staff, to remind Hitler of Spain's wish to enter the war, but Hitler kept Vigón waiting a week before receiving him, and then he was cool to him. Confident of final victory, Hitler had little interest in Spain's entry into the war.

The summer of 1940 marked the apogee of Hitler's power. Most of Western Europe had fallen to his attack. A ten-year nonaggression pact with Russia protected his eastern flank. At the same time not all was going according to plan. To Hitler's surprise and chagrin Britain had not followed France in capitulating, and it looked as though only a successful invasion, for which Hitler had no prepared plan, would bring her to her knees. In order to soften up the island Hitler ordered an all-out air attack on London and other strategic targets, but the British were tougher than he expected. German losses in men and planes were extremely heavy, and Britain showed no signs of giving up. It began to appear that the war might last longer than Hitler had anticipated. Gibraltar, at the tip of the Iberian peninsula and, with Suez, a key to control of the Mediterranean, took on new importance.

Franco, on his part, was still confident of German victory and still wanted to be listed on the winning side when the spoils were divided, but he was no longer in a hurry. He decided to send Serrano, who was then interior minister, to Berlin to establish high-level contact with Germany. In expressing agreement to Serrano's visit Joachim von Ribbentrop, Germany's foreign minister, made clear that Hitler did not share Franco's deliberateness. "What we want is Spain's entry into the war," he warned the German ambassador.

Replying to a letter from Franco introducing Serrano, Hitler expounded in succinct language his plan for closing the western end of the Mediterranean, a plan in which Spain was to have a key role. He said:

"1. The war will decide the future of Europe. There is not a country in Europe that can avoid the political and economic effects. The end of the war will also decide Spain's future, perhaps for centuries. But even today Spain is suffering, though she is still not a participant in the war. . . .

"2. Spain's entry into the war on the side of the Axis Powers must begin with the expulsion of the English fleet from Gibraltar and immediately thereafter the seizure of the fortified rock.

"This operation must and can be successfully carried through within a few days, if high-grade, well-tried, modern means of attack and attack troops are employed. Germany is willing to provide them under Spanish command in the quantities needed.

"3. Once Gibraltar is in Spanish possession the western Mediterranean is eliminated as a base of operations for the English fleet. Aside from the threat from isolated British submarines, then possible only to a limited extent, a sure connection will have been brought about between Spain and North Africa (Spanish Morocco). The Spanish Mediterranean coast itself will then no longer be endangered. . . .

"[Protection of Spain's Atlantic coast] consists in placing [German] dive bomber units in the vicinity of the coast; these are more effective than heavy coastal batteries, as experience from Narvik to the Spanish border has shown. . . .

"6. It is more probable, however, that after losing Gibraltar England will try instead to seize a naval base on the Canary Islands. Therefore the defensive power of the islands in the Canary group which might be considered for naval bases must be strengthened in so far as possible *before* the start of the war. Either before or at the latest at the same time as the beginning of the war it will in my opinion be necessary to transfer German dive bombers or long-range fighters to Palmas. Past experience has shown that they provide the *absolute* certainty of keeping the British ships far away. Preparations for this should best be made before the beginning of the war."

Hitler's plan was clear and it was logical. If it were successfully carried out it would change the course of the war in Germany's favor.

On September 15 Serrano arrived in Berlin for conversations with Hitler and Ribbentrop. Hitler was friendly and courteous but Ribbentrop asked Serrano abruptly when Spain could enter the war. Serrano replied by speaking of Spain's friendship for Germany, and also of its hopes and its needs, its deplorable economic situation, its shortages of wheat, of fuels, of rubber, of fertilizers, of transport—of just about everything in fact. He assured Ribbentrop that Spain was unshakable in its desire to enter the war but he said that it could not enter then—or even soon. It could not enter until its economy had been restored to a point where entry would be feasible and helpful. When that would be, he suggested, would depend on Germany's willingness to assist.

Ribbentrop spoke of possibly recognizing Spain's claim to all Morocco provided that Spain would enter into commercial agreements which guaranteed Germany a share of the raw materials of the area, and provided also that Germany could occupy Moroccan harbors for use as naval bases. The concessions Germany sought would have given her effective economic, and probably political, control over Morocco. In a letter to Hitler Franco said later that occupation of the harbors was unnecessary in peacetime and superfluous in time of war.

Even while the Civil War was going on the Germans had made clear that they expected special privileges during the postwar period; nevertheless, Serrano was alarmed at what he now heard. Equally alarmed was Demetrio Carceller, a Spanish businessman who had accompanied Serrano to Berlin. Carceller remembered what the Germans had said when he later became minister of industry and commerce and had numerous and fruitful conversations with representatives of the British and American embassies. I participated in a number of them.

During a subsequent conversation with Serrano, Ribbentrop said that Germany would like Spain to cede it one of the Canary Islands for use as a military base. An indignant Serrano said that the Canaries were a part of metropolitan Spain, and that if the Americans should try to take them the courage of Spain's soldiers would defend them. He refused to transmit the request officially (he transmitted it privately and Franco turned it down.) Serrano later informed Ribbentrop in a letter that Spain had sent one of her bravest generals to take command in the Canaries. He seemed to be suggesting that one brave Spanish general would be as effective as squadrons of German dive bombers.

To say that Hitler and Ribbentrop were disappointed at the results of Serrano's visit would be an understatement. Shortly after Serrano had left Berlin, Hitler, describing the visit, said to Italian Foreign Minister Galeazzo Ciano:

"The Spanish proposals to Germany, somewhat crudely expressed, were as follows:

"1. Germany is to deliver for the coming year 400,000–700,000 tons of grain;

"2. Germany is to deliver all the fuel;

"3. Germany is to deliver the equipment which the Army lacks;

"4. Germany is to supply artillery, airplanes, as well as special weapons and special troops for the conquest of Gibraltar;

"5. Germany is to hand over to Spain all of Morocco and, besides that, Oran, and is to help her get a border revision south of Rio de Oro;

"6. Spain is to promise to Germany, in return, her friendship."

When Hitler met Mussolini at Brenner Pass on October 4, he remarked that Spain demanded much but gave nothing. In Berlin Serrano had indeed asked for much but had yielded nothing. He left Berlin with mixed feelings toward Hitler but filled with animosity toward Ribbentrop. If the Germans had hoped that his visit would bring the two countries closer together they were to be disappointed. Dr. Paul Schmidt, Hitler's interpreter, noted that both Hitler and Mussolini were soon referring to Serrano as a "crafty Jesuit."

Shortly after his return from Berlin, Serrano was named foreign minister. Responding to a suggestion that Hitler had made to him in Berlin, on October 23, Franco and he met with Hitler and Ribbentrop in Hendaye, just over the border in occupied France. It was the only meeting the two dictators ever had and it did no more to improve relations between the countries than Serrano's meetings with Hitler had done. The Spaniards made a poor first impression by arriving late at the Hendaye railroad station where Hitler and Ribbentrop awaited them with some impatience. Serrano tells us that the delay was involuntary; he blames it on Franco's private car and its ancient locomotive, and on the bad conditions of the Spanish railroads. He is probably right. Few things worked as they should in wartime Spain. And yet, and yet, being a little late was a Spanish habit, and the punctilious Germans knew it.

At the meeting Hitler was all confidence. He said that with two hundred divisions at his disposal he was now master of Europe. Recalling Germany's "material and spiritual" association with Spain during the Civil War, he said that the time had come for Spain to enter the war and to take her place in Europe's New Order in which she was to play an important role.

Franco assured Hitler of Spain's desire to enter the war when she was able to. He reminded him that she had already shifted from neutrality to nonbelligerency, and he assured him that if it were not for the economic, political, and military problems she faced she would already be fighting on Germany's side. He made a strong pitch for greater aid from Germany and also for Spain's right not only to Gibraltar but to Morocco and Oran as well. He asked for a prior commitment that Spain would be awarded those territories.

Hitler was not prepared to make such a commitment however. He noted that for Spain the recovery of Gibraltar was a matter of honor; indeed Spain should have the principal role in that operation. He noted also that because of history and other circumstances Spain was destined to acquire all Morocco and Oran, and that if she entered the war they would be awarded to her. Nevertheless, he added, for Germany to offer those territories to Spain she must first have them in her possession, and since they were not yet in her possession she was not yet in a position to dispose of them.

Franco knew that Hitler was holding Morocco back as a prize for France should that country, with its still powerful navy, decide to come over to Germany's side, but he did not mention that. Instead he began to comment on Hitler's campaigns and to offer unsolicited (and obviously unwanted) advice on campaigns to come. He wondered about the reasons for Germany's failure to take Britain out of the war. He suggested that even though England were defeated her government and fleet would move to Canada and continue the war from there. He recited the litany that Serrano had already given to Hitler in Berlin. He talked on and on, explaining Spain's ambitions and her problems in minute and monotonous detail.

Hitler became increasingly bored with Franco's monologue and began to yawn openly. He instructed Ribbentrop to hand the Spaniards copies of a draft secret protocol which provided, in effect, that Spain would join the Axis and would enter the war when Germany considered it opportune. There was no mention in the protocol of Morocco or Oran. Franco read the draft rapidly and said that he could not accept it; that it did not reflect the sense of the meeting they had had. Hitler asked Franco to study the draft and think it over. He invited the two Spaniards to dinner that night in his car. As they left, the Baron de las Torres, Franco's genial chief of protocol, heard Hitler say, "With those characters we can do nothing." Hitler was not far wrong.

At dinner the four continued their discussion but without result. Franco, in his own mind, was indignant that Hitler wanted to decide when Spain should enter the war. A born trader, he was equally indignant that Hitler had offered no compensation to Spain. "After victory, whatever they say now," he had said to Serrano earlier, "if they don't put it down in black and white they won't give us a thing." Hitler and Ribbentrop escorted their guests to Franco's private car. While Franco was waving a courteous good-bye from the car's platform his locomotive, in a clumsy maneuver, backed into the car with some violence. Only Franco's agility and his presence of mind saved him from being thrown to the ground or possibly under the car's wheels. Spain had been in no less peril during the Hendaye conversations.

Back in San Sebastián Franco and Serrano worked through the night amending the protocol to reflect Spain's position. As finally agreed to, it committed Spain to enter the war *after* the Axis powers had "provided her with the military support necessary for her preparedness, at a time to be set by common agreement of Germany, Italy and Spain, taking into account military preparations to be decided upon." The protocol provided also that Germany would grant economic aid to Spain by supplying her with food and raw materials, "so as to meet the needs of the Spanish people and the requirements of the war."

So far as Spain's possible participation in the war was concerned there was nothing in the protocol that Franco had not already offered. Germany's commitments to Spain, on the other hand, were more specific than they had been. As it turned out they were beyond Germany's ability to carry out. Franco had outtalked and outfoxed Hitler.

(Spaniards have an amiable habit of sometimes saying things they do not mean but are pleasing to hear. When a Spaniard tells you that his house is yours, he does not expect to be taken literally; he wants to make you feel good. After Franco had exhausted Hitler with his explanations, his reservations, and his demands, he suddenly took Hitler's large hand in both of his and declared, "In spite of everything I have said, if the day should come when Germany truly needs me I shall be unconditionally at her side." Serrano felt a chill go up his spine. He was certain that Hitler, a first-class actor, would embrace Franco and tell him that the day had already arrived. Even though Franco should slip out of Hitler's grasp the incident would produce new tensions and perhaps new problems between the two countries. Happily Hitler's interpreter, doubtless because he knew that Franco's promise was meaningless, did not translate it and a crisis was averted.)

Hendaye became of crucial importance to Hitler when, on October 28, 1940, Mussolini, without prior notice to him, invaded Greece. Results for the Axis were disastrous. The Greeks not only repelled the assault but also they sent the feckless Italians reeling back through their recently conquered colony, Albania. Operating from North Africa the British quickly established air bases in Greece. Hitler wrote to Mussolini that he hardly dared think about the consequences of those events. "From the military standpoint this situation is threatening," he said, and he added, "from the economic standpoint, as far as the Rumanian oil fields are concerned, it is positively terrifying."

Hitler was not exaggerating. On November 12 he issued Directive 18 calling for military action in Southwestern Europe and North Africa. Dubbed Operation Felix, the objective was to take Gibraltar and close the Straits. Hitler abruptly summoned Serrano to another meeting, this time at Berchtesgaden, his mountain retreat. Discussing the summons with Franco, Serrano said, "If we don't go to Berchtesgaden we run the risk of meeting them in Vitoria." Vitoria is the first city of any size south of the Spanish-French border.

On November 19 Serrano met again with Hitler, but a different Hitler from the one he had known in Berlin and Hendaye. After noting that Mussolini's unsuccessful attack on Greece had made it necessary to close the Mediterranean to the Allies, Hitler said, "I have decided to attack Gibraltar, and the operation has been meticulously prepared. All that remains is to carry it out, and it must be carried out." He said that participation in the attack was an honor that belonged to Spain.

Hitler, surrounded by his military and political aides, spoke more than an hour, rapidly and with increasing insistence and emotion. Serrano, outnumbered but not overwhelmed, listened intently and then replied. He told Hitler that when he had received his invitation he did not know what Hitler planned to discuss, and for that reason he could only give his personal reactions to what he had heard. He reminded Hitler that the Hendaye Protocol provided that Spain should enter the war not when Hitler so decided, but when Spain was in a position to enter. Hitler replied that in any case a joint operation against Gibraltar was necessary.

Serrano noted that closing the Mediterranean at Gibraltar meant that Britain would close the Atlantic to Spain. That would be fatal, he said, because of Spain's desperate need of supplies from overseas. Hitler remarked that if Spain were belligerent Germany would supply it just as it supplied its own needs, but Serrano countered that Germany underestimated Spain's needs. Hitler asked Serrano if it were not true that Spain had decided that it could improve its economic situation by staying out of the war. Serrano said that the Spanish government did not have that view but that the Spanish people did, and they believed further that a large part of their shortages came from shipments of foodstuffs and other commodities to Germany. He said that to ask the Spanish people for new sacrifices only a few months after the end of the bloodiest of civil wars was beyond the powers of the Spanish government. He added, significantly, that Spaniards would resist a new invasion in the same manner they had resisted the armies of Napoleon. Hitler then asked if Spain would give German troops free passage through the country but Serrano replied that it could not. Playing for time, Serrano asked Hitler to send technicians to verify Spain's needs.

Serrano talked until Hitler began to show signs of annoyance and fatigue. Finally Hitler said, "I know Spain has many difficult problems. I think she might take another month to prepare and decide." This gave Serrano new opportunities, and he pursued them doggedly.

The interview lasted four full hours. At the end an unabashed Serrano said, "When I return to Madrid the British and American ambassadors are going to ask me the purpose of this visit. . . . I suggest that I tell them I came here to ask you to ship us cereals . . . , and that will make them hurry up their own shipments to us." Hitler agreed to that suggestion so readily that Serrano added, "And [the deception] would be complete if you would ship us some wheat." Hitler replied tersely that he would look into that. That night Serrano slept, or tried to sleep, in Berchtesgaden where Austria's Kurt von Schuschnigg and Czechoslovakia's Emil Hacha had tried without success to preserve their countries' independence. One can imagine his thoughts.

Hitler adopted Serrano's suggestion that he send technicians to Spain. He sent Admiral Wilhelm Canaris, his intelligence chief who knew Spain well. Canaris talked to Franco on December 7. He was more specific than Hitler had been. He said that Hitler wished to send troops into Spain on January 10, 1941, in order to initiate an attack on Gibraltar. He explained that economic aid to Spain would begin as soon as the troops entered the country. Franco explained patiently that for a number of reasons Spain could not enter the war that soon. Furthermore she could not wage a long war without imposing unbearable sacrifices upon her people. Canaris then asked him if he could fix a date later than January 10. Franco replied that since removal of the difficulties did not depend upon the will of Spain alone he could not set a definite date. He asked that Hitler send an economist to examine conditions in Spain and report to Hitler. As always, he sent Hitler effusive greetings.

The protocol of the Franco-Canaris conversation that the German embassy transmitted to Berlin had been prepared by General Vigón who, like Franco himself, was an old friend of Canaris and had attended the meeting. What it did not reveal was that immediately after his arrival in Madrid Canaris had conveyed to Vigón the crucial information that Franco could safely refuse Hitler's demands. He had explained that Hitler's other military requirements were such that he could not attempt to take Gibraltar in the face of Spanish opposition. (Canaris, it was later revealed, was involved in attempts to assassinate Hitler. Shortly before the war ended Canaris himself was assassinated by Hitler henchmen. The Spanish government granted his widow a pension.)

The Spaniards had worn Hitler down. Without knowing it

they had brought about a turning point in the war. On December 18 Hitler ordered that serious preparations for Operation Barbarossa, an attack on Russia, be undertaken. Gibraltar was to be put on the back burner. Nevertheless nine days later Hitler's naval staff reported that in the light of Mussolini's fiasco in Greece and other Axis setbacks, the significance of taking Gibraltar had increased rather than diminished. The Fuehrer agreed, but he said that Franco was not ready. He promised that one day he would try again to influence him. That day came sooner than he may have anticipated.

Hitler's naval advisors continued to maintain that the Operation Felix should not be delayed. Admiral Raeder, the Navy's commander-in-chief, argued that if the Straits remained open the British, who controlled Malta and Suez as well as Gibraltar, and had numerous mobile land forces in northern Africa, would try to isolate Italy, the weaker of the Axis partners, before attacking Germany itself, and that this might well be within their capability, particularly if they should receive help from the United States.

Hitler recognized the force of the admiral's arguments. Also it continued to rankle him that Franco, the "bourgeois" figure who had the "mentality of a subaltern," was deterring him while his own advisors continued to insist on the need to take Gibraltar. On January 21, 1941, eleven days after German troops were to have crossed into Spain, Ribbentrop instructed German Ambassador Eberhard von Stohrer to read verbatim to Franco a message from Hitler that was probably as insolent as any national leader has ever sent to a presumptive ally.

After noting that the war was already won, Hitler reminded Franco that the capture of Gibraltar and the closing of the Mediterranean would be strategically useful only if they could be carried out during the next few weeks. Otherwise, he stated (quite correctly in the light of what we now know was Hitler's plan to attack Russia), it would be too late because of other military operations.

Hitler went on to say that he and the Reich government were deeply disturbed by the equivocal and vacillating attitude of Spain, which was incomprehensible in the light of the help they had given Franco during the Spanish Civil War.

"Without the help of the Führer and the Duce there would not today be any Nationalist Spain or any Caudillo," the message said. One can picture the hapless Stohrer repeating those words, even in slightly modified form, to Franco's face, and Franco's thoughts as he heard them.

Franco told Stohrer that the message he had received was extremely grave and contained untruths, and that he would reply to it as soon as he could. But before he had time to reply Hitler sent him another message saying, "Only Spain's immediate entry into the war is of strategic value to the Axis." Hitler offered to supply Spain with 100,000 tons of wheat and other aid once she had entered the war. "If General Franco nevertheless does not enter the war," he said, "this can only be ascribed to the fact that he has doubts about ultimate Axis victory."

Franco denied Hitler's charge and asked that still another high-ranking military man come to Spain to appraise the situation. He suggested that Field Marshal Keitel, Hitler's chief of the Armed Forces High Command, would be a good man to send.

Hitler was truly furious—at Stohrer as well as at Franco. In a telegram to Stohrer, Ribbentrop said, "I regret that in the conversation you have given General Franco the opportunity to divert your demarche from its purpose. . . . I request you therefore to state precisely whether General Franco has understood unmistakably from what you said that we expected an immediate entry by Spain into the war." The truth is that Franco understood that all too well. A bewildered and chastened Stohrer answered Hitler as best he could.

On February 6 Hitler sent Franco an extraordinary letter. He may have intended it for the record. Franco had said that January 10 would be a poor date for Germans to enter Spain because, among other reasons, the roads might be blocked with snow. Hitler's comment might have been amusing in different circumstances.

"I do not understand why one should first want to declare an event impossible on economic grounds which is now said to be impossible simply for climatic reasons," the Fuehrer said, and he added, quite logically, "I do not believe that the

German Army would be disturbed during its march in January
by a climate which in itself is nothing out of the ordinary for
us." "In any case," he went on the say, "from the participation of German soldiers and officers in your campaign, Caudillo, the climatic conditions of Spain are nothing unfamiliar
to us."

"The attack on Gibraltar and the closing of the Straits
would have changed the Mediterranean situation in one
stroke," Hitler continued. "On January 10, if we had been
able to cross the Spanish border with the first formations,
Gibraltar would today be in our hands. That means: Two
months have been lost, which otherwise would have helped
to decide world history."

Hitler was making, accurately, the awesome charge that
Franco had interfered with his plan of conquest, a charge that
would have plagued Franco and Spain if that plan had succeeded. But happily it did not.

On June 22, 1941, Germany invaded Russia. Serrano immediately informed Stohrer that the Spanish government had
noted with the greatest satisfaction the beginning of the
struggle against Bolshevist Russia. That was an understatement on Serrano's part. The Spanish government had noted
the invasion not only with great satisfaction but with enormous relief. Following the invasion German pressure on
Spain to enter the war diminished almost to the vanishing
point. The march on Gibraltar had not been abandoned, however; it had merely been postponed.

On September 19, 1941, a top-secret military memorandum
from the Fuehrer's headquarters decreed: "Our political and
military relations with Spain must not break off before next
spring, but on the contrary must be expanded. Military actions on the Iberian Peninsula are, however, undesirable until
the eastern campaign has been concluded and sufficient German forces are available—in spring 1942 at the earliest." The
Fuehrer was determined, once Russia was defeated, to march
through Spain to Gibraltar whether or not the Spaniards
agreed to it.

Meanwhile the Wehrmacht was developing a plan to resist
a possible British invasion of the Peninsula. At the same time

the head of one of Hitler's intelligence groups was drawing up a list of Spanish leaders who were thought to favor removal of Franco and of Serrano as well. But that too proved to be a Nazi chimera.

When Hitler reminded Franco that without the help of the Fuehrer and the Duce there would be no Nationalist Spain or any Caudillo he must have offended Franco beyond repair. Nevertheless what he said was true, and Franco could not show indifference to those who had made his victory possible. And even if he had been inclined to turn on his old friends and helpers he could not afford to indulge any such inclination because of the certainty of prompt and savage retaliation by Hitler, whose submarines could sink Spanish ships at will, and who was not playing marbles.

Nor were the Allies playing marbles. Franco was not exaggerating the power the Allies had to punish him if he entered the war on the Axis side, or if he was otherwise excessively helpful to the Axis. They, like the Germans, could cut off Spain's imports from overseas, and that was a severe constraint on Spain because she continued to be heavily dependent on overseas supplies of food, petroleum, and other products that she needed for survival, and that she had no confidence Germany could or would supply, even if Spain should enter the war on the Axis side.

So Franco continued his balancing act. When the Germans tugged him in one direction the Allies would tug him back. The tugs were annoying to the Spaniards but useful at the same time because they helped Franco to maintain the equilibrium he desperately needed to maintain and, since each side knew the other was pressing him in ways he could not fully resist, it overlooked acts that in other circumstances might have brought severe reprisals.

The test arrived when Ambassador Hayes, with me accompanying him as interpreter, got Count Jordana, who had replaced Serrano as foreign minister, out of bed at two o'clock in the morning of November 8, 1942, and informed him that at that very moment Allied troops were landing in French Morocco in an area which the ambassador and I knew was only a few miles from Spanish forces that were numerous and powerful enough to place great difficulty in the way of the landings if ordered to. At nine o'clock that morning Hayes handed General Franco a letter from President Roosevelt assuring him that the landings were in no shape, manner, or form directed against the Spanish government or people. "Spain has nothing to fear from the United Nations," the president said.

The government-controlled Spanish press published the United States' guarantee in bold letters, and Franco asked the Germans for a similar guarantee. The Germans replied that guarantees were not needed among friends, but they finally offered guarantees of a sort that the Spaniards did not bother to make public. The Spaniards did, however, publish their decision to resist invasion from any side, which meant from Germany of course. From that time on I never had any doubt that Spain had moved decisively in the Allied direction, nor did I have any real fear of a German invasion.

Following the invasion of Russia Spain sent a "volunteer" "Blue Division" to support Hitler's armies at the front. Many, possibly most, of its members were in fact volunteers, and the Nationalist government was content to see them expressing their Falangist zeal in Russia rather than in Spain. Scholars have reported that the Blue Division fought against the Soviet Union with courage and élan. Back in Madrid, however, it was the butt of sardonic humor. It was a token contribution to Germany's war against Russia. Most Spaniards, in and out of government, hoped devoutly that it would be the only military contribution they would have to make.

Germany tried to induce Spain, at the time the Blue Division was dispatched, to declare that a state of war existed between Spain and Soviet Russia, but Franco did not go along. Franco, in turn, considered that sending the Blue Division to Russia canceled out the debt that Spain owed Germany for military aid during the Civil War. Hitler considered that a debt still existed. He sent the Spaniards detailed bills for materials supplied and services rendered. They were settled after a good deal of bickering.

In addition to substantial aid that was directly useful to its war effort, Spain had given Germany great influence over the Spanish press. Nazi influence over the press boomeranged, however. The British Broadcasting Company (BBC), the Voice of America, and the British and American information services in Madrid kept Spaniards pretty well informed of the course of the war, and the latter soon reached the conclusion that the Nazis and their own government were lying to them. That was a plus factor for the Allies, and it was not too much resented by the Spanish government because, in the oblique manner in which things happened in Spain, it strengthened its hand against German pressure to force it into the war.

Following the North African landings Hitler removed Ambassador Stohrer, whose mission had clearly failed, and replaced him with Hans-Adolf von Moltke who had earned a reputation for toughness as ambassador to Poland. But von Moltke soon died. At any rate it was a little late for toughness. Hitler was deeply concerned at the lack of progress in Russia. Franco, on his part, was more and more convinced that Spain's future lay on the side of the Allies.

Did the Spanish government ever want an Axis victory as it so often said or implied in public statements of its officials and press and as it clearly conveyed to the Axis powers? It certainly did not want a Russian victory, and it was difficult to reconcile that with an Axis defeat. But it is also difficult to believe that Spain wanted a Nazi-dominated Europe, which would have meant a Naxi-dominated Spain.

Hitler's nonaggression pact with Russia had come as a distinct shock to the ostentatiously Catholic Spanish government. Following the blitzkrieg against Poland Franco repeatedly expressed his concern for that country as a Catholic bulwark against godless communism. From then on it was fear (and for a brief time cupidity), not gratitude or loyalty, that principally dictated Spain's attitude toward Germany.

Spaniards, despite their reputation for romanticism, can be a cold, realistic people. It is true that there would have been no Nationalist Spain and no Caudillo without Hitler, as Hitler himself had said, and Franco knew it. He knew also that there would be no Nationalist Spain and no Caudillo in a

Nazi-dominated Europe unless Hitler willed it, and I have found no reason to believe that Franco ever wished Spain to be a part of such a Europe if there was a better alternative. Early in 1943 the Spanish Foreign Office initiated a series of conversations with representatives of neutral countries looking to the formation of a bloc that might influence the belligerents to negotiate an early peace. No success attended that effort, which effort was interpreted by many observers (although not by Germany which by then had little trust in Spain) as a means of saving Germany from total annihilation. And that is what it was, although the Spaniards had in mind frustrating total Russian victory more than saving Germany.

For a long time trade was the Allies' only weapon in Spain. It continued, until the war's end, to be their principal weapon. It was the British of course who first applied the policy of influencing Spain through trade, and the policy paid off handsomely in 1940 and 1941 when it enabled Franco to resist Hitler's pressure to enter the war. At that time we were tail to the British kite. We sold Spain what it could pay for, which was not much; we gave her a small Export-Import Bank credit for the purchase of surplus cotton in 1938, and the American Red Cross carried out a limited program of distributing U.S. government-donated flour and milk to the very needy in the early 1940s. But until we ourselves were forced into the war we were far from having any plan to insure her against dependence on Germany.

In a book he wrote after retirement, Herbert Feis, a State Department official who was intimately involved in relations with Spain, said: "But when France fell . . . all of Britain's strength was needed in the desperate struggle to defend its island and to keep the sea lanes open. There was none to spare to meet an attack by or through Spain. A strong and free German Army camped along the Pyrenees frontier. Gibraltar could not defend itself against a well-organized assault. Even though the Rock was held, the airfield and naval base could be made useless and passage through the western Straits impossible. If Britain lost the entry into the Mediterranean, the battle for Malta, Suez, and the whole of the East would be lost.

"Thus the Spanish government seemed possessed of the power to decide whether Britain could continue to resist outside its island—perhaps even of the power to decide whether it could continue to fight at all. For if Germany could use the Spanish coasts in Africa and the Spanish islands in the Atlantic, the sustaining flow from the United States might be broken.

"The British and American governments took the measure of these dangers. The struggle to influence or control Spanish action became crucial to their battle plans and hopes. To quiet the specter, or keep it confined, they used all their arts and powers. Spain became the focal point of their diplomacy. Every day the Rock remained unsurrounded was a day gained—until there was no further need to count the days gained."

That is stirring rhetoric, and it accurately records the awesome power Spain had to influence, and possibly to alter, the course of the war. It also accurately reflects British policy toward Spain at that critical moment. But contrary to what Feis thinks he remembers, the United States lagged far behind Britain in the attention it gave to Spain. Before I left Washington for Madrid, in June, 1941, a year after France had fallen, Feis' superior, Undersecretary of State Sumner Welles, told me that the United States had no intention of engaging in an elaborate program to supply Spain with goods, and I repeated his statement at the first British-American economic meeting I attended in Madrid. The statement was received with weary inattention by the representatives of the British embassy, who went on with their work. By that time the United States was engaged in an undeclared naval war against Germany. It was giving Britain all possible aid short of declared war, and an embattled Britain, in turn, was extending credit to Spain at some sacrifice to itself. But the United States was reluctant to go along. Alexander Weddell, our first ambassador to Nationalist Spain, was sending appeal after appeal to Washington to show some recognition of Spain's importance to us and to the war against Hitler and Hitlerism, but Washington paid little attention to him.

With tiny Gibraltar performing a heroic and indispensable

service to the cause of freedom, guarding the Straits, dispatching convoys to Malta and Suez, keeping open the Empire's lifeline, the British regarded Spain with cold realism. Americans, more emotional, more ideological, and more influenced by what they read in the press, disliked Spaniards in government and distrusted them.

It was our entry into the war, a full year and a half after the fall of France, that forced us to reexamine our Spanish policy. We at last joined the British in a well-considered trade program. We set up in Spain, and also in next-door Portugal, a government-owned United States Commercial Company (USCC) to match the United Kingdom Commercial Company (UKCC) which had long been operating effectively in those countries, and to cooperate with it in 1) making available to Spain the food and materials it required if it were to avoid dependence on Germany, and also in 2) depriving the Germans, to the extent possible, of commodities of strategic importance they might wish to acquire in Spain. The most important of those was wolfram (also known as tungsten), used in the hardening of steel. Spain and, especially, Portugal, were Germany's principal suppliers of wolfram. The United States had the resources that were needed for diplomatic victory in Spain, and at last it was putting them to full use there. It was no longer tail to the British kite.

The British-American economic program not only pleased the Spaniards, it gave them a feeling of euphoria, an almost hysterical enthusiasm for neutralism and even for the Allied cause, because our device for depriving the Germans of wolfram was to offer higher and higher prices for it, and we raised prices to what must have seemed to the Spaniards (and to the Germans) astronomical levels. Since we had dollars to spare, and since the sums were chicken-feed to us, there was almost an element of unfair competition in what we did—particularly since we doubled and tripled the price of the petroleum we were selling to Spain in order to recover a part of our costs.

Finally, in October, 1943, with the Wehrmacht retreating in Russia, we decided to use compulsion more than dollars to deprive the Germans. We interrupted petroleum supplies to Spain, and told the Spanish government that we would resume them only when it placed an embargo on exports of wolfram to all countries, including the United States (which had no need of Spain's wolfram). Spain finally agreed to a near-embargo but it must have been one of the most difficult decisions it ever had to make. It not only put an end to the wolfram bonanza; it also brought German wrath down on Spanish heads. Happily it was too late for the Germans to do much about it.

From the beginning Washington was schizophrenic on the subject of trade with Spain. On January 12, 1942, in a telegram to Ambassador Weddell, the State Department remarked, smugly, that it did not regard the effects of its economic proposals upon the Spanish government's policy (toward the war) as a major factor; that it would base its decisions regarding the movement of supplies to Spain on whether it could obtain a tangible and valuable quid pro quo. An economic quid pro quo it meant. That was a repudiation of the whole Anglo-American attitude toward Spain, an effusion from desk-bound diplomats and bureaucrats, and the Department did not remain long on that limb. Less than a month later, in a telegram addressed to me as chargé d'affaires, it said, "While our economic relations with Spain are important . . . it should not be overlooked by the embassy in its reporting activities that it is the Spanish political situation in which the Department is principally interested." Far from overlooking the relationship between trade and politics (or rather between trade and military victory), the embassy had been urging Washington to recognize that relationship since the outbreak of World War II; it was Washington itself that had often appeared to overlook the relationship.

Using trade to attain political and military ends in Spain never became popular in Washington. There was a nagging fear that the Spaniards would betray us. The American press, especially ideologically inclined papers such as Ralph Ingersoll's *PM* in New York, warned repeatedly that this would occur. Officials in Washington read *PM* religiously, and often the Department of State's replies to our cables reflected the attitudes of *PM* more than those of the embassy. Our officials, especially those in political life, were fearful of public criticism if they went too far in "appeasing" Spain or if they seemed to be going too far.

Time magazine, of which Ingersoll had been publisher before setting up *PM*, was not far behind *PM* in urging a hard line toward Spain. During an automobile trip I made from Algiers to Casablanca in 1944 I met a young American Air Force officer whose duty, he explained, was to make reconnaisance flights over the Mediterranean between Morocco and the Iberian Peninsula. Openly anti-Franco, he mentioned a small island off the Spanish coast he was sure the Germans were using, although he admitted he had no evidence of that. "One of these days I'm going to bomb that island and claim it was an accident," he said. After listening to his anti-Spanish and anti-Franco rantings I asked him where he got his information concerning Spain and its relationship to the war. "I get it from *Time* magazine," he replied. Millions of other Americans also got their information and their opinions concerning Spain and its relationship to the war from *Time, PM,* and other American publications.

Nor could the media really be faulted. Since the Spanish government was concealing and even misrepresenting its true attitude toward the Axis, news coming out of Spain was almost uniformly unfavorable to the government. The German-influenced Spanish censorship saw to it that no news that was favorable to the Allies was sent out. Franco's speeches were freely transmitted of course, but those were almost uniformly pro-Axis. Other than them, and some Falange propaganda that was equally badly received in the United States, news coming out of Spain concerned little more than bullfights and religious ceremonies. Most of what passed for Spanish news came not from Spain but from Mexico City, Montevideo, New York, and Moscow, and nearly all of it was anti-Franco propaganda. Most of it was Spanish Republican or Communist in origin. A common reaction among readers was that if the Spanish government was that bad we shouldn't have relations with it.

Ideology also tended to make the wish father to the thought. Franco's pro-Axis statements became so annoying to Americans, including persons in government who were not familiar with our Spanish policy or who disagreed with it, that many wished for his downfall totally apart from the effect that might have on the course of the war. When the embassy reported that, saving untimely death, Franco seemed destined to lead Spain a long time, some Washington officials charged it with localitis, with being too close to the scene, with having little perspective. We tried to report objectively from Madrid, and it is clear now that we achieved a high degree of objectivity, but our reports were often interpreted in the light of the readers' biases, of their own concept of what was true and untrue.

For people in the United States, even many in government, the Spanish problem was largely an impersonal one, a problem on paper. For the embassy, however, it involved human beings, not only Spaniards within the government and outside it who were our friends and wanted to help our cause, which also was theirs, but the mass of Spaniards whose health, well-being, and lives in many cases depended in part on decisions made in Washington by persons who were influenced by newspapers and magazines, and by the radio, and who had the predilections that were inevitable in those circumstances. Few Spaniards were our enemies, but millions were enemies of our ally, Russia. While the American media were vilifying Franco a book written by Joseph E. Davies, a former U.S. ambassador to Russia, which praised Stalin to the skies and portrayed the infamous Moscow trials as models of justice, was being widely read and favorably commented on in the United States. Most Americans saw no inconsistency in that, but many Spaniards did.

The fact that Russia was our ally was a continuing problem for our Spanish friends, who believed that we underestimated the Communist threat. They knew what we sometimes forgot, or put out of our minds, that only a trick of history had made Russia our ally, that she might willingly have become our enemy, as in fact she later did, and that in such case the attitude of Americans toward Spain might have been quite different.

Our government, including those officials who were fully committed to our Spanish policy, had the same problem the Spanish government had, of not being in a position to explain its policy publicly, because to explain it would be to defeat it. Like all other parties it was doing its share of deceiving. It was concealing much of what it knew and what it was doing; it was applying the lessons of jujitsu—letting its enemies defeat themselves and letting the Spaniards help defeat them— and it was best to be silent in those circumstances. When I thought the time had come to explain our Spanish policy to the public I wrote an article attempting to do that. It was held up in Washington for months. Later, after I had fished it out of the Department's files, it was used by the authors of a much longer article in *Harper's Magazine*. The *Harper's* article was the first authentic report on our Spanish policy to be published. It caused little adverse public reaction. By that time of course the effects of our policy were becoming apparent. Nevertheless many persons in political life were still reluctant to acknowledge that Spain had been helpful to us.

The tensions and at times the discord that characterized relations between Washington and the embassy in Madrid were not unique of course. They were more nearly characteristic of situations such as our government faced in Spain where problems were grave and solutions not always apparent. The British have a saying that illustrates the relationship that so frequently exists between the Foreign Office and the field. They say that people in the Foreign Office often suspect that people in the field are crazy, while people in the field know that people in the Foreign Office are crazy. The relationship is even more difficult when not only the Foreign Office (the State Department in our case) but a dozen other offices and committees have to agree to policies and decisions, as often seemed to be the case during the war.

Of course many things are clear now, but it was not a simple task at the time to evaluate Spain's attitudes and acts and to fit them into our conduct of the war. Keeping the Iberian Peninsula free from war, protecting Gibraltar, maintaining a foothold on the Continent were of immediate importance. But how important were the pro-Axis speeches of Franco and Serrano? What lay behind them? What were Franco and Hitler, and Serrano and Ribbentrop, saying to each other? What promises were being made, and with what intentions? What surprises awaited us? What was the importance of the help we were sure the Spaniards were giving the Axis submarines? The Germans had a merchant vessel in Vigo that we felt was in the refueling business, and it turned out that it was. There were two such vessels in the Canary Islands. Italy had a vessel in the Bay of Algeciras that we strongly suspected was sabotaging Allied shipping in Gibraltar, and it became known later that we were right.

What was the importance of such phenomena? We couldn't be complacent about them. Britain's ambassador, Sir Samuel Hoare, gave particular importance to them and badgered the Spanish government constantly about them, sometimes with good effect. But would German submarines have respected Spanish shipping if Spain had been unwilling, for a time at least, to give some facilities to the German war effort? How could Spain keep from throwing itself into Hitler's arms if Germany cut off its supplies from overseas? Were the facilities it might be giving Germany too high a price, too large an installment, to pay for staying out of the war?

We had to balance the minus factors against the gains we were making in Spain and that we hoped to make in the future. Following the total occupation of France, Spain, defying German protests, permitted some thirty thousand French military men to pass through its territory to North Africa. They formed the core of General de Gaulle's new French army. Thousands of Allied airmen and military escapees came out of France and through Spain to Gibraltar and North Africa, most of them to return to duty. One American airman we came to know crossed the Pyrenees into Spain three times.

The military airfield at Gibraltar was indispensable to the success of our North African landings. Using Spanish workers who commuted daily from next-door La Linea, the British gradually, almost stealthily, extended it into the "neutral" zone that connected Gibraltar with Spain. Both it and the adjacent naval base were within range of Spanish guns that were capable of knocking them out in minutes. The naval base made it possible for our great armada to assemble and prepare for the landings. From their rooms in Algeciras' Maria Cristina Hotel the Germans could see what was going on in Gibraltar, but they could do nothing about it.

Naturally the Germans had to do the same kind of soul-searching that we were doing, particularly as the war progressed and their problems multiplied. They trusted no one in Spain, suspected everyone, and they were right. In retrospect the Allies got immeasurably more out of Spain than the Axis did. We in Madrid believed that this would be the case, but we couldn't be sure, and we frequently had trouble convincing the doubters, the hard-liners, and the play-safers at home. Happily the United States could make a great many mistakes and still win. It had a built-in insurance policy, which was Spain's own determination to stay out of the war if that were possible.

One is tempted to speculate at this point as to whether Spain would have entered the war if Hitler had met her demands in full. I believe that this could not have occurred because Germany was unwilling and probably incapable of meeting the open-ended demands that the Spaniards advanced, presumably with straight faces. In a memorandum of the Spanish General Staff which Germany's Ambassador Stohrer cabled on February 4, 1941, two months after Franco had withheld permission for German troops to enter the country, Spain requested, in addition to a very large amount of war materials, 3,750 tons of scarce copper, 1 million tons of grain, 8,000 trucks, 16,000 railroad cars and 180 locomotives, as well as 13,000 additional trucks for military purposes. Spain of course wanted all this *before* she would agree to enter the war. She also reserved the right to make further requests according to how matters proceeded. One can visualize matters proceeding in such manner as to make Spain's requests endless.

The director of the German Foreign Office's Economic Department, after studying the message, reported that "the most important parts of the memorandum contain requests that are so obviously unrealizable that they can only be evaluated as an expression of the effort to avoid entering the war under this pretext."

What were the limitations on the effectiveness of our Spanish policy? In general they were the limitations that are normal in a free society and that tend to be offset by the many advantages our system offers.

There was the influence of a large number of wartime officials, ready with their oversimplifications, thrilled with the importance of their jobs, earnest, hardworking, patriotic, prepared to win the war by themselves if others would not cooperate. And there was the influence of those who disagreed with our policy and tried to defeat it.

There was our own anti-Axis propaganda, and British propaganda, that sometimes boomeranged and influenced many Washington officials—such as the old chestnut that Spain was exporting foodstuffs to the Axis, which was true but less and less significant as time went on.

There was also the charge that the United States was sacrificing by letting scarce gasoline go to Spain—a charge that was useful if the Spaniards believed it but was not true because our tank farms in the Caribbean were bursting with the low-grade gasoline Spain bought and that we had little use for. Gasoline was scarce in the United States not because of shortages of gasoline but because of shortages of transport, and Spain furnished her own transport. She carried away gasoline we didn't need.

We in Madrid felt there was little to lose from the policy we recommended. It might fail but no other policy could succeed, so it was no great act of courage to press for its acceptance even in the face of resistance from Washington. A compliant Spain might be the key to Axis victory in Europe. It would be ridiculous, we felt, not to use the means we had to defeat that possibility. We argued that the worst result of our policy, if it should fail, would be that the Germans, should they enter Spanish territory, would have available to them a small amount of materials that we had supplied, and we might be made to look stupid or worse by the media and some persons in political life. But in terms of the national interest those were slight risks.

Administration leaders in Washington, and many officials who were not leaders, regarded the problem from a different angle, however. They feared, for some time at least, that if Franco should reward our "generosity" (or naïveté) by entering the war on the side of the Axis, as he sometimes suggested he might, it could not only cost them the next elections, it could also lesson support for our overall wartime policy. It took more courage to support our Spanish policy in Washington than it did in Madrid.

2 FRANCO

It was not General Franco's Nationalists who first rebelled against the Republic; it was Communists and other leftists who rebelled against a right-leaning government, and it was Franco and his friend, General Goded, who led the Republic's defense.

The rebellion, which began in October, 1934, with a nationwide general strike, had three principal centers: Madrid, Barcelona, and Oviedo, the last an important mining city in the northern province of Asturias and that province's capital. The rebellion was quickly put down in Madrid and Barcelona but it continued in Oviedo where the miners (who it might be noted in passing were among the highest paid workers in Spain) were well supplied with dynamite and of course skilled in its use.

Whereas in the rest of Spain there was little cooperation among the groups opposing the government, in Oviedo Anarchists, Socialists, Communists, and Trotskyists worked together effectively, and soon much of the province was in their hands. Arms factories in the area were seized and made to operate day and night. In what was to become a pattern in Spain some churches and convents were burned, and some middle-class women were raped and murdered.

Faced with an emergency of critical proportions, the government in Madrid named Franco and Goded joint chiefs of staff with the mission of restoring order in the province. The two were quite equal to the task. They brought a contingent of Legionnaires and Moors from Morocco, and with local help the "Africans" quickly and brutally brought an end to the rebellion. Before surrendering, the miners, who had used the centuries-old University of Oviedo as both headquarters and storehouse, blew up the university together with several surrounding blocks of houses.

Following his success in helping to quell the rebellion in Asturias, Franco was named army chief of staff, but when a Popular Front government came into power he was relieved of that post and assigned to the distant Canary Islands. After many church burnings and the assassinations of bishops, priests, nuns, and others that the new government made little or no effort to prevent, he helped to plan the Nationalist revolution of which he quickly became the leader.

In Spain's long history there have been only two republics, and both were short-lived. The second was inaugurated in 1931. Civil war broke out five years later and ended in the Republic's overthrow in 1939. To discover the origins of the Civil War one would have to delve deeply into Spanish history. But its proximate causes were the events that took place following the election of the Republic's Popular Front government in 1936. Hugh Thomas, an eminent and eloquent authority, tells us:

"[On June 16, 1936] an anxious group of middle-aged, middle-class liberals were gathered on the blue government bench at the front of the semi-circular debating chamber. Honest and intelligent men, they and their followers hated violence. They admired the pleasing, democratic ways of Britain, France and America. In both this hatred and this admiration, they were, however, unusual among Spaniards of their time, solitary even among the four hundred other deputies sitting or standing around and above them, as best they could, in the crowded debating chamber. . . .

"The nature of the crisis in Spain was described . . . by Gil Robles, the sleek, fat and almost bald, but still young leader of the Spanish catholic [sic] party, the CEDA. . . . Now he recalled that the Government had had, since the elections in February, exceptional powers, including press censorship and the suspension of constitutional guarantees. Nevertheless, during those four months, 160 churches, he said, had been burned to the ground, there had been 269 mainly political murders and 1,287 assaults of varying seriousness. Sixty-nine political centres had been wrecked, there had been 113 general strikes and 228 partial strikes, while 10 newspaper offices had been sacked. 'Let us not deceive ourselves!' concluded Gil Robles, 'A country can live under a monarchy or a republic, with a parliamentary or a presidential system, under communism or fascism! But it cannot live in anarchy. Now, alas, Spain is in anarchy. And we are today present at the funeral service of democracy!' "

What Gil Robles described had taken place *before* the Civil War had begun. Thomas tells us what happened after it had broken out a month later.

"So now there was to spread over Spain a cloud of violence, in which the quarrels of several generations would find outlet. With communication difficult or non-existent, each town would find itself on its own, acting out its own drama, apparently in a vacuum. There were soon to be not two Spains, but two thousand. The geographical differences within Spain were a prime factor in the social disintegration of the nation. Regional feeling had sown the wind, and now reaped the whirlwind. Sovereign power ceased to exist and, in its absence, individuals, as well as towns, acted without constraint, as if they were outside society and history. Within a month, thousands of people would have perished arbitrarily and without trial. Bishops would be murdered and churches profaned. Educated christians [sic] would spend their evenings murdering illiterate peasants and professional men of sensitivity. These events inevitably caused such hatreds that, when order was eventually established, it was an order geared solely for the rationalization of hatred known as war."

The two sides in the Civil War appealed for foreign aid almost at the same time, and the war's outcome was largely determined by the amount, the quality, and the timeliness of the aid they received. Neither Franco nor his Republican opponents could have chosen more disreputable helpers than Hitler, Mussolini, and Stalin, but little other aid was available to them. Portugal favored the Nationalists in ways that were open to her, but the help she could give was very limited. The Republicans appealed first to France, which, like Spain, had a Popular Front government at the time, and France very timorously made some planes available to them but, later, a French-proposed Non-Intervention Agreement, aimed at preventing hostilities from spreading beyond Spain, quickly put an end to aid from the democracies. Nearly all European countries signed and, in general, respected the agreement. Totalitarian Germany, Italy, and Russia signed it but openly violated it.

Franco and other Nationalist leaders had hoped they could carry out a swift coup d'etat but it did not turn out that way. On July 17, 1936, the Nationalist rebellion broke out prematurely in Melilla, a Spanish enclave in North Africa. Two nights later Republicans set fire to fifty churches in Madrid alone. In that city, too, a frenzied mob attacked the Montana barracks, which had declared for the rebellion, and finally penetrated it. Its occupants were dealt with summarily. Some were chopped to death on the spot. Others were hurled from the highest gallery of the barracks to the street below. The tone of the Civil War had been set.

Finding himself in Morocco's capital, Tetuán, without funds or planes, or even plans, and separated from peninsular Spain by the Straits of Gibraltar, Franco, on July 22, appealed to Hitler for help. Hitler responded promptly; between July and September German planes flew more than 20,000 Spanish and Moroccan Nationalist troops from Morocco to southern Spain. With that ready-made army Franco moved quickly northwest to cut Republican Spain off from Portugal and continued on to join up with the Army of the North while some units advanced

up the Tagus valley in the direction of Madrid itself. Hitler was
to remark later that Franco ought to erect a monument to the
glory of the Junkers 52 because it was that aircraft that the
Spanish Revolution had to thank for its victory.

But Hitler also did much more. By November a 6,500 man
"Condor Legion" of German bombing and fighter planes plus
some tank units had been assembled at Seville. The Condor
Legion was to give the Nationalists invaluable help during the
remainder of the war. In addition some 36,000 Spanish officers passed through the hands of German instructors. The
total number of Germans, including instructors and some civilians, who helped the Nationalists reached 16,000.

Hitler gave different reasons at different times for supporting the Nationalist revolution. He said once that his purpose
was to divert the attention of the western powers to Spain in
order to permit German rearmament to continue unobserved.
Later he said it was to prevent the Red Peril's overwhelming
Europe. At another time he said he wanted a fascist state
athwart the sea communications of Britain and France. On
still another occasion he indicated that Germany needed
Spanish iron ore, which a leftist government could not be
depended upon to supply. The possibility that German submarines might one day be refueled in Spanish waters may also
have been in his mind, as it surely was in the minds of his
naval advisers.

In general, German aid was unobtrusive. German advisors
did not try to run the war for the Nationalists, as they might
have been tempted to. General Hugo von Sperrle, the Condor
Legion commander, respected the Franco government and got
along well with it. Germany's first ambassador to the Franco
regime, General Wilhelm Faupel, was a different kind of person however. A colonel of the regiment in which Corporal
Adolf Hitler had served during World War I, and a former
inspector-general of the Peruvian army, he wore a cap and
gown rather than a uniform when he presented his credentials
to the Caudillo, and acted just as strangely during the remainder of his brief mission. Finding Franco likable but
unable to measure up to the needs of the situation, he soon
began to tell Berlin, and the Spaniards as well, how Franco

should carry on the war and how he should organize the Falange. Faupel and Sperrle hated each other and showed it. Franco, himself, resented Faupel's heavy-handedness and did not delay long in requesting his withdrawal. Berlin promptly complied.

In numbers of troops furnished Italy exceeded both Germany and Russia. At their maximum they probably reached 50,000. Italy's fighter planes covered the merchant ships that carried 2,500 Nationalist troops from Morocco to Spain in August, 1936. Italian pilots supported the Nationalists in combat, and Italian surface vessels and submarines also played an active role. But Italy's contribution to Nationalist victory is not remembered as glorious.

Mussolini was flattered when Franco asked him for aid, and he responded eagerly. His enthusiasm waned, however, as casualties mounted and Italian ground troops failed to distinguish themselves. Early in the war some 30,000 Italians plus 20,000 Nationalists took part in the Battle of Guadalajara, which was supposed to open up the northern entrance to Madrid, the Republicans' capital. In that battle alone the Italians suffered some 2,000 killed, 300 taken prisoner, and 4,000 wounded, and they were finally routed.

Ernest Hemingway, a Republican sympathizer who arrived in Spain about that time, wrote, "I have been studying the battle for four days, going over the ground with the commanders who directed it, and I can state that Guadalajara will take its place in military history with the other decisive battles of the world." Herbert Matthews cabled the *New York Times* that Guadalajara was to fascism what the defeat of Bailen had been to Napoleon. These were exaggerations but they reflected Republican opinion at the time. During the three years I lived and worked in Madrid the mere mention of Italy brought to mind the rout at Guadalajara. Mussolini's "crusaders" continued to be the butt of scornful jokes spread by supporters as well as critics of the Franco regime. Franco himself once said that the whole history of Italian troops in Spain was a tragedy.

Germany and Italy responded promptly to Franco's plea for military assistance, but it was three months before any Soviet aid reached the Republicans. Also, while most of Germany's and Italy's role in the Civil War was overt, for many to see, the Russian government long maintained that it had no role at all. In fact it was not the government but the Russian Communist party and the Comintern under Russian direction that principally arranged the aid. The distinction was specious, but for a long time it helped to blur the full scope of Russia's involvement. Both Germany and Italy eventually submitted bills to the Nationalist government for goods, supplies and services rendered, and they were eventually paid, but Russia took no financial risk at all. Stalin declined to authorize aid until the Republican government had dispatched its entire gold reserve to Moscow for "safekeeping" and as a guarantee of reimbursement for aid.

Unlike the Nazis and the Fascists, Russian and other foreign Communists were already involved in Spain's domestic politics before the Civil War began, and involvement was greatly intensified during the war. Indeed before long the effective leader of Spain's Communist party was not a Spaniard but the Italian Palmiro Togliatti, one of international communism's most skilled and most ruthless leaders. There were never more than 2,000 Russians in Spain, but all of them were in key positions. And the fact that the Republic was totally dependent on Soviet Russia for military support gave the Communist party a very important role in the conduct of the government as well as of the war.

In mid-1937 the Russians vetoed a plan which Prime Minister Francisco Largo Caballero supported to launch a major attack on Estremadura. They said that planes would not be available for it. Shortly afterwards, at the meeting of Spanish Communist party leaders, Togliatti demanded that Largo Caballero be removed. Largo Caballero soon resigned. Compared with the Germans and Italians the Russians were "in charge."

Although Russians, themselves, did little fighting, other foreign Communists, particularly the Comintern-organized International Brigades, had an important role. Some observers claim that their timely arrival in Madrid, in October, 1936, only three months after the war had begun, and the élan with which they defended against besieging Nationalist forces, were crucial in encouraging Republicans to hold out in the capital and prevent what might have been a much quicker Nationalist victory.

Of the approximately 40,000 members of the International Brigades a possible 3,000 were Americans, who made up the "Abraham Lincoln Battalion." The Americans arrived in Spain too late to participate in the early defense of Madrid, but they served later, often with courage if not always with distinction. Like their European counterparts, the members of the Abraham Lincoln Battalion were recruited by Communists, and most were Communists or Communist sympathizers. And when they arrived in Spain, they were placed under Russian Communist control.

The first sixty "Lincolns," as the Battalion members came to call themselves, arrived in Barcelona on January 6, 1937, some six months after the Civil War had begun, and in order to demonstrate their Americanism they marched straight to the American consulate general where, lined up in military formation before the building, they sang the "Star Spangled Banner." Their Communist connection was clear to persons inside when they sang not only the first stanza but the second and third stanzas as well. Then, as now, few average Americans knew those stanzas; Communists, on the other hand, studied such matters.

Before two months had passed, a still untrained and poorly equipped Battalion, now numbering some 400 men, was thrown into a battle it could not possibly win. The battle was later referred to, correctly, as a massacre. And the Battalion's subsequent record was little more impressive. Its history was one of enthusiasm, bravery, inadequacy, disillusionment, and of course for many, death; probably one-half of its members were killed.

Except for their early help in defending Madrid, the military accomplishments of the International Brigades were less than sensational. Their greatest achievment was to give the impression throughout the world that freedom-loving people everywhere supported the Rupublican cause. It is ironic that this should have occurred while Stalin, who had authorized creation of the brigades, was destroying whatever small remnants of freedom remained in Russia.

Paulino Hermenegildo Teodulo Francisco Franco y Bahamonde (b. December 4, 1892), Nationalist Spain's Caudillo, was a *Gallego,* and that tells a good deal about him. Gallegos occupy the northwestern corner of Spain. Some are sailors and fishermen. Others till the steep slopes of the Galician mountains. Many are canny businessmen. All of them are stubborn. Franco remained a Gallego all his life.

Franco's father was a naval officer, and Franco himself wanted to follow in his footsteps, but since there was no room in the Naval Cadet School he entered the Army's Infantry Academy instead. As a captain of infantry in Morocco he was seriously wounded by a Riff sharpshooter. Restored to health he quickly rose to be commander of the Foreign Legion. At thirty-three he became Europe's youngest brigadier general.

"Every Spaniard," Salvador de Madariaga wrote, "is a dictator at heart." Madariaga knew his people well, but whether Franco conformed to that norm we do not know. That he was a strict disciplinarian we do know. In Morocco, one day, when he was inspecting the meal his troops had just been given, a soldier threw a plate of food in his face. Franco calmly wiped the food away and continued the inspection. The next day the soldier was executed. (Some commentators maintain that the food was thrown not at Franco but at the officer who accompanied him. There are no differences regarding the rest of the story.)

Franco had no record of being a plotter, a common breed among the Spanish military. He never joined the *Juntas de Defensa,* a labor union-type group among the military which paved the way for the Primo de Rivera dictatorship in 1923. He did not participate in the abortive Sanjurjo rebellion which preceded the Civil War.

In any case Franco was difficult to characterize. Few persons beyond his family and his immediate associates knew him well, and others tended to find in him what they wanted to find. I myself saw him only on ceremonial occasions, and there were two kinds of these—and two Francos. His most

important public appearace was probably his review of the
annual July 17 parade commemorating the entry of Nationalist forces into Madrid. The parade was always well organized,
and the Falange party claques also were well organized. But
Franco appeared to be little impressed, as though it were all
déjà vu, as indeed it was. His fascist salute was limp. He
seemed bored, almost distracted.

He gave the same impression when he read his speeches.
Until the end of 1943 many of them were in praise of the
Axis, and when they were published Allied sympathizers
reacted with anger. But Franco himself seemed incapable of
emotion. He read the speeches in a monotone, as though he
were seeing them for the first time, and he rarely took his
eyes from the text.

At social functions Franco was quite a different person.
Every year, at Epiphany, he had the chiefs of diplomatic missions and their principal aides to lunch at La Granja, the royal
palace far up in the Guadalquivir mountains. To emphasize
Spain's neutrality all chiefs of mission were seated at a single
table, with neutrals placed between belligerents. The luncheons presented problems particularly since the guests could
not always distinguish friend from foe, but Franco was an
attentive host. He was gracious to both sides, not only to
chiefs of mission but also to subordinates. On one occasion he
engaged Caroll, my wife, in lively conversation for several
minutes while chiefs of mission waited to talk to him. Caroll,
for whom Franco was a remote and lonely person, could
hardly believe her eyes or her ears.

Time magazine portrayed Franco as stupid and overbearing.
He was neither. *Time* referred to him during World War II as
"fat-bottomed Franco." That was not only unhelpful to the
Allied cause; it also was inaccurate. Franco was on the plump
side, but he was well-proportioned, light on his feet, and ath-
letic. He was an expert horseman, and an avid hunter and
fisherman. He also played golf—with what skill I do not
know. To the disappointment of some of his detractors, his
health was excellent and remained excellent for many years.

Emmet Hughes, who headed the American Embassy's information section during World War II, said in a book he

wrote after he had joined *Time* magazine, that in Morocco Franco "learned the need of playing off one envious Moorish chieftain against another, allying himself with one, warring upon a second, betraying a third, preparing to betray the first. It was a relentless game of governing by conspiracy, cabals, caprice, conquest. This is what he learned and this is what he practiced, for this is all he knows."

Franco knew much more than that of course. Hughes, like most other writers, underrated him. Hughes was much closer to the truth when he suggested that Franco had a kind of "intelligence that is crafty, a sincerity that is fanatic, a tenacity that is ruthless, an integrity that is cruel." Hughes suggested, correctly in my opinion, that a politically mature people should be unafraid to remember the nouns as well as the adjectives in that characterization.

British Ambassador Hoare said that Franco looked insignificant among military men. He was much more impressed by the German ambassador, Eberhard von Stohrer, who was six feet seven inches tall but had a reputation for timidity and badly misjudged the Spaniards, than he was by Franco, who was below average height, had been cited more than once for bravery, and was handling the Germans with masterful skill.

But other Spanish generals did not consider Franco insignificant. In July, 1943, a group of imprudent generals, businessmen, and Cortes members circulated a petition calling upon Franco to restore the monarchy. Hughes says that when two generals and an admiral, none of whom had signed the petition, had summoned enough courage to face Franco and ask him to deal leniently with the petitioners, Franco rose from his chair and, placing himself immediately in front of the startled officers, said in tones that were not measured: "You too! You do not understand that Monarchy is *lo parcial*—and my regime is *lo total*. I am here to fulfill a divine mandate, and any contrary maneuver is an act against Spain."

We never knew exactly what Franco's words were; there were various versions of what he said. I doubt that he used the word "divine." But the references to his manner and his meaning are authentic. The incident was amply confirmed.

The officers wilted under Franco's attack, and the pressure to restore the monarchy quickly subsided. Franco later called in the petitioners, one by one and convinced them they were wrong in their petition.

I am convinced that Franco, at the time, was just as monarchist as the men who petitioned him but that he thought that it was much too early to restore the monarchy; that only a nonmonarchical authoritarian government (Franco's government that is) was capable of surviving the resentments, the animosities, and the hatreds that then divided Spaniards, and the great new war that still threatened to engulf them. And if that was his opinion I believe he was correct in holding it.

Franco had none of the provincialism that characterizes most Spaniards. He was born a Gallego and remained a Gallego, but before anything else he was a Spaniard. A member of his cabinet once said to me, with some vehemence, "I am a Spaniard but first of all I am a Basque." There were millions of Spaniards who, similarly, were regionalists before they were Spaniards. This stubborn regionalism was one of the reasons Spaniards had had so much trouble living together in peace through the centuries. But Franco's loyalty was to Spain, not to any portion of it.

A quality of Franco's that impressed people—and annoyed some—was his monumental calm, his easy assumption that the first place belonged to him. This had nothing in it of arrogance, but it infuriated the nobility who suspected, doubtless with abundant reason, that Franco considered himself at least as good as royalty and better than nobility. When he sat in a chair formerly reserved for royalty he did it as though he were quite used to it, as though he gave it no importance, while the monarchists chattered and protested among themselves although never to Franco.

Franco met Hitler at Hendaye and returned to his palace without having given up anything that mattered. Hitler was near the height of his power at that time, and his plans included bringing Spain into the war and taking Gibraltar. Franco agreed to the plan in principle but not in fact.

Franco was low third among the European dictators, but the other two courted him. Mussolini was not above asking the Caudillo to meet with him since he had already met with Hitler. Pétain didn't want to be left out either. He also asked Franco to visit him and Franco did. Ambassador Hoare once made the point that Franco's opposition was weak and divided, and he was right. Indeed all Spain was weak and divided, and those who supported Franco also opposed him many times and in many ways, just as they opposed one another. Leftists criticized him for catering to the forces of reaction, but reactionaries considered him too liberal. Monarchists were impatient with him for not bringing back the monarchy, but his policies and acts led directly to the restoration of the monarchy. Conservatives detested his closeness to the Falange, but he never permitted the Falange to have any real power. At the same time most of his critics were grateful for the peace that Spain enjoyed. The editors of *PM* might consider it the peace of the tomb, but they were comfortable in their editorial chairs; they had not been through the Civil War, and they did not know Spaniards nearly as well as Franco did.

A story that was widely circulated while I was in Spain concerned a Catalan who indulged in a lengthly tirade against Franco. When a friend, who was listening, asked, "And whom would you like to have in power now?" the Catalan replied, "Why Franco, of course." Franco was close to being the indispensable man.

Alexander Weddell, our first ambassador to the Nationalist regime, told me of being with his wife in San Sebastián shortly after they had arrived in Spain when a car bearing General and Mrs. Franco appeared in the great plaza there. Without a sound or a signal the thousands of Spaniards who were in the plaza knelt down until the car had driven away. Weddell said that he and Mrs. Weddell knelt down too. He doubted that they would have left there alive if they had remained standing. Happily the Jack Anderson of the times never got wind of that bizarre episode in the life of an American ambassador.

Ambassador Hayes judged Franco more accurately than Ambassador Hoare did, or at least he described him more accurately, but neither Hoare nor Hayes may have given him full credit. Both commented on the good fortune that befell the Allies prior to the North African landings, with the appointment of Jordana to replace Serrano as foreign minister, and both gave full credit to Jordana for his attitude in relation to the landings and to the democracies in general. But neither recognized sufficiently that both Serrano and Jordana spoke for Franco.

Serrano ridicules Hoare's speculation as to what would have happened if he, Serrano, had remained as foreign minister. He says, "Franco did not entrust me with any portion of his power, and in the final analysis it was he who decided everything." In my view Serrano did not overstate the case. Franco presided over what often appeared to be anarchy, coordinated it, and made it serve his purpose, which was to promote Spain's interest. There was a kind of flexibility in regimented Spain that made it possible for Beigbeder and Jordana, Franco's foreign ministers, to follow an apparently sincere policy of friendship toward the Allies while Serrano, Franco's interior minister and later Beigbeder's successor as foreign minister, followed an apparently sincere pro-Axis policy.

When, late in May, 1939, newly appointed Ambassador Weddell called on President Roosevelt before departing for his post in Madrid, he asked the president whether he had any message for Franco. Roosevelt replied, "Yes I have. Tell him I don't like dictators." Roosevelt did not mean for Weddell to deliver that messages of course, but he was expressing the attitude that he and most other high officials of the United States government had toward Franco, who was seen less as a person who might help to bring down the tyrant, Hitler, than as a tyrant himself, a dictator, and what was worse, a fascist dictator.

The United States press, on its part, regarded Franco as an all-powerful despot who could work his will in Spain without restraint, and Franco did little to alter that image because it was helpful to him in some ways. But it was not the image he had of himself. He told Ambassador Hayes once that if he had the authority of a Franklin D. Roosevelt he would do a lot of things that were in fact beyond his power to do. At that time many Americans were referring to Roosevelt as "that man in the White House."

There is little doubt that Franco spoke to Hayes with sincerity because what he said was true. He presided over a rickety structure whose main support came from the Army, the Church, big business, and big wealth. One of those groups, or several working together, may have had the power to topple Franco, but for any of them such action might be suicidal. Hitler also may have had it within his power to topple Franco, as Napoleon had toppled a Spanish monarch a century and a half earlier, and some of Hitler's supporters played with that idea. But Hitler was never persuaded that such a course was in his interest.

Yet Franco could never be sure that some person, or some group, would not tire of him and bring about his downfall. Far from being the tyrant he often appeared to be he was a master maneuverer who gave Spain a kind of fragile unity, in part by helping to keep his supporters as well as his opponents divided. Perhaps he had learned important lessons in Morocco, as Hughes suggested. Or perhaps he was just a good politician.

Carceller, the businessman turned politician, once told me that Franco was less a dictator than a chairman of the board, and there is a lot to what he said. Franco provided stability, which in Spain was not a common commodity. No Spanish leader in his senses probably thought seriously of getting rid of Franco once the latter had established his leadership. Serrano, I do not doubt, at one time dreamed that Franco might some day content himself with being chief of state, leaving him, Serrano, as active chief of government. He tells us that Mussolini once asked him if that might take place. And it appears that General Agustín Muñoz Grandes, while he commanded the Blue Division, talked with Hitler about such a possibility, with Muñoz Grandes, not Serrano, becoming chief of government, but nothing came of that either.

Hoare said that Franco would start to burn his ships and then put the fire out. He was quite correct in that too, and I believe Franco planned it that way. He had the faculty of pleasing everyone and no one. He would make a speech that infuriated the Allies and created angry headlines in the free press of the world, and then turn round and give the Allies a concession that had the Nazis tearing their hair. On July 17, 1941, the

anniversary of the Nationalist uprising, and a month after Hitler had invaded Russia, Franco, his mind on German tanks that
were already two-thirds of their way to Moscow, denounced
"out-worn democracy" and praised the "New Order" in Europe. He said that if Russian Communists should succeed in
invading Germany (a doubtful possibility at the time) a million
Spaniards would rush to the defense of Berlin. A year later,
with the Germans bogged down before Stalingrad, Franco said
the million Spaniards would take their stand not before Berlin
but at the Pyrenees. Little attention was paid to that speech in
the democracies, but to Franco-watchers in Madrid it marked a
giant step in the Allied direction.

On the day he signed the Treaty of Friendship with Nazi
Germany Franco also signed a Treaty of Friendship and Non-
Aggression with Spain's anti-Nazi neighbor, Portugal. Tiny
Portugal was not a military power but it had a vast empire,
and its territory, like Spain's, had great strategic importance.
Besides, it was Britain's oldest ally.

While Spain's relations with Germany became increasingly
strained, her relations with Portugal were strengthened. In
February, 1942, Prime Minister Oliveira Salazar visited
Franco in Seville, and the two arrived at what Spanish diplomat José M. Doussinague later called a "true verbal treaty."
Nor did Franco rest there. In November, shortly after Allied
forces had landed in North Africa, he told Jordana, who had
succeeded Serrano as foreign minister, that he wanted him to
return Salazar's visit. A month later, in Lisbon, the "verbal
treaty" of Seville was converted into a formal treaty that
joined the two countries together in what became known as
the "Iberian Bloc." On the very day Franco began to withdraw
the Blue Division from Russia, Ambassador Hoare informed
Jordana that Portugal had granted air and naval bases to Britain. Jordana promptly called in the German ambassador and
told him the Anglo-Portuguese agreement was no reason for
bringing the war into the Iberian Peninsula. That evening,
after a Columbus Day dinner, Franco assured the Portuguese
ambassador that his country need not fear for its back door;
Spain would guard it.

Hitler was so elated when German tanks reached Hendaye,

on the Spanish border, leaving a defeated France behind them, that during his first and only visit to Paris he danced for the newsreels. It was the last time he had occasion to dance. Hitler had conquered Poland in twenty-one days, Norway in a month, and France in two weeks. His next obvious target was Britain, but although his troops could clearly see the cliffs of Dover, he had no prepared plan for invading that island nor, except for planes, the equipment he would need to accomplish the task. Moreover he nurtured a hope that invasion would not be necessary, that Winston Churchill could be convinced that Britain and Germany, racially similar nations, could live in peace and cooperation. But after Churchill, in a speech that was heard around the world, had asked the Britons, defiantly, "What kind of people do [the Nazis] think we are?" and British fighter planes had repulsed Germany's best efforts to soften up the island by aerial bombardment, Hitler's thoughts were directed increasingly toward Russia, the country he most feared and hated. Nevertheless Gibraltar was first on his list.

As noted earlier, on November 1, 1940, six days before his talks with Serrano at Berchtesgaden, and without prior consultation with the Spaniards, an overconfident Hitler issued Directive 18 which called for Operation Felix, the occupation of Gibraltar. More specific orders concerning Felix were issued on November 14. The assault on Gibraltar was to have four phases. First of all, while attack formations were assembling in France at some distance from the Spanish border, German reconnaisance troops wearing civilian clothing would enter Spain, complete final assault plans, and seal off Gibraltar against any British sorties. Next, as the bulk of German forces were crossing the border into Spain, there would be an aerial attack on British fleet units; the planes would take off from France but would land in Spain and be available to support the attack on the Rock. The troops would consolidate their positions and close the Straits; naval support, especially submarines and coast artillery batteries, would participate. Once Gibraltar was secured, heavy batteries and infantry would be moved over to Africa. Possibly Spain's Canary Islands would be occupied.

With German help the Spaniards had built a new and stronger bridge at Hendaye. Roads and bridges within Spain also had been strengthened. On November 2 the first staff sections left Munich for Besançon, in France. Soon troops were moving from virtually every major command to training grounds in the Orleans-Anger-Poitier-Niort-Besançon area. Following Admiral Canaris' conversation with General Franco on December 7, however, everything stopped. Franco had refused to agree to the plan. Nor did all of Hitler's and Ribbentrop's importuning and insults cause him to change his mind, as we have seen.

At the same time, on the theory that Germany might one day march through Spain to Gibraltar, German officers continued to discuss plans with the Spanish military. Following his talk with Franco, Canaris and his companions went on to Algeciras, across a narrow bay from Gibraltar. An almost carefree Canaris, himself very doubtful that the attack on Gibraltar would ever take place, said the exercise would be a vacation for them. In Algeciras they were joined by another group led by General Hubert Lanz, who had been selected to command the Gibraltar invasion.

Wearing ill-fitting Spanish uniforms, the Germans examined the Rock from all angles. They had a near view of it from the neutral zone that connects Gibraltar with Spain. They also embarked on the Spanish mine-layer *Jupiter* for a look at it from the seaward side. Lanz, fearing capture by the British, was hesitant about going along, but Canaris laughed at his concern. He told him that the British were fully aware of what was going on, but that for them to remove him from a Spanish vessel would be a casus belli, which the British wanted to avoid. While the Germans examined the Rock from the *Jupiter*'s deck, a British aircraft hovered overhead.

That was as close as the Germans ever got to Gibraltar. Hitler could have invaded Spain without Franco's consent, of course, and some of his advisors urged him to do that. But he decided that, while taking Gibraltar was quite feasible if Spain cooperated, making the effort in the face of Spanish resistance was not. The need to bail out the Italians not only in the Balkans but also in the Mediterranean and North Africa, plus the enormous requirements of the attack on Russia that he now planned, precluded Hitler from committing the forces required for Felix, if Spain resisted. It was that vital information that Canaris, doubtless in general terms, had conveyed to General Vigón, and Vigón had passed on to Franco. Following a talk with General Jodl on January 28, 1941, the Fuehrer ordered the final cessation of preparations for Felix. He would win additional victories, but the path he was now taking would lead inexorably to defeat.

Nevertheless Hitler had not yet given up on Spain. Confident of victory in Russia, he ordered the military to prepare a new plan for taking Gibraltar, and on March 10, 1941, such a plan, dubbed Felix-Heinrich, was submitted. It provided that when German forces reached the Kiev-Smolensk line in Russia the troops needed for the Gibraltar operation would be withdrawn and assigned to that project. But that proved to be still another Hitler chimera. Instead of taking Gibraltar, the German military were soon making plans to defend against possible British landings in Spain. Landings took place on November 8, 1942, but they were British-American landings and they were in North Africa rather than in Spain. And of course Hitler was unable to interfere with them.

In the democracies it was widely charged that Spain was on the Axis side, and Franco's speeches, as well as the news that was permitted to come out of Spain, certainly supported that charge. Opposition to Franco was also based on four additional charges: 1) that he had been placed in power by Nazi Germany and Fascist Italy; 2) that he had destroyed Spain's democracy; 3) that he was the fascist head of a fascist state; and 4) that his government had indulged in gross violations of human rights. How valid were those charges?

It is true that Franco could not have won the Civil War without the aid he received from Hitler and Mussolini. But that did not make him a creature of those totalitarian leaders. Replying to a criticism of United States' alliance with Soviet Russia, President Roosevelt, who yielded to no one in support of democracy, once said that if he were confronted by an assassin on a narrow bridge he would accept assistance from the devil. The statement is apt, and Hitler was as much a devil as

Stalin was. But Hitler's attack on Russia and Stalin's resistance made the latter a hero throughout the free world. If Hitler had invaded Spain, and Franco had resisted as he indicated he would, he also would have been a hero. He would have been "our brave ally," as Stalin was. Like Stalin he would have been glorified and romanticized instead of vilified.

Furthermore the little democracy that existed in Spain had already been destroyed when the Nationalist rebellion began. What Nationalists saw in Spain was anarchy that threatened to open the way to communism, and they were right. Salvador de Madariaga, who never ceased to attack Franco, said that the 1934 leftist revolt which Franco, as a general of the Republic, helped to put down, had deprived the left of any right to criticize the later Nationalist rebellion. If Spain's left had no right to criticize the rebellion, there was little basis for foreigners to criticize it.

Answering the third charge is not so easy. Nationalist Spain was a one-party state, and many commentators, inside as well as outside Spain, compared the country's political party, the Falange, with the Nazi party in Germany and the Fascist party in Italy. Were they justified in doing that? Was Nationalist Spain in fact a fascist state, and was Franco, himself, a fascist?

There were two Falanges: the pre–Civil War Falange and the new, vastly enlarged Falange that was born of the Civil War. Both were Catholic-oriented. The leader of the pre–Civil War Falange was José Antonio Primo de Rivera. A tall, pleasant, well-educated man of good family and good will, José Antonio, as he was familiarly known throughout Spain, had little of the zealot in him. He despised Marxists and mistrusted Republicans—Spanish Republicans that is—but he also had little confidence in either the conservatives or the military (his father, General Miguel Primo de Rivera, had been Spain's dictator under the monarchy). He admitted to his close friends, who included many liberals, that his views differed little from those of the moderate Socialist leader, Indalecio Prieto, with whom he tried unsuccessfully to achieve a working relationship.

José Antonio's Falangists were uniformed and used a fascist-type salute, and for some time José Antonio referred to the party as "fascist," but he changed his view after he had glimpsed fascism in action. In the spring of 1934, on his way to England on vacation (he and his family admired the English and felt at home with them), he stopped off in Berlin to look around. What he saw there dismayed him; he was never again tempted to call himself or his party fascist. In any case his career was coming to an end. Some six weeks before the Civil War broke out a suspicious Republican government imprisoned him. On November 20, 1936, he was executed.

Before the Civil War broke out the Falange had no more than 25,000 members, most of them very young, but its capacity for provocation was great. Following the election of the Popular Front some Falangists exacerbated the disorder that was going on, confident that government supporters would get the blame. Immediately after the Civil War broke out there was a rush, in Nationalist territory, to join the Falange. Many joined it for what they considered patriotic reasons; others regarded the Falange as a safe-haven from political persecution. Government officials and military officers and petty officers were automatically enrolled in it. A majority of the new members probably did not know what the Falange stood for except that it was something vaguely "social."

On July 25, 1936, the Nationalists, now aware that their failed coup d'etat had brought about a civil war, set up a *Junta de Defensa Nacional* which named Franco chief of state as well as generalissimo of the armed forces. But they still had no political party or political program, and how those were to be created under war conditions was not clear. The rightist parties had practically ceased to function; in any case the right had not developed a mystique adequate to attract adherents. The Falange constituted a possible solution to the regime's problems, but not alone.

A smaller unofficial group which supported the Nationalists but disagreed ideologically with the Falange in many ways, was the *Comunión Nacionalista*. The "Carlists," as its members were commonly called, were conservative Catholics and monarchists who supported a dissident monarchist line. When Ramón Serrano Suñer, after escaping from Republican territory, arrived in Burgos and was assigned by Franco to look after political matters, he undertook to bring about a union of the two groups. At midnight, April 19, 1937, Franco, on his own authority, decreed their amalgamation into the *Falange Española Tradicionalista y de las Juntas de Ofensiva Nacionalista* (its awkward name itself indicated its mongrel origin). Franco named himself National Leader.

The Nationalist regime was still not fascist—in the conventional sense certainly—or totalitarian as it claimed to be, but it was authoritarian, and Franco, not the Falange or any institution or ideology, wielded authority. The statutes of the new Falange, which were adopted as State Doctrine, provided:

"Our State shall be a totalitarian instrument dedicated to the service of the national integrity. All the Spanish people will participate in the State through the families, municipalities and syndicates. No one shall participate through the medium of a political party. We shall radically abolish the political party system with all its consequences: inorganic suffrage, representation by warring parties, and a parliament of the kind that is only too well known."

The Falange was made the state party, or "movement," as it was officially referred to, because it was ready-made and available, and because it was authoritarian. It never acquired political power but it supplied a bureaucracy that became known chiefly for its arrogance. Republicans detested the Falange for ideological reasons. They, and many Nationalists as well, resented it because it was an agent of oppression. But for Franco it was a useful instrument for carrying out certain social programs, and for appeasing, and sometimes deceiving, Hitler and Mussolini.

The final portion of the Falange's name indicated that it was national syndicalist, and the expression evokes memories of Italian syndicalism (and also of Spanish anarchism). The government did organize industrywide national syndicates, but the action had little social significance. Its principal effect was to enable the government to deal with workers in a given industry as a whole. So-called national syndicalism was little more than an instrument for controlling labor.

A small group within the Falange did try to introduce orthodox national syndicalism, which has been described as equidistant between Marxism and the Catholic company unions, and General Juan de Yague Blanco, who was widely known as "the Falange general," in part because he was one of the very few generals entitled to that epithet, supported the effort clandestinely. After his role was revealed, Franco called him for a little chat. Instead of punishing Yague, however, he promoted him, leaving the general weeping and broken, without influence within the Falange or outside it. Orthodox national syndicalism had ended before it was born.

It was in the field of propaganda, of control and manipulation of the media, that the Falange became notorious for appeasing the Axis. Its Vice Secretariat of Popular Education was so blatantly on the Axis side that it sometimes sickened even the few who admired Hitler and Mussolini. Emmet Hughes tells of the manner in which it censored an American motion picture, *The Vatican of Pius XII.* The distributors were ordered to:

"1st. Suppress all reference to persecution of the Catholic Church in Germany.

"2nd. Suppress dialogue and scenes, referring to the presence of a representative of President Roosevelt at the Vatican.

"3rd. Suppress all dialogue and scenes referring to the existence of an American College in the Vatican."

This in Catholic Spain!

Gabriel Arias Salgado, vice secretary of popular education, who was responsible for the censoring, was close to one extreme of the Franco government. General Francisco Jordana, the liberal, God-fearing Spanish gentleman who served twice as Franco's minister of foreign affairs, represented a quite different extreme.

Was Franco a fascist then? He was first and foremost a military dictator, a familiar figure in Spain's history. But he was also El Caudillo, Spain's Fuehrer, its Duce. The Falange had all the fascist trappings—blue shirts, black boots, red berets, the straight-arm salute, bully-boys, and carefully prepared "spontaneous" demonstrations in honor of Franco and of the Falange—but it was made up of discordant groups. While the Carlists were pro-monarchy and pro-Church, the "old-shirt" Falangists were anti-monarchy, anti-capitalist, and frequently anti-Church. The Falange had not achieved power, as fascism had in Italy and Nazism had in Germany. It was Franco's military who had achieved power. The little power the Falange had Franco had given it. The Falange was Franco's creature, and it died when Franco died.

If Franco was a fascist he was a "rice-and-beans" fascist, as the Cubans would have said. He may have been, for convenience, a national syndicalist but he was a military dictator by inclination and by necessity, and as dictators go he was an effective one. He outlasted Hitler and Mussolini as well as many of his democratic critics.

Franco and Hitler met only once—at Hendaye—and neither enjoyed the experience. Hitler told Mussolini, when he saw him a few days later, that he would rather have three or four teeth pulled than repeat the conversations he had had with Franco. He also told Mussolini that Franco undoubtedly had a stout heart, but that only by accident had he become generalissimo and leader of the Spanish state. He said Franco was not a man who was up to the problems of the material and political development of his country. Later he changed his mind about the stout heart. In his letter to Franco of February 6, 1941, after Franco had denied him free passage to Gibraltar, he asked for a "stout heart rather than prudent caution," which he intimated Franco and his advisers possessed in excess. General Jodl said at Nuremburg that Hitler used more violent language against Franco than against Roosevelt or Churchill.

German propaganda continued throughout the war to stress the regime's close association with Spain, but Goebbels, Hitler's minister of propaganda, recorded in his diary Germany's increasing disillusionment with the Caudillo.

February 1, 1942. "Franco has delivered a speech, intended chiefly for home consumption, in which he declared that the Spaniards are God's chosen people and will remain faithful to the Catholic Church. It would be more fitting for Spain to remain faithful to the Axis. . . . That's a nice revolutionist we placed on the throne!. . ."

February 16, 1942. "Franco delivered a very aggressive speech against Bolshevism. It would be far better if he declared war on Bolshevism."

March 2, 1943. "[Goering] especially blames Ribbentrop for not succeeding in drawing Spain over to our side. Franco is, to be sure, cowardly and irresolute."

July 28, 1943. "This would-be big shot and inflated peacock owes it to the Duce alone that he is sitting on his pretender's throne."

September 9, 1943. "The Spanish Government has initiated a new press campaign with a twelve-point declaration that inclines more toward the English than the German side. The dirty thing about it is that the Franco Government has not even deemed it necessary to give us any detailed reasons for it."

We know that Hitler's attitude toward Franco was one of increasing resentment and disdain. But what were Franco's feelings toward Hitler? One is tempted to suggest that Franco had no private feelings, that his feelings were those of Spain's chief of state. And as chief of state he saw Hitler as both friend and threat. But friendship weakened with time whereas the threat remained. During 1940 and 1941 it was acute.

There is little reason to believe that Franco felt indebted to Hitler for making it possible for him to be Caudillo of a Nationalist Spain. Donald S. Detwiler, an acute observer, said:

"[Franco] and a great number of his followers fought the Civil War in the sign of the cross as a struggle to preserve Western Chistendom from atheistic Bolshevism in sinister alliance with Asiatic barbarism. They were particularly offended by the pedantic exactitude with which the Germans set out to total up and present their bill for a half billion *Reichsmark* even before the graves of the fallen were covered with grass. In Spanish Nationalist perspective, Hitler had actually been participating in a Holy War, not a business enterprise. How, then, after the final victory, won at such terrible cost, could he demand further sacrifice from desolated Spain in the form of monetary compensation, from that very same Spain which had accorded him the extraordinary opportunity to honor the Lord of Hosts on the battlefield."

Detwiler adds that while no responsible Spaniard put it quite so extravagantly many Spaniards "tended to regard themselves not as military rebels or reactionary conspirators, but rather as soldiers of Christ, and as such, they felt more or less the same gratitude for Hitler's and Mussolini's support as the pastor does for the Sunday collection."

Hitler was familiar with that attitude and he resented it. In conversation with Ciano he noted that when the Germans demanded payment of the debt incurred during the Civil War the Spaniards often regarded that as a tactless confusing of economic and idealistic considerations; that they made the Germans feel almost like Jews who want to make business out of the holiest possessions of mankind.

In the last analysis, of course, Franco's attitude toward the war was determined not by any feelings he might have toward Hitler but by his calculation of what was good for Spain. The Hitler-Stalin pact and Hitler's attack on Poland were cruel blows to Franco. Hitler's attack on Russia, in contrast, was an enormous relief; it offered hope of a Communist defeat or, even better, a stalemate which might restore a power balance in Europe that would permit weak countries such as Spain to live in peace. Whatever Franco might say after that he never again had complete confidence in German victory.

Cruelty was one of the charges most frequently leveled against Franco, and it was contrasted to the piety that he often seemed to exhibit. Indeed Nationalist reprisals during the Civil War became a source of so much public comment that, in 1938, Stohrer, then Nazi Germany's representative to the rebel Nationalist regime, was impelled to ask Jordana, Franco's foreign minister at the time, if it were true that the regime had a list of two million "Reds" who were to be punished for crimes committed. He reported that Jordana was evasive in his reply but acknowledged that there was a long list of "Reds" who would have to be punished.

The figure Stohrer mentioned was a gross exaggeration, but there is no doubt that the Nationalist forces, with Franco's knowledge, engaged in severe, sometimes savage, reprisals against Republicans in areas they conquered, and it was general knowledge that imprisonments and executions continued during the three years I served in Spain. But the provocations were great, even in Spanish terms, indeed so great as to be beyond the comprehension of most Americans.

As has been noted, the Republic was inaugurated amid an

orgy of church burnings and assassinations of Catholic clergy and their followers, and of monarchists and conservatives in general. The election of a Popular Front, in 1936, was followed by another plague of church burnings and assassinations. It is little wonder that in July, 1936, nearly all Spain's bishops signed a collective letter supporting the Nationalist cause, and that the Vatican was among the first to name a representative to Franco's rebel government.

Herbert L. Matthews, who covered the Civil War for the *New York Times* and was an avid supporter of the Republic, has nevertheless described Franco more accurately than anyone else I know. Speaking of the Civil War Franco, he tells us that it was silly to think of him as a tool of the Germans and Italians, that Franco was never anybody's tool. It was equally foolish, he says, to think of him as the servant of forces such as the Church, the Army, the Falange, or big business; Franco was nobody's servant. Matthews describes Franco as a man of oriental patience and iron self-control. He says it was nothing for him to make up his mind to a policy and keep it to himself for a year or two; that it was not a matter of mental or physical laziness, or indecision or weakness, but of patience, the ability to wait, to let time work, to dominate himself, to exercise will-power. Within natural human limitations one could say that Franco had no nerves, he tells us; that while the normal Spaniard is the most undisciplined of men, Franco was as disciplined as a Prussian general; that he had the classic military characteristics raised to an almost inhuman degree.

Was there an alternative to the Franco whom Matthews describes? Spain is a land of extremes. There is a middle sector, politically speaking, but it is not dominant. At least it was not dominant during Franco's time. If Spain was to maintain its independence of World War II, and contribute to the defeat of Nazism, its government had to be authoritarian, and it had to be on the right. No other government could have held Hitler off. A leftist or centrist Spain would have become a captured nation, an Axis puppet, possibly a part of a greater Reich. And in practice Spain's leader had to be Franco, who had no rival among military men. Those who wished that Franco were more liberal were wishing that there were no

Franco, and such persons were wishing against their own interest and, paradoxically, against the interest of freedom in the world.

Once every few months for more than fifteen years, it seems to me now, the *New York Times* had an article by its Madrid correspondent, whoever he might be, concerning Franco's attitude toward the monarchy. Those reports differed little from the reports the American embassy was writing in the early 1940s. There was a consistency in Franco's attitude from the beginning. It was the monarchy's flag that replaced the flag of the Republic. Franco was moving toward restoration of the monarchy, but at a snail's pace, and I do not doubt that he considered that pace to be the most helpful one from the viewpoint of Spain's future stability. As the end of his regime approached he probably wished he could govern Spain another twenty or thirty years, not only because he enjoyed the experience but because he believed that in twenty or thirty additional years Spain would be better prepared to give the monarchy a trial. If he believed that he was probably wrong, but it was probably fortunate for Spain that he lived and governed as long as he did.

Under Franco, the dictator, Spain evolved from a fractured, backward, nineteenth-century nation, tied to the Axis by history and to political reaction by instinct and fear, to one that was united at least in its desire to enter the twentieth century; a nation that pursued, compared to what preceded, liberal trade policies; was on its way to conducting free elections; and, with its network of American bases, was one of the free world's military bastions.

In April, 1961, some seventeen years after I had left Spain, I led a National War College study group to the country and talked to Franco in Madrid. He was a wrinkled counterpart of his old self, dim of eye and soft and slow of speech. His manner was more benign than it had been but just as assured. Franco had grown old but Spain was a younger Spain, dynamic, relatively prosperous, growing in confidence. The old pre–Civil War Spain was more romantic, at least in the eyes of foreigners who did not know it well, but the new Spain, and what it promised, was better for Spaniards.

3 BEIGBEDER

Two developments contributed decisively to Nationalist success in the Civil War. One was massive German and Italian aid; the other was Spanish Morocco's prompt and even enthusiastic support of the rebellion. Colonel Juan Beigbeder Atienza, a subordinate of Franco's during Moroccan War days, played a prominent role in both of them.

On July 22, 1936, four days after the rebellion had broken out prematurely in Melilla, the German consul in Tetuán sent the following telegram to his Foreign Office for relay to General Kühlental, a friend of Beigbeder's dating from the latter's long service as military attaché in Berlin. "General Franco and Lieutenant Colonel Beigbeder send greetings to their friend, the Honorable General Kühlental, inform him of the new Nationalist Spanish Government, and request that he send them ten troop-transport planes with maximum seating capacity through private German firms.

"Transfer by air with German crews to any airfield in Spanish Morocco. The contract will be signed afterwards."

It was Franco's first request for aid from Nazi Germany, and Hitler responded to it promptly and favorably.

(Among the spectators who witnessed his arrival in Tetuán from the Canary Islands, Franco spotted Johannes Bernhardt, a German businessman and local Nazi functionary whom he knew well. Franco arranged for a Spanish Air Force officer to fly Bernhardt to Berlin in order to reinforce his request for planes. Bernhardt was to play an important role in economic relations between Nationalist Spain and Germany.)

Beigbeder, a charismatic Arab-speaking officer with a deep interest in Islam, had already played an active role in the Melilla uprising. He had told the *Jalifa* and the *Gran Visir* of Tetuán what was afoot, and had obtained their support. He had taken command of Spain's Department of Native Affairs in Melilla. From there, addressing the 69 tribal chieftains by telephone and radio in their local tongues, making frequent references to the Koran, he had obtained the backing of all of them. The German consul in Tetuán, reporting to Berlin, marveled that even the cities, most of whose Arabs were on the leftist side, had been brought over easily.

Beigbeder was soon named secretary general to the high commissioner, and shortly afterward he himself became high commissioner. In that post he had the leading role in assuring that Morocco would remain on the Nationalist side. He built and repaired schools and mosques. He made Arabic the sole language of the schools, and arranged for the curricula to be "Arabized." He subsidized trips to Mecca. And he did many other things to satisfy Moroccans' needs and desires. He also fostered dissension among leaders and stamped out trade unions; nevertheless his popularity remained high. By 1939 some 70,000 mercenaries had gone to Spain, this despite the fact that Franco was professing to lead a Christian crusade. One out of every ten or eleven Nationalist soldiers was Moroccan, and Moroccans proved to be the Nationalists' fiercest fighters, always in the vanguard and always reliable. Chief of State Francisco Franco selected Moroccan cavalrymen to be his bodyguard.

In August, 1939, Beigbeder was named foreign minister. In an emotional send-off by Moroccans, Beigbeder was acclaimed "a beloved brother, and on many occasions a father, whose

positive protection has not been lacking for an instant."
Among others seeing him off was the *Jalifa* Muley el Hasan
himself. Beigbeder responded to the ovation by shouting,
"Viva Muley el Hasan; Viva Franco." He had been careful to
mention the *Jalifa* first.

Serrano has given us his version of how Beigbeder's appointment as foreign minister came about. He says that
Franco had often spoken to him about Beigbeder and his good
work as high commissioner in Morocco. Serrano, himself,
during a trip he made to the area, had been impressed not
only by Beigbeder's work with the Moroccans but also by the
manner in which he had fostered support for the Falange
among the Spaniards. Upon his return to Madrid, aware that
there was some pressure to replace Count Jordana, who was
then in his first term as foreign minister, Serrano said to
Franco, "Why don't you name Beigbeder foreign minister?
That would be a great move. A military man of prestige, a
high commissioner, and besides a fervent Falangist. He'd be
the ideal man. He'd have support all around."

Franco's response was, "But don't you know that Juan Beigbeder, in addition to all you have said, is also crazy?" "Why
do you say that?" a startled Serrano asked. "Well look,"
Franco replied, "when we were in Africa, every now and then
Beigbeder would disappear from circulation, and we would
ask, 'What's happened to Juanito Beigbeder?' Some times it
would turn out that he had been in a brothel; other times he
had been engaged in spiritual exercises with the Franciscans."

Franco nevertheless accepted Serrano's suggestion. Beigbeder, idiosyncrasies and all, became foreign minister and remained foreign minister during fifteen critical months in the
history of Spain, of Europe, and of the world.

Although Beigbeder had become foreign minister at Serrano's recommendation, as cabinet officers the two never got
along. Their personalities, their ideas, and eventually their
sympathies clashed. Germany's ambassador Stohrer, who
knew Spaniards well, and reported on them in detail, informed Berlin that socially as well as officially the Beigbeder
and Serrano camps had to be dealt with separately. The two
cabinet officers were rivals more than collaborators.

Beigbeder, like other Spanish foreign ministers of the period, gave first priority to obtaining advantages from both the Axis and Allied sides while conceding no more than was necessary to either. But he also engaged in some bizarre diplomacy aimed at gaining territory in North Africa from a defeated and humiliated France. On June 18, 1940, just five days before the Franco-German armistice was signed, he asked France to deliver over to Spain two provinces of French Morocco, and he suggested to the French ambassador in Madrid that he hurry France's compliance because delay would deprive Spain of what it was seeking. Complying with his request would have greatly worsened France's already deplorable situation vis-à-vis Germany; among other things it would have imperiled the precious economic and military position it still maintained in Africa. Beigbeder knew that, of course, but he apparently saw nothing strange in his request. He argued strenuously that if France was to lose its African empire in any case it were better that Spain rather than France's enemy, Germany, should profit from it.

Nothing came from those efforts by Beigbeder, which approached the irrational, but Spain did have a victory of sorts when it occupied Tangier. The accomplishment was a temporary one, and it was only a small accomplishment while it lasted, but it revived Spain's dream of imperial conquest, and for a while it made Beigbeder himself feel like a conqueror. And it was aimed principally at Italy.

Early in the war Beigbeder was pro-German; later, for whatever reason or reasons, he became pro-British. But he was never pro-Italian, principally because Italy and Spain were rivals in North Africa. Both were alert to the possibility of obtaining territory in that area at France's expense. They already shared with Britain, France, and several other countries responsibility for the administration of Tangier, an International Zone on the Moroccan coast near the entrance to the Straits of Gibraltar and for that reason regarded by the Great Powers as having considerable strategic importance. Geographically, Tangier was a part of Spanish Morocco, and Spain had never ceased to believe that it should also be politically a part of that protectorate. For many Spaniards, and particularly for the "Africans," control of Tangier was almost as emotional an aim as recovery of Gibraltar.

On June 4, 1940, one day before Hitler launched his final offensive against France, Beigbeder outlined to Ambassador Stohrer the territorial rewards Spain would expect to receive in partial compensation for her entry into the war. They included not only all of French Morocco but Tangier as well. Beigbeder noted that recent Italian troop movements had aroused concern in Spain, and that his government would "regret it" if the Italians should install themselves on territory Spain expected to receive. Four days after Mussolini had declared war on Britain and France, Spain occupied Tangier.

Beigbeder had taken care to warn the French ambassador of Spain's intention to occupy the zone. Explaining that there was a great risk that the war might be brought even closer to Spain, he assured the ambassador that the occupation would be temporary and that Spain's official announcement would make clear that it was carried out in order to insure the zone's neutrality. Nevertheless when the announcement was made the Falange-controlled press characterized the occupation as the beginning of a Spanish project to conquer Morocco and as an Allied defeat.

Hitler, on his part, lauded the occupation of Tangier. Following its defeat in World War I Germany had been denied any role in the administration of the zone. Hitler was content that for the time being Tangier should be in Spain's hands. In March, 1941, five months after Serrano had succeeded Beigbeder as foreign minister Germany was permitted to open a consulate in Tangier. It became a valuable espionage and sabotage instrument for the Axis.

From the beginning of World War II both the British and American governments strongly suspected that Spain was permitting Axis submarines to refuel and resupply in its waters, and their suspicions were fully justified. Indeed even before the Civil War had ended and the new war in Europe had not yet begun, Franco, concerned that such a war might cause Germany to withdraw or greatly reduce its military assistance to Nationalist Spain, let Hitler know that in the event of a European conflict Spain would be willing to make such facilities available to it. On September 25, 1938, with war clouds plainly visible over the Continent, a worried Franco complained to the German liaison officer at his headquarters that he knew nothing about Hitler's political and military intentions in the event of a European war. Spain was not a great power, he observed; nevertheless she was in a position to help Germany in one way or another if her help were needed. Franco asked, for example, what Germany intended to do with her fleet, and whether she wished to use Spanish ports for refueling purposes. In Berlin an alert Naval Staff, fully aware of the Peninsula's importance in the event of war, asked the Foreign Office to adopt a positive attitude toward Spain, but German diplomats paid little heed; they had more urgent things to attend to.

Franco was in a perilous situation. If war should break out while German and Italian troops were in Spain, there was not only a grave possibility that crucial German and Italian aid might be interfered with; it also was possible that France and, perhaps Britain as well, would invade the Peninsula, and Spain would find herself directly involved in the war. Hitler, on the other hand, who improvised more than he planned, was in no position to tell Franco anything. On September 27 Franco issued his formal declaration of neutrality; almost immediately afterward, however, Neville Chamberlain, Britain's prime minister, and France's Edouard Daladier, agreed to meet with Hitler at Munich, and for Franco the immediate danger was soon over. But Hitler did not forget Franco's offer to help although at times during World War II it appeared that Franco himself might have forgotten it.

In July, 1939, some three months after the Civil War had ended, Germany's Admiral Canaris, who was to have an extremely important role in relations with Spain, visited General Franco to talk about long-range plans, but Franco now showed little interest in them. German interest continued, however, and two weeks before Hitler's tanks crossed into Poland a special courier carried to Commander Kurt Meyer-Döhner, Germany's naval attaché in Madrid, instructions to prepare plans for resupplying submarines in Spain.

The rationale for obtaining facilities in Spain was simple. If

Germany's submarines could refuel at places closer to the battle zones than Germany they could be spared the time-consuming voyage back to their home bases. With submarines in short supply and at the same time so important to Germany's conduct of the war, that consideration had enormous importance. The most practical device would be to use German tankers that were interned in neutral ports. Spain, including the Canary Islands, was the most promising prospect.

Meyer-Döhner, who spoke fluent Spanish and liked Spain and its people, subsequently had a long discussion with Spain's naval minister, Admiral Salvador Moreno Fernandez. The admiral was sympathetic to Germany's request for cooperation, but said that any arrangement would have to be approved by Foreign Minister Beigbeder. To the gratification of the Germans, Beigbeder immediately agreed to give consideration to their request. He said he would speak to General Franco and would meet with the Germans again soon.

German troops had barely begun to cross into Poland when Meyer-Döhner met with Beigbeder again. After indicating that General Franco was ready to grant Germany's request, Beigbeder suggested not only that a Spanish supply organization be set up but that it should operate under his, Beigbeder's, authority. The personnel might include two Spanish naval officers and Meyer-Döhner himself. An enthusiastic Beigbeder went on to suggest that the group might have a Spanish gunboat or submarine assigned to it for its own use. He also agreed that the German tanker, *Nordatlantik*, then anchored in Vigo harbor, might serve immediately as a source of supply.

Meyer-Döhner promptly informed Berlin of his unexpected success and began to make arrangements for refueling to take place. It turned out, however, that Beigbeder had gone farther than the Germans themselves were willing to go. While Meyer-Döhner was busy carrying out Beigbeder's suggestions he received a cable from Berlin instructing him that neither the Spanish Navy nor the Spanish government should be involved in supplying German vessels, that Spanish neutrality must be fully protected. The supply project, the cable stressed, must be carried out entirely by Germans and behind

the backs of Spanish officials. At that point, too, Franco himself had second thoughts. Citing the close watch the British
were maintaining, he decided that he did not want German
naval units in Spanish harbors, nor did he want the supply
efforts to be discussed further. He indicated that some day he
hoped to be able to accommodate the Germans in the matter,
but that for the moment he wanted all steps toward that end
stopped. The German authorities again instructed Meyer-
Döhner to make his own preparations, using German ships
that were already in Spanish ports. That meant of course that
he would be compelled to work clandestinely, probably in
violation of Spanish law.

While Meyer-Döhner was pondering his problem, aid came
to him from Poland. With the rapid victories of Hitler's
blitzkrieg in that country Franco's position softened. On September 8, while Ambassador Stohrer was talking to Beigbeder
about totally unrelated matters, the latter volunteered the information that Spain was now willing to help Germany to
build up an adquate supply organization. A surprised Stohrer
thanked Beigbeder effusively but noted at the same time that
not all Spanish officials were as prepared to help as Franco
and he appeared to be. Beigbeder promised that Franco would
take care of that, and the following day Admiral Moreno visited Vigo and Ferrol in order to inspect personally the facilities available in those ports. Upon his return he reported to
the German Embassy that preparations for the supply operation in the two ports were in good order. He said the Germans
could go ahead and supply their submarines; he had instructed the Vigo harbormaster to be more cooperative than
he had been.

Meyer-Döhner was of course pleased at this new change in
Spain's attitude, but knowing the vagaries of Spanish politics,
and having in mind Berlin's earlier cautionings, he continued
preparation of his own supply organization outside official
channels. In a short time he had collected some 44,000 tons of
heavy fuel oil. Not all the oil was immediately available but
neither was it all immediately needed.

Meyer-Döhner continued to have problems with local
Spanish officials, however, and under some pressure from the

Naval Staff in Berlin he persuaded Ambassador Stohrer to speak to Beigbeder again. The Naval Staff no longer had qualms about involving the Spanish officials in the operation. Beigbeder immediately agreed to help, and even suggested that the refueling process begin immediately; Franco later concurred. Meanwhile Meyer-Döhner had acquired material for seven supply units; two on the Biscayan coast, one on the Atlantic coast, two on the Canary Islands, and two in southern Spain. The operation was given the code name Moro.

On January 24, 1940, Meyer-Döhner informed Beigbeder that the first refueling operation would take place in Cadiz, utilizing the German vessel *Thalia*, and Beigbeder expressed his pleasure. At 8:00 P.M. on January 30, the U-25 entered the port of Cadiz, with decks awash, in covering darkness. By 2:00 A.M. the refueling and resupplying was accomplished and the U-25 had departed without having been detected. Moro had had a successful baptism.

By July, 1941, the British undoubtedly knew of the refuelings, but naval leaders in Berlin were eager for more killings. In October, shortly after the U-564 and the U-204 had refueled in Cadiz, the British sent up star-shells that illuminated a large part of the harbor. On December 18, 1941, the British destroyers *Blankney* and *Stanley* caught the U-343 on the surface. The next day the sloop *Stark* destroyed the U-574. Prisoners from the two submarines revealed that their vessels had refueled in Vigo.

After Britain had lodged a strong protest and threatened to curtail oil shipments to Spain, the Spaniards placed guards on the supply ship in Vigo and asked Meyer-Döhner to halt his supply activities. They indicated that they might permit a resumption in the future if the British should relax their vigilance. Subsequently they denied permission for a renewal of such activities.

There were twenty-four recorded refuelings of German submarines in Spanish ports between January 30, 1940, and September 5, 1942. In addition there was one probable loading. There were also five loadings of Italian submarines. The resulting gain in the effectiveness of the submarine fleet was great. Beigbeder was a principal actor in arranging those re-

loadings. Great Britain was the direct loser. Beigbeder was
still foreign minister when Sir Samuel Hoare arrived in Madrid as ambassador of a beleaguered Britain on June 1, 1940.
Four of the landings occurred between that date and October
17, when Beigbeder was replaced by Serrano. But by that time
"pro-German" Beigbeder had switched to the British side.

American Ambassador Alexander Weddell, in informing
Washington of Beigbeder's appointment as foreign minister,
referred approvingly to his powerful personality and energetic
spirit. The Portuguese ambassador, who knew Spain better
than any other foreign representative did, was struck with
Beigbeder's intelligence and friendliness. But Serrano, who
knew him better than the diplomats did (although he was less
objective than they), noted, in retrospect, that Beigbeder was
"a strange and unique person, cultured beyond the ordinary,
capable of a thousand follies, a passionate Germanophile in
the early days of the World War, and later Anglophile due to
the seduction of Sir Samuel Hoare and one of Hoare's staff."
General Francisco Salgado, a cousin of Franco's who served
the latter as secretary for many years, suggests that the staff
member was a woman, and that it was she, rather than Sir
Samuel Hoare, who converted Beigbeder to the Allied cause.
Beigbeder was undoubtedly all or most of the things he was
charged with being. He was, well, Beigbeder and even those
who knew him intimately were not sure they understood
him.

Following the fall of France, Spain's leaders moved quickly
to adjust their policies to the new situation. Franco, Beigbeder, and other military leaders, and Serrano also of course,
now were convinced that, like it or not, Spain's future, and
even their own futures, would depend to a considerable degree
on Hitler's plans and wishes. By the autumn of 1940, however, when it was apparent that England was not about to
surrender, they decided that the war would be longer than
they had estimated a few weeks earlier. Nevertheless most of
them were still confident that Germany would win. Beigbeder
did not go along. He professed to believe not only that the war
would be longer, but that it would be much longer. And he
went further than that; he maintained that there also was an

excellent possibility that the United States would enter the war on Britain's side, and that ultimately Germany would be defeated.

Beginning with Franco and Serrano, most Spanish observers saw Britain's flight from the continent at Dunkirk not only as disgraceful but also as a sign that its defeat was imminent. Beigbeder, in contrast, noted that Britain had rescued some 400,000 Allied soldiers to fight another day, that it retained the support of a worldwide empire rich in natural resources, that its powerful navy was intact, and that British morale was high. To Ambassador Hoare he said, "The British bull has not yet come into the arena. Will it fight? And if so, how will it fight? No one can say that it is dead until the *corrida* is over."

Much to Hoare's surprise he and Beigbeder immediately struck up a close friendship. Hoare was fascinated by the mixture of Latin and Arab manifested in the man, by the fact that, in the middle of a political discussion he could, for example, burst forth in an Arabic chant from the Koran, a copy of which he kept in his office. North Africans sometimes refer to Spaniards as "Moors who wear hats." Beigbeder fitted that description. But his strange ways only added to the fascination he held for Hoare, the cold, calculating, deliberate Englishman who, it developed, was quite as capable of emotion as Beigbeder was. The two men understood each other from the beginning and both despised German tyranny and the idea of a police state.

So Beigbeder, who had helped to obtain Hitler's support of the Nationalist revolution, who had arranged for the refueling and resupplying of Axis submarines which were even then taking place in Spain, who, at the very time he was assuring Hoare of his devotion to the Allied cause was telling the German ambassador that Spain was prepared, under certain conditions, to enter the war on the Axis side, became Hoare's intimate friend and, in Hoare's view, his close collaborator.

Collaboration between the two officials, to the extent it existed, was close, but it also was short-lived. On October 15, 1940, Beigbeder had a long and, he professed to believe, a very satisfactory conversation with Franco. Twelve hours later he learned from a single paragraph in the controlled press that

Serrano had replaced him as foreign minister. Beigbeder said he was surprised at his dismissal, yet it had been predicted for months. Doussinague tells us that as early as May Beigbeder himself had told him that Germany's military victories had made a change of foreign ministers necessary, that he, Beigbeder, would have to be replaced by someone more pleasing to Berlin. When, in September, Franco sent Interior Minister Serrano rather than Foreign Minister Beigbeder to talk to Hitler it was generally assumed in Madrid that Serrano would soon be named foreign minister.

Two years later, when the tide of battle had turned in favor of the Allies, Serrano himself would be as indignant at his dismissal as Beigbeder professed to be at his.

During my three years in Spain I got to know Serrano and Jordana well, but I knew Beigbeder only casually. When I arrived in Madrid in June, 1941, he had been out of office nearly a year, and the possibility that he would one day return to active service in the Franco government was remote. Nevertheless on August 11, 1942, I met with him at his request. Beigbeder told me, among other things, that the Germans still maintained contact with him; that his relations with Spain's Ambassador Cárdenas in Washington, whom he said he had once tried to have fired, were bad; and that he, Beigbeder, had survived two attempts to assassinate him. He said also that Franco still believed implicitly in German victory; that although Franco detested the Nazis he courted their favor in the hope he would be permitted to remain chief of state. More to the point, Beigbeder said that the government, for reasons he did not reveal, was trying to exile him to the Americas, and that to avoid exile he would like the embassy to deny him a visa.

Later the embassy informed Washington that Beigbeder had postponed his departure for the United States until September 15. The minister of war, Beigbeder claimed, was willing to appoint him a one-man mission to certain American governments. He expected also that Ambassador Cárdenas would try to prevent his entry into the United States. The embassy, in its telegram, noted that there there was a good chance that Beigbeder would never reach the United States; that he probably wanted to remain in Spain in the event of political change.

Five full months later, in a note to Caroll who was back in Pawtucket with the children, I said, "I gave a dinner for Beigbeder last week and had the Hayeses. Beigbeder is supposed to be going to Washington but keeps putting it off." I don't recall all the circumstances of that dinner but it is evident that Hayes, who had been ambassador since May, 1942, wanted some courtesy shown to Beigbeder but that he did not want to associate himself too closely with him. He must have asked me to give the dinner. I don't recall that Beigbeder ever reached the United States. If he did, the trip had no meaning. Beigbeder's brilliant and erratic official career had already ended.

4 SERRANO

Ramón Serrano Suñer made an extremely important contribution to defeating Germany's purposes in Spain, but in doing so he acquired a reputation as a Nazi appeaser.

Serrano achieved high position in the Nationalist government in part because he was Franco's brother-in-law. More accurately, he and Franco were married to sisters. The Spanish name for brother-in-law is *cuñado*. Franco had the military rank of *Generalísimo*. Serrano became popularly known as the *Cuñadísimo*. The name indicated the power Spaniards thought he had and where it came from.

A prominent lawyer from Saragossa, Jesuit-educated and with a flair for politics, Serrano was in many ways the opposite of the stolid Franco. Slender, blue-eyed, prematurely gray and emotional, prior to the Civil War he had been a member of Gil Robles' CEDA, and head of *Juventud de Acción Popular* (JAP), its youth movement, whose members wore green shirts and used a modified fascist salute. The pre–Civil War Falangists ridiculed JAP as too tepid to be useful. The Falange's founder, José Antonio Primo de Rivera, although he was Serrano's friend, said of JAP, "This is the only case in which the debris of a party has been in its youth."

Tepid or not, for Serrano JAP was a step in the direction of authoritarianism. Shortly after the Civil War began he permitted some JAP members to switch their allegiance to the Falange where they were incorporated into its militia. Soon JAP members and other Catholic youth were joining the Falange in droves. Serrano himself never became a member of the original Falange however.

Before Serrano left Madrid for his historic talks with Hitler in September, 1940, Ambassador Stohrer supplied Berlin with a sketch of him. He said:

". . .Serrano Suñer is today undoubtedly the most influential and also the most important Spanish politician. He is, however, just as surely the man with the most enemies in Spain, especially among the military. . . .

"Serrano Suñer's attitude toward us has always been friendly. That his friendship for Germany, however, has come about more by way of the Axis, that is, by way of Italy, which he knew from his youth and esteemed very highly, I have stressed. . . . In his inmost heart, however, Serrano Suñer, who is a strict, not to say intolerant Catholic, may still have certain reservations with regard to the Third Reich. That he nevertheless believes in and hopes for a German victory I have stressed at various times. His hatred of England is our absolute guarantee of this."

Stohrer was correct in saying that Serrano believed in German victory, as indeed nearly all Spaniards, and nearly all Europeans, did in the early 1940s. But seventeen months earlier, while the Civil War was still going on, Stohrer had reported, "Although, or perhaps precisely because, [Serrano] always emphasizes his great sympathy for Germany in his meetings with me and tries to prove it by examples, I am inclined to believe, as I always have, that he is no friend of ours." Serrano never was as easy to judge as most people thought he was. Stohrer was also correct in saying that Serrano was the man with the most enemies in Spain. The military resented Serrano because of the influence he had, or they

feared he had, over Franco. The masses resented him because
he was the government's most visible and most articulate
proponent of close relations with Germany. Both military and
civilians resented him because of his role as active leader of
the Falange.

As interior minister, Serrano had been responsible for seeing to it that the Spanish press published nothing that the
Germans disliked. Serrano maintained that when he became
foreign minister others took over that disagreeable chore, but
in the minds of many Spaniards, and most foreign diplomats
as well, Serrano was still responsible for it, to some degree at
least.

In short, Serrano was so unpopular that Franco, in compari-
son, was popular even among those who disliked his government, and I sometimes wondered whether that was not one of
the reasons Franco kept him on. And to cap it all, Serrano was
not a very likable politician. In private life he could be a
charmer; as a politician and a diplomat he could be opinion-
ated, intolerant, and abrasive. And many who agreed that circumstances required Spain to cozy up to Nazi Germany
thought that Serrano carried coziness too far.

Serrano had hitched his wagon to the German star because
he believed in German victory and wanted Spain to be in a
position to profit by it, or at least not to lose needlessly as a
result of it. Even today he has no apologies for his pro-Germanism. He has said that he and his friends were quite aware that
Germany was planning to create a New Order, a new empire
that is, and they thought that Spain could play a more important role in that empire than the one to which it had been
reduced under French-British hegemony—that of a poor relation. Serrano himself thought that Spain might become the
most important province in the new German empire, as it was
during the period of the Roman Empire. But there was also
another reason for Serrano's pro-Germanism. His two brothers
had been killed during the Civil War—assassinated by Communists, Serrano has maintained—and the Germans and the
Italians had helped to defeat the Communist threat in Spain.
According to Hoare, Serrano attributed his brothers' deaths to
the refusal of the British Embassy to give them refuge, but

Hoare said that although he took great pains to sift that allegation he found no evidence to substantiate it.

Serrano persisted in his pro-Germanism even after the tide of battle had turned against the Axis. Like O'Henry's beachcomber who refused to drink with the man he was planning to blackmail, Serrano, out of a perhaps perverse sense of honor, would not turn against the side he had long been publicly supporting merely because circumstances had changed. Concerning Hitler and Mussolini, in an astounding admission, he said: "I would venture to say that [they] were great men, men who believed in something great and wished it, men who wanted above all to make their fatherlands great. The world, which today has a jealous hatred of strong men and zealously elects mediocrities—it is the law of fatigue—will undoubtedly admire them again."

In contrast, Serrano was repelled by many Nazi leaders he met. Goebbels' grand palace, and the special train which Goering was said to have given to his wife, convinced him that those leaders were venal and drunk with power. He especially detested his opposite number, Joachim von Ribbentrop. That former champagne salesman had most of the qualities that Serrano, the middle-class Spanish lawyer, depised. Serrano refrained from criticizing the Axis leaders for their ideologies or their politics. His complaints had to do with their personalities and their attitudes toward the Spanish government.

Serrano's dislike of Ribbentrop was so intense that he had to search for words to express it. He has told us that Ribbentrop was blown up with affectations, that even his facial expressions were put on for effect. The stiffness he exhibited was not the spontaneous stiffness of the Prussian, Serrano said; it was cultivated and abrasive. Serrano could not understand how Ribbentrop had ever got anywhere in politics. In short, Serrano hated Ribbentrop's guts, and Ribbentrop returned the feeling with enthusiasm. He once referred to Serrano as a "Jesuit swine."

Serrano related that during his visit to Berlin, in the middle of a reception in Serrano's honor, Ribbentrop had the bad taste to tell him that Spain's equivocal position was displeasing to the Fuehrer. He went so far as to charge that "a certain

Spanish minister" (Beigbeder, who was then foreign minister, he clearly meant) was taking his orders from England. When Serrano retorted that Spanish ministers served only the national interest Ribbentrop retreated somewhat, but he still maintained that there was a lack of clarity in Spain's foreign policy.

Berlin charged Serrano with being a "verbalist Germanophile." He was more than that, of course. Nevertheless there was substance in the charge. Serrano, himself, has reminded us that while all his speeches were Germanophile not one was interventionist, and it was his resistance to Hitler's war plans that disillusioned Hitler with him. Serrano's attachments to Germany certainly had their limitations, and those limitations, as well as the attachments themselves, proved to be important to Allied victory. Serrano might also have reminded us that every time he made a pro-German speech, Spaniards who disliked him, most Spaniards that is, became even more determined to keep out of the war. But he has chosen not to mention that.

All Franco's aides supported his wartime policies. What distinguished Serrano was the intensity of his public identification with the Axis cause. Demetrio Carceller, minister of industry and commerce and, like Serrano, a member of the Falange's hierarchy, engaged in quite a different tactic.

Like many other Spanish lawyers, Serrano considered himself an intellectual. Authoritarian-minded, he visualized a Spain in which elites like himself would lead the masses to a better life. He disliked Englishmen, Frenchmen, and foreigners in general except Italians. Carceller, in contrast, was a self-made businessman with a businessman's common sense. He was without pretense, and he knew the United States and was at ease with Americans and Englishmen. He undoubtedly thought that there was no present alternative to authoritarian government in Spain, but he wished that were not true, and he hoped it would change.

Both Serrano and Carceller were deceivers, but Carceller was franker in his deceptions—franker to the other side that is. When I called on him shortly after my arrival in Madrid and complained about Spain's excessive friendliness toward

Germany, he said that Franco would be doing the democracies the greatest possible disservice if he took any other attitude. He would be inciting the Germans to come into Spain, and the Spaniards would be unable to resist.

Carceller said that a more intelligent American policy would be to cooperate with Spain in organizing a system of smuggling imported commodities into Germany. He suggested, for example, that the democracies should make a thousand tons of coffee available to Spain. Then the Spanish government, in a spontaneous gesture of cooperation, would make five hundred tons available to the Germans. Five hundred tons of coffee were worth very little, he said, but the gesture would give the Germans the impression that Spain was sincerely cooperative with them, and they would be less tempted to disturb the status quo. "There is not an intelligent man in the German Embassy, and I can fool them all," he said. "In fact I'm fooling them today."

A few weeks later Carceller was in Berlin, telling the Germans how he could fool the Americans and the British. He explained that Spain was going to have to patch up its relations with the United States. She would probably have to cut down press and radio attacks against the United States and Britain, for example. But such things should not disturb the Germans, because they would enable Spain to add to its war-making capacity. Besides, he said, he could pass some of the materials on to Germany. This time he mentioned not coffee but tin. Carceller served Franco well. He was popular with Allied representatives, and he got along well with the Germans too. Whether he was as useful to the Allied cause as Serrano was is questionable however.

The Franco government freely acknowledged, and sometimes even boasted, that its nonbelligerency was intended to favor the Axis, and for some time it did favor the Axis, often in ways that the government denied. In his books Serrano generally is silent concerning clandestine aid to the Axis, and as foreign minister he sometimes denied that such aid was being extended. (Neither Serrano, Hoare, nor Hayes related in their respective books the clandestine activities of their respective governments, and in that sense all three accounts are

one-sided.) In February, 1942, after Allied newspapers had reported that German submarines operating in the West Indies
had refueled at a German base in the Canary Islands, Serrano,
as foreign minister, issued a statement which he prepared in
his own handwriting, denying the charge.

"In none of Spain's ports are there bases or installations of
any belligerent power, or armed forces that are not exclusively Spanish," Serrano said. He then pointed out that German submarines had no need to use Spanish ports because
they now had French ports at their disposal. Serrano was
nearly correct about that. German submarines had indeed
been refueling and resupplying in Spanish ports, but following
Serrano's statement they abandoned the practice at Spain's
insistence.

Nevertheless Serrano, himself, had once authorized the
refueling not of Germany's submarines but of its destroyers.
In a telegram to Berlin dated December 5, 1940, while Hitler
was pressing Franco to join him in an attack on Gibraltar,
Stohrer reported: "In reply to proposal made by Embassy as
instructed, Foreign Minister has now informed that Spanish
Government has agreed to the placing in readiness of German
tankers in out-of-the-way bays of the Spanish coast for the
supplying of German destroyers with fuel. Foreign Minister
vigorously requested observing greatest caution in carrying
out measures." The foreign minister was Serrano.

Serrano had a "thing" about Portugal, in part because of its
centuries-old alliance with the Britain he hated, and he sometimes shared his thoughts with the Germans. When he was
trying to convince Ribbentrop that for security reasons alone
Spain had to be given all of Morocco, he noted that in addition to her 600 kilometer border with France and her 300
kilometer border with French Morocco, Spain's 1,200 kilometer border with Portugal had at times been equivalent to a
border with England. Besides, he added, Portugal did not believe in German victory. He said further that when one
looked at the map of Europe he could not avoid the conclusion that geographically speaking Portugal had no right to
exist, only a moral right, and he obviously gave little importance to that. He expressed confidence that Germany and

Spain, working together, could easily influence Portugal. He had explained to the Portuguese ambassador in Madrid, he said, that Portugal's fear of Germany was justified only to the extent that Portugal let her policy be influenced by England; that if the Portuguese policy were no longer subject to English influence then every reason for fearing Germany would disappear. When Ribbentrop spoke of Spain's ceding one of its Canary Islands for use as a German military base, Serrano suggested that he think in terms of Portugal's Madeira instead.

Serrano maintained that Franco's meeting with Prime Minister Salazar in Seville in February, 1942, had not the slightest importance. He says that Salazar talked to Franco only briefly; that he was much more interested in talking to him, Serrano, who had dealt with Hitler and Mussolini. "What kind of man is Mussolini?" he said Salazar asked him, "and how are his relations with the King?" But José M. Doussinague, the Foreign Office's director general of foreign policy who was there and was a more objective observer than Serrano, has told us that it was Franco (who spoke Gallego dialect which is closer to Portuguese than it is to Spanish) who led the way and did the talking. "I am completely alone," he said Serrano told his subordinates. In Seville Serrano was a foreign minister without a role. Seven months later he was no longer foreign minister.

In Seville the two Iberian dictators, bent on closing ranks before a common danger, understood each other perfectly, but Serrano was not sure he understood either of them. Serrano's statement that the Seville meeting had not the slightest importance does not jibe with the description of the meeting he gave to me upon his return to Madrid, a version which was later confirmed by the Portuguese ambassador to Spain.

Serrano's lack of enthusiasm for closer relations with Portugal fitted into his general effort to placate and even to deceive Germany. At the same time I have little doubt that in some of his dreams of the New Spain which might emerge from the war that Germany was going to win, Portugal would be united to Spain, as it had been a mere three hundred years earlier, hardly more than the day before yesterday in a Spaniard's mind. I doubt that Serrano ever thought such a thing would happen, or that he even wanted it to happen, but that probably did not prevent him from dreaming, and Serrano's dreams tended to be grand.

Serrano could dissemble and deceive; he could also be frank when frankness was impolitic and even offensive. What one frequently could not tell was whether his frankness, or appearance of frankness, was itself a means of deceiving, or even which side he was trying to deceive.

Late in January, 1941, Ambassador Weddell took William ("Wild Bill") Donovan, whom President Roosevelt listened to very respectfully and who was to become head of the wartime Office of Strategic Services (OSS), to call on Serrano, and the latter avowed Spain's friendship for Germany and its hostility to Britain and France. "We hope for and believe in the victory of Germany in the present conflict," Serrano said. When Donovan asked him why, he replied that it was out of gratitude for help received during the Civil War and the belief that Spain's natural rights would be safely guarded by Axis victory; that Spain would regain Gibraltar and that its rights in Africa would be recognized.

Serrano has given us a vivid description of his conversation with Donovan. He said, in liberal translation: "Donovan had come to demand explanations of everything, to censure everything, and to threaten. And I responded in kind. I asked myself, Who does this guy think he is? All of a sudden he shows up here and ticks me off. What are ambassadors for anyway? From the moment he arrived Donovan was offensive. And I was offensive too. When he left I did not accompany him to the door as I usually do with visitors. I don't believe I even shook hands with him." Serrano evidently put "Wild Bill" several notches below Ambassador Faupel on the diplomatic scale. His indignation was not lessened by the conviction he harbored but could not express that by helping to resist Hitler's demand for free passage through Spain to Gibraltar only a few weeks earlier he had performed a priceless service to Great Britain and also to the United States, even though the latter was not yet a belligerent.

I have no doubt that Serrano told Stohrer of his conversation with Colonel Donovan. At the time, a literally starving

Spain was a supplicant for American aid, but it was still not sure that pressure from Hitler to enter the war would subside.

Serrano was a better diplomat than his detractors gave him credit for being. His rudeness was sometimes calculated; it was a part of his diplomacy. With Stohrer he got along very well, and by doing so he furthered Spain's purposes and, on balance, the purposes of the Allied countries too.

Stohrer, a career diplomat, had served in Spain as a junior secretary during World War I; he had succeeded the detested Faupel as ambassador in 1937. He liked Spain, and he knew, and did not hesitate to report to Berlin, that many of the reasons Spain gave for not entering the war when Hitler wanted it to were valid. Stohrer also came to like Serrano, for the latter's consistently pro-Axis attitude for one thing, but he seemed to have liked him as a person too. If Stohrer had represented a democratic country Allied ambassadors would have considered him a very nice guy, and it is clear that Serrano had that view of him.

On December 11, 1940, at the height of the Hitler-Franco confrontation over Gibraltar, Stohrer explored with Berlin possible new action by Germany. He noted that starvation in Spain was "terrible," that people were dying in the streets of starvation. The real reason for Spain's refusal so far to enter the war, he said, was the critical food situation.

Stohrer went on to list and comment on four possible lines of action by Germany.

"1. Eliminate the cause of Spain's attitude. That would entail massive support of Spain's economy.

"2. Carry out the operation against Gibraltar without Spain's cooperation. That would be very difficult.

"3. Suggest to Franco that he protest against Germany's entry into Spain but go along with it. Spain would probably not be able to maintain order in that event.

"4. Conduct a surprise action. That would be extremely dangerous. It would be an action against a friendly people; besides Spain might turn on Germany."

Only the first course, giving greatly increased support to Spain's economy, was practical, Stohrer said. He suggested that negotiations with Spain should be started over again.

Stohrer's attitude did not sit well with either Hitler or Ribbentrop, who were convinced by that time that it was much more than a critical food shortage that was holding Spain back, but it may have influenced them. Hitler, at that point, was tottering on the edge of invading Spain even in the face of Spanish resistance, and he might easily have been moved either way. The fact that Stohrer stood up for Franco's and Serrano's thesis is a tribute to Serrano's diplomacy as well as to Stohrer's courage.

Serrano, in turn, was often open, if not completely so, with Stohrer. On April 20, 1941, only a day after he had an acrimonious meeting with Ambassador Weddell that led to a five-months' estrangement between the two, Serrano told Stohrer a part of what had gone on. Weddell, he said, had asked in a threatening and impudent tone whether rumors regarding imminent accession of Spain to the Tripartite Pact were true. He said that Weddell had also complained about some of the articles in the government-controlled press, and that he, Serrano, had answered him abruptly ("since Serrano, himself, had inspired many of the articles," Stohrer interjected in his report to Berlin). Serrano said that Weddell seemed either to have acted in accordance with very sharp instructions from Washington or to have completely lost self-control. He went on to say that he would have thrown Weddell out, or, better still, slapped his face, if he had not been the representative of a foreign power.

Stohrer was undoubtedly happy to be able to send that report to Berlin because it demonstrated his closeness to Serrano. Serrano, in turn, was clearly anxious for him to send it because it conveyed the impression that Spain did not tolerate any nonsense from the powerful United States. The information was far from compensating for Spain's stubborn refusal to cooperate in an attack against Gibraltar, but it was something—a crumb perhaps, but a crumb that both Serrano and Stohrer were happy to provide.

I strongly suspect that the Serrano-Weddell incident, which I shall refer to in more detail later, and Serrano's action in promptly informing Stohrer of it, were in the end helpful to the Allied cause. The best-laid plans of diplomats do often go awry while apparent failures turn out to be helpful. The Serrano-Weddell incident may well have been an example of the latter.

Serrano's friend, Stohrer, was not the only high German embassy official with a genuine liking for Spain. Stohrer's trusted counselor, Erich Heberlein, like Stohrer a career diplomat, had even closer ties to the country. Ordered back to Berlin when Stohrer eventually was recalled, Heberlein, who was married to an attractive Spanish lady, was later granted permission to return to Spain with his wife for medical treatment and to visit a country home they owned in Toledo, not far from Madrid. After Heberlein had refused orders to return to Germany, two Gestapo agents, on the night of June 17–18, 1944, knocked at his door and carried him and his wife away to Germany where both were interned in a concentration camp. Spain protested those arbitrary acts of the German government but without visible effect. Following the Allied occupation of Germany, the American authorities freed the Heberleins and they returned to Spain to live.

Although Serrano identified himself publicly with the Axis cause, he also maintained close if not always friendly relations with the Allied side through his personal contacts with ambassadors and chargés d'affaires, and especially through the contacts that career diplomats in the Foreign Office, most of whom were pro-Allied, had with them. In general these were the same career officers who served under foreign ministers Beigbeder and Jordana, and regardless of who headed the Foreign Office they maintained helpful relations with the Allied representatives.

The case of José Pan de Soraluce, a career diplomat who, in effect, "ran" the Foreign Office, is an interesting one. Pan was of the type of pure Spaniard than whom there is no purer. Serrano tells us that one of the first things he planned to do when he became foreign minister was to fire Pan (probably because of Pan's known pro-Allied leanings). He says that minutes after his arrival at the Foreign Office he asked the chief of protocol to bring him the person who knew most about what was going on. The chief of protocol brought him Pan de Soraluce, and Pan soon became Serrano's principal adviser.

Serrano has said he developed a special liking for Pan. He has told us that, after he had had a number of discussions with him, Pan told him he wanted Serrano to know something. "While I understand the reasons for your foreign policy," Pan said, "I believe it is fair for you to know that I am an Anglophile." "That's just fine," Serrano says he told Pan, "because my relations with the British and American embassies are bad, and I shall be happy if so far as possible you will conduct those relations." "There is another thing I should like you to know," Pan then said, "I am a liberal and a democrat." Serrano said he replied, "Well look, that doesn't matter to me. You are loyal, and that is all that matters." Pan was my principal contact in the Foreign Office during the three years I served in Spain. There were few subjects involving relations between Spain and the United States that we did not discuss. At no time was I less than candid with Pan, nor was he ever less than helpful to me.

Pan's attitude required great courage, a kind of courage that diplomats in happier countries than Spain are seldom called upon to show. I don't have the slightest doubt that Pan would have given his life joyously if that would help to make Spain free and democratic. The fact that pro-Axis Serrano was foreign minister much of the time I was in Spain had no effect on Pan's attitude toward me or toward the United States. It was another example of Spain's balancing act. Serrano's relations with Allied ambassadors, however, were often less pleasant than my relations with Pan.

Serrano was a principal architect of Nationalist Spain. He had been a leader in converting what was in effect a failed coup d'etat into a nationalist state that probably suited Spain's immediate requirements better than any other that might have been devised. He had fashioned a "totalitarian" state that was more authoritarian than totalitarian, a fascist state in which the fascists had no more power than Franco permitted them to have, a state that was pro-German while it helped to frustrate Germany's ambitions. And he had done all that while not only Spain but all Europe was in mortal danger from German aggression.

With such a background of achievement, and given his natural egotism, Serrano was not overimpressed by the world-famous statesman Sir Samuel Hoare, who seemed to have filled most of the highest offices in the government of Great Britain but who necessarily had an incomplete view of what was going on in Spain, or the United States ambassadors, career diplomat Alexander Weddell and historian Carlton J. H. Hayes. Compared to himself he undoubtedly considered the ambassadors to be minor participants in the fearful contest that was going on in Europe, one in which he was playing a direct and, he might have considered with some justice, a crucial role. All the Allied ambassadors were convinced that Spain, if it were to serve Allied purposes, had to assume an overt attitude of friendship toward Hitler's Germany, but all of them resented Serrano, who pursued that attitude with consummate success. The irony of that did not escape Serrano.

Nor did it escape Serrano that Turkey, which had signed mutual assistance agreements with Britain and France in 1939, has also signed a non-aggression pact with Germany only four days before that country invaded Russia, and that it continued to supply badly needed chrome to Germany throughout the war. Serrano knew also that Sweden had permitted the passage of an entire armed division of German troops from occupied Norway to Finland following the outbreak of the Russo-German war, and was also supporting the German economy in many ways. There were reasons, good reasons no doubt, for those actions of the two countries, but there were good reasons for Spain's actions, too, Serrano thought, although one would not have guessed that from the attitude toward Spain of many Allied officials.

When Weddell left Spain and I remained as chargé d'affaires, Serrano showed me considerable deference, possibly in order to make up for his estrangement from Weddell. He had Caroll and me to dinner at his home, a courtesy he never showed to a British or American ambassador, and to the theatre as well. He could not have been more genial.

I never hesitated to raise subjects that I knew were disagreeable to Serrano, and he never failed to respond courteously. On one occasion when I called on him to protest against a pro-Axis stand that Spain had taken, Serrano listened to me with some impatience and asked, "Would it be helpful to the United States if Spain, at this moment in history, should begin to make faces at Germany?" I thought the question was an excellent one, and I admired Serrano for asking it. I agreed that it would do us no good. I could have added that it might do the Allies a good deal of harm. What I did not know then, of course, was that shortly before the Serrano-Weddell quarrel—which had brought me from Havana to Madrid—Spain, by refusing to enter the war at that time, or to permit the passage of German troops through Spain, had not made faces at Germany; it had spit in Germany's face.

On a number of occasions Serrano told me truthfully, in response to my questions, things that were important to the United States. I knew of course that he was quite capable of deceiving me. I knew also that as time went on the need for deceiving either Americans or Germans was diminishing. Spain was increasingly able to stand on its own two feet, precariously it is true, without leaning too far toward either side. Our policy was helping it to do that.

Following the Franco-Salazar meeting in Seville there was much press speculation concerning its content. When I failed to inform a deeply worried Washington promptly concerning the substance of the meeting I received a rather peremptory telegram from the State Department instructing me to report on the subject. No report had been made public, and neither Franco nor Serrano had yet returned to Madrid. I asked Sir Samuel Hoare if he knew what had taken place in Seville and he said he did not. I tried in other ways to learn what had gone on but without success.

When Serrano returned to Madrid I called on him and asked him if he could fill me in on the content of the meeting. He was quite ready to talk. He told me that the meeting had been held because of rumors that the United States was planning a military attempt against the Azores (if the rumors had referred to the Canaries rather than the Azores they would have been close to the truth). He said that Salazar did not believe the rumors but had nevertheless assured Franco that Portugal would defend against any invader. Salazar was apprehensive about a possible German invasion of Spain, Serrano said, but

Franco had told him that there was no danger of that occur-
ring so long as Spain maintained its policy of friendship toward Germany. I knew, of course, that the content of such a
high-level meeting had to be broader than that, but Serrano
had given me the tone of the meeting, and its meaning.

I told Serrano that I nevertheless regretted that Franco, immediately after his meeting with Salazar, had made a strong
pro-German, anti-Russian speech. Serrano said that Franco was
doing nothing more than reiterating his well-known attitude
toward communism and Communist Russia. Feeling Serrano
out a little more, I suggested that Franco's reference to the
possibility of Germany's being overrun by Russians was not
flattering to the Germans and did not reflect Spain's earlier
opinion that Germany was invincible. Serrano's reply was to
assure me that Spain's policy was directed at staying out of the
war. That was the opposite to what Franco had said in his
speech. It more nearly reflected authentic Spanish policy.

While Franco was alive Serrano was, in general, circum-
spect in what he wrote concerning relations between the two.
In his 1977 memoirs, however, he was more outspoken. Serrano alleged, among other things, that his dismissal, on September 2, 1942, was due to domestic political considerations,
not to a desire on Franco's part to signal a change in the
direction of his foreign policy, as he, Serrano, said some interested parties maintained. That, he claimed, was a cynical in-
vention conceived some years after the event. He pointed out
that when he left office the time for a change in policy had
not yet arrived; that Franco, his ministers, and particularly
his military advisers, all remained convinced of Axis victory.
The turnabout in Africa, Rommel's defeat at El Alamein, had
not yet occurred, he reminded us, nor was the German disaster at Stalingrad foreseen.

Serrano was not completely frank. The version that his
dismissal was due to Franco's desire to signal a change in the
direction of Spain's foreign policy was not conceived years
after the event, as he alleges; it was the version accepted
immediately by British and American diplomats, by Foreign
Office officials in whom we had confidence, and by most
other Spaniards whom we knew. And in supporting his thesis

Serrano, writing many years after the event, described the state of the war, and probably Franco's attitude toward the war, in terms that were far from accurate.

The military situation had changed much more than Serrano indicated. The difficulties of the Russian campaign had turned out to be far beyond Hitler's calculations. The United States, by that time, had been at war some nine months. The battle of Midway, which turned the tide against the reckless Japanese, had already taken place, and the formidable United States economy was now totally geared to war. Britain was no longer the isolated, beleaguered island it had been in 1940. As early as May, 1942, 1,000 British planes had dropped 2,000 tons of bombs on Cologne in a single raid. Also, while it is true that El Alamein had not yet taken place, the British, under Montgomery, were doing well in North Africa. Indeed on the day following Serrano's dismissal Rommel began the withdrawal that ended in Axis defeat at El Alamein.

Serrano pointed out as further evidence that he was not dismissed for his association with the Axis the fact that General Alfred Jodl, one of Hitler's closest military advisers, wrote in his diary that Serrano's resistance had frustrated Germany's plan to bring Spain into the war and take Gibraltar, and that at Nuremberg *Reichsmarschall* Hermann Goering had said that the Gibraltar operation would have permitted Germany to fortify Africa, and in that case the Allies could not have disembarked there.

Serrano could also have cited other examples of German distrust of him. Hitler himself had said that from his first meeting with Serrano he was conscious of a feeling of revulsion in spite of the fact that Ambassador Stohrer, with abysmal ignorance of the truth, had introduced him as the most ardent Germanophile in Spain. But that was not the point. The point was that Serrano had held himself out as a Germanophile and he was generally regarded as a Germanophile. Serrano had the unenviable distinction of being disliked and mistrusted by all sides.

By the summer of 1942 Franco had lost much of the confidence he had once had in Serrano. It is probable, too, that he had never had as much confidence in him as Serrano thought.

Germany's Admiral Canaris, as we have seen, had an extremely important role in Franco's decision to reject Hitler's demand that Spain enter the war in January, 1941, but Serrano did not mention that in his writings. Even today he disclaims any knowledge that Canaris had a role in helping to keep Spain out of the war. On June 18, 1982, after I had reestablished communication with him, Serrano wrote to me: "I know absolutely nothing of the conversation in which Canaris assured General Juan Vigón that Franco could, without reprisal, deny permission for Hitler to send German troops through Spain for the purpose of taking Gibraltar." I cannot, therefore, affirm or deny that it took place.

What Serrano does know, and doesn't mind saying, is that he never liked Canaris. He tells us that he talked to Canaris a few times but never became intimate with him. Canaris, he suggests, never felt at home with persons such as Serrano who had dealt with the greats in political life; that Canaris was more comfortable with "isolated" (inexperienced and unsophisticated he doubtlessly meant) persons such as Franco and Vigón.

Franco could have revealed a quite different Canaris to Serrano (possibly a Canaris who distrusted Serrano), but he apparently chose not to. And there were probably other things that Franco refrained from revealing to him. Franco was closer, in many ways, to General Vigón and a few other military leaders than he ever was to Serrano. The Nationalist government, after all, was a military dictatorship and remained a military dictatorship until Franco died. Serrano's role in that dictatorship was a very important one but Serrano, himself, was increasingly expendable. His departure gave added strength and acceptability to the dictatorship.

What Serrano had particularly in mind when he said that his departure was due to domestic political considerations, however, was Franco's refusal to go along with a plan he had long urged upon him to create a new Spanish state on a juridical basis. Serrano revealed that a number of months before his dismissal, during a meeting with Franco at which he, Serrano, had exhibited his customary frankness, Franco had said, "It seems to me that you have grave doubts concerning my qualities as political leader," and that he, Serrano, had made no reply. He said that shortly afterward he was invited again to El Pardo where a nervous Franco told him that he wanted to speak to him about a very serious matter, and that after much beating around the bush Franco had told him that he was going to replace him. Serrano said he retorted that if that was all Franco had to say he needn't have frightened him so, that Franco knew very well not only that he had offered to resign more than once but also that he had lost faith in his work since he and Franco obviously differed on Serrano's plan to create a juridical state that would meet Spain's future needs. Serrano said he then told Franco that there were a few things he would like to say and that he thought Franco would want to hear, but that Franco had said, "Look, I have General Jordana waiting to see me. He is the one who will replace you." With that Serrano left.

A few days later, in a letter to Franco, a thoroughly alienated Serrano said, "I am sick and tired of the intrigues, the maneuverings, the pettiness, and all the rest that has caused me to know a world I should have preferred not to know." Serrano has told us that shortly after that Franco asked, indirectly, if he would accept the post of president of the Council of State. He has said he turned the suggestion down abruptly.

For three years after that Serrano had almost no contact, even of a social character, with Franco. Following Mussolini's assassination, Hitler's suicide, and Allied victory in Europe, however, Serrano sent Franco a letter urging him to take steps to adjust Spanish politics to the new anti-Nazi, anti-Fascist world that had come into being. Serrano said this about the new Spanish State he had in mind: "The State requires continuity. . . . It is a question of orienting the regime in the only direction possible—toward a national government resting on a popular, broad and apolitical base which will begin at the extreme right and end in the moderate left. All non-Red Spain will be integrated into this National Government composed of eminent men (beginning with the most respectable monarchists, then politicians of exceptional worth such as Cambó, and ending with political-intellectual types such as

Ortega and Marañon) who are known throughout the world and will be able to convince it that a majority of Spanish people, for fear of the communist revolution with which they have had a cruel experience, is united in creating the state while adjusting to world realities."

What Serrano wanted, then, was an "apolitical" state which would be "popular" and "democratic" while at the same time excluding the "Reds" who may still have constituted a majority of the population. That might be described as nice work if you can get it, but trying to get it would have revived all the hostilities, all the divisions, of the Civil War that had ended only six years earlier. The very length of the Franco regime, the healing effect of time itself, together with the dramatic improvement in the Spanish economy which was to take place, were the best possible preparation for an institutional government that might have a chance of surviving. Serrano, more than any other person with the exception of Franco himself, was the architect of the Nationalist State. Happily for Spain, that state never became the New Spanish State that Serrano later envisaged.

Serrano remained bitter about his departure from government. He has related that at his final official interview with Franco, standing, and on the point of departing, he said to the Caudillo, "I wish for your own good and the good of the country, that you would get firmly in your head the idea that the loyalty of a counselor, of a minister, lies in being not an unconditional follower but a loyal critic." He has not told us what Franco said in reply. Like Beigbeder before him Serrano did not receive the usual letter thanking him for services rendered. All he saw was a couple of lines in the *Official Gazette* reporting that Jordana had replaced him as foreign minister.

History may not deal kindly with Serrano. He was not an easy man to like. But he had qualities that helped to save Spain, and possibly the free world, from imminent disaster. Serrano bore the burden of dealing with Hitler and Ribbentrop. Hitler was a fearsome person once he had his mind set on an objective. Neither men nor nations stood in his way. Mussolini was sometimes mute in his presence. But when

Hitler told Serrano, "I have decided to attack Gibraltar," and made it clear that he expected Spain to participate in the attack, Serrano went on the offensive. Furthermore he remained on the offensive, and Hitler never attacked Gibraltar. A man who could stand up to Hilter with such success is not devoid of character nor unworthy of respect.

5 WEDDELL

Alexander Weddell was our first ambassador to Nationalist Spain. Although the United States was officially neutral during nearly all the period of his mission, the danger that Spain, by joining the Axis in its war against Britain, would add immeasurably to the peril in which the free world found itself was never so great. Weddell worked persistently and with some effect to reduce that peril. Even a five-month period during which he was denied contact with Franco, and had no contact with Foreign Minister Serrano, proved to be the prelude to a rapidly improving relationship between Spain and the United States. It might even be said that Weddell won, in part, by losing, not an unprecedented phenomenon in diplomacy, where many things (and some persons) are far from being what they appear to be.

Weddell had been a career Foreign Service officer but ·he was not a career ambassador. He had retired after reaching consul general rank and had later been named ambassador following generous contributions to the Democratic party. A Virginian, son of an Episcopal clergyman, Weddell had mar-

ried a very estimable and wealthy widow from Missouri
whose name, happily, was Virginia. Weddell was a Virginia
gentleman of the old school. Tall, handsome, debonair, he
was mildly fond of bourbon whiskey and happy in fashionable
society. Everyone liked him. Even Serrano says that as interior minister he knew and liked Weddell and Mrs. Weddell.
He refers to them as a very attractive couple, which they
were.

The Madrid embassy's living quarters, and its chancery as
well, were in the rented Palacio Montellano, Madrid's finest
private residence. A Nationalist shell had exploded in the embassy grounds during the Civil War, but it had caused little
damage to the palacio itself. The palacio contained, among
other treasures, six Goyas housed in a hexagonal room built
especially to display them, two additional Goyas, and five
Guardis. The Weddells were quite at home in the Palacio
Montellano.

Back in Richmond, Virginia, the Weddells lived in an historic Tudor mansion that they had brought over, brick by
brick, from England. Equally fascinated by Spanish architec-
ture and art, they made leisurely trips to all parts of Spain,
visiting castles, palaces, monasteries, and other historical and
cultural monuments, and incidentally purchasing choice spec-
imens of antique furniture and Spanish art that they shipped
back to their Tudor home.

Weddell, in a dilettantish way, was a scholar, a student of
history and literature. Politics interested him, but economics
did not. He told me once that if he should learn tomorrow
that Spain exported X thousand tons or barrels of olive oil a
year he would not remember the number the following day,
but that he recalled what the author of *Peck's Bad Boy* had
written on page 64 of that remarkable book although he had
not read it in thirty years. Uninterested in details, he was
fascinated by the big picture. He gave his subordinates great
leeway in carrying on the embassy's business.

Before coming to Spain, Weddell had been ambassador to
Argentina, and following his mission there he had published a
book concerning that country, a kind of tourist guide for elite
travelers. It attracted little attention, but it did reveal what

his subordinates already knew—that Weddell sincerely liked the Latin people he had lived and worked with. When he later concluded that Serrano had dealt harshly with him he felt betrayed.

Mrs. Weddell shared the ambassador's liking for Spaniards, although her attitude was less sentimental than Weddell's. She not only contributed generously to Spanish charities but also conducted a charitable program of her own from her office in the embassy residence. She gave special attention to the *"pobres distinguidos,"* literally the distinguished poor, persons who had once been affluent but whom the Civil War had impoverished. There were many of them, and in some ways their lot was more difficult than that of persons who were long accustomed to poverty. Mrs. Weddell did a great deal to relieve suffering, and she did it quietly. But the Spaniards knew of her work, and many appreciated it.

The Weddells had no children, but Mrs. Weddel had two Pekinese dogs who had the run of the embassy. Unfortunately they were inadequately housebroken, and the results caused some distress to Mrs. Hayes after the Weddells had departed and she had become the embassy's doyenne.

Sir Samuel Hoare, like most others, was fond of Weddell, although he gives him only a few lines in his book. He probably liked him because Weddell looked and acted like an aristocrat, and also because Virginia Weddell was a lady and very rich. He undoubtedly liked him, too, because Weddell supported him consistently, out of conviction, and never threatened his leadership. Weddell played a distinctly secondary role in Madrid, as was natural since the United States was not at war during most of his tour. Nor, despite ringing messages that occasionally came out of Washington, was the United States really committed to Britain's program of trading with Spain in order to keep her out of the war.

Although Weddell's role was secondary to Hoare's, it was in some ways more difficult. Hoare, despite his critics, enjoyed enormous prestige from having occupied some of the highest offices in the British government. He was still a Member of Parliament; he could communicate directly with his foreign secretary when he wished to, and could even get a

message through to Mr. Churchill if he thought that was
needed. Furthermore Spain's ambassador in London, the Duke
of Alba, who through family connections also was a British
peer and himself had easy access to Churchill, knew that—
which meant that Franco knew it too.

More important still, the British government was thoroughly committed to the policy that Hoare was carrying out.
Hoare had no need to be continually justifying his recommen-
dations, no need to reinvent the wheel every day or every
week, as it often seemed Weddell had. Weddell, on his part,
was a respected ambassador but not an influential one. He
could write to the president and the secretary of state, and he
did write to them occasionally, but whether they paid much
attention to what he wrote was another thing. Weddell had to
fight harder than Hoare in order to gain less.

Hoare had one practice that annoyed Weddell. Fiercely sup-
portive of Britain, especially when she was fighting alone,
Weddell kept Hoare informed not only of his actions but also
of his thinking. If Hoare disliked some idea of Weddell's he
might, through the Foreign Office in London and the British
Embassy in Washington, arrange for the State Department to
instruct Weddell along the line of Hoare's thinking rather
than of Weddell's. Even more annoying, the British Embassy
in Washington would sometimes inform Hoare of views
expressed by the State Department before the latter had communicated those views to Weddell, and Hoare, without
informing Weddell, would transmit them to tthe Spanish Foreign Office as coming from the State Department.

Hoare was by no means the only British ambassador to act
as he did. His tactic was much more common in Britain's
agile wartime diplomacy than it was in American diplomacy.
But Weddell thought, with some justice, that Hoare overdid
it.

Except for such instances, Hoare and Weddell got along
well with each other; nevertheless they had little in common.
Hoare was the tight-fisted, calculating banker, in spirit if not
in fact. He gave nothing unless he got something in return.
He cared little for Spaniards unless they were monarchists,
and he didn't like monarchists all the time. He complained

that he was "shocked by the mode of life that gets up very late, never has luncheon before two, nor dinner before ten and sleeps for most of the time between luncheon and dinner." Hoare evidently had difficulty finding Spaniards to do business with, and that annoyed him, as many other things in Spain did. To Hoare, Spaniards were pawns in a very important game that Hoare was determined to win. To Weddell they were also people he was genuinely fond of and sometimes romanticized.

Weddell looked like an aristocrat, and often acted like one, but he never acted superior. He treated his subordinates as equals. He rarely gave me a direct instruction. He told me what his policy was and gave me considerable freedom in carrying it out. Weddell had the same relationship with Ralph Ackerman, our commercial attaché. Our principal weapon in Spain was the economic weapon, and Ackerman handled economic affairs with superb skill. He was an unsung hero of our World War II diplomacy in Spain.

Weddell and Ackerman played golf, as I did, and every other week or so the three of us would go out to the Puerta de Hierro course, where one did well to stay in the fairway because there still might be unexploded Civil War mines in the untended rough, and we hacked away with delight. On the golf course Weddell discarded rank and sometimes decorum. Proud of his slender figure, he would sometimes engage in a hip-slimming exercise that he could practice better in the open than within the embassy residence. As he cavorted down the fairway he appeared less the ambassador than a well-trained hoochy-koochy dancer. Ackerman and I would watch him in stitches. No others observed him. Few Spaniards had time for golf and most of them had no way of getting out to the course.

Mrs. Weddell, relatively self-sufficient in her wealth and her personality, was respected and appreciated. Weddell was held in affection.

In 1939, before the European war had started, Weddell induced the State Department to support Spain's request for an Export-Import Bank credit to make possible the purchase of cotton that the United States had in surplus and Spain desper-

ately needed. Such was the low repute of the Franco government, however, that even that small transaction, when it
took place, was strongly criticized in the United States, and
the State Department played it down as though it were something it should probably apologize for. Following the outbreak
of war, moreover, when the need for mutually advantageous
trade had become vastly greater, American resistance to trade
with Spain actually increased. The belligerent countries, in
contrast, early recognized Spain's economic and military importance and acted accordingly.

By the end of January, 1940, Germany and France had
signed trade agreements with Spain, and in March Britain followed suit. The United States, on its part, was selling the
Spaniards what they could pay for and the British would navicert, but that was far from meeting even their minimum
needs. "Starving Spain" was more than an expression; for mil-
ions of Spaniards it was a reality.

On June 22, shortly after France's Marshal Pétain had sued
for an armistice with Germany, and only days before German
troops reached the Spanish border, Britain, fearful that Hitler
would press through Spain to Gibraltar and North Africa,
asked the United States to restrict the supply of petroleum to
Spain, and the United States hastened to comply. In contrast,
when a desperately weakened Spain did not move quicky to
the Axis side, and Britain, taking heart, asked the United
States, out of its bounty, to send Spain a modest amount of
relief, the United States was slow in responding.

(In the summer of 1941 Caroll, my wife, and I drove from
Madrid to Vigo, Santander, Bilbao and return, a distance of
nine hundred or more miles, without meeting a single pas-
senger car or truck outside the vicinity of cities. We were able
to make that and other similar trips because a condition for
permitting Spain to import petroleum and its products from
the Western Hemisphere, which was Spain's only source of
supply, was that we and the British would have all the gasoline we wanted. The Germans and Italians supplied gasoline
for their embassies' use. Other foreign diplomats made out as
best they could with minimum allotments. Some Spaniards
traveled in crowded trains; most of them stayed at home.)

Weddell, from his vantage point in Madrid, implored Washington to provide relief to Spain and also to increase trade. He flew back to the United States and made his arguments directly, but with little effect. Nor, for a while, did events help him to make his case.

Weddell had long been insisting that the Spaniards return the properties of the International Telephone and Telegraph Company that they had taken over at the Civil War's end, and he had the State Department's full support. The Department, war or no war, was not about to extend substantial aid to a Spanish government that did not respect private ownership. Protection of American properties in Spain was a right the Department was determined not to relinquish. Among other merits it was good psychology.

ITT's Spanish operation was a model of American enterprise and efficiency. Even during the long siege of Madrid, when its "skyscraper" headquarters was a special target for cannonading by Nationalist forces, the telephone system had continued to operate. That was helpful to the city's defenders, and when the Nationalists finally took Madrid they charged the company with having been overfriendly with their Republican enemies. ITT's owners protested that the company was only doing its job in circumstances it had not helped to create, but the Nationalists seized the company's properties anyway. Meanwhile the ever-helpful Nazis had presented a plan for reorganizing the company under German management. The telephone system, it appeared, was destined to become a German-Spanish showpiece within the New Order.

I have no reason to believe that Franco, as confident as he was of German victory at the time, had any desire to see Spain's telephone system under German control. On May 14, 1940, Serrano, as interior minister, signed an agreement that would permit ITT to regain control of its properties. On June 2, however, with the French forces routed and the Allied evacuation from Dunkirk nearly completed, he told Weddell he considered the agreement invalid.

Even more ominous were Spain's shift to nonbelligerency on June 12 and Italy's entry into the war on June 19. When Weddell asked Franco the meaning of Spain's shift, Franco replied that it was an expression of national sympathy with the Axis. He went on to tell Weddell, however, that the United States was closer to war than Spain was. That was true, but few persons in Madrid or Washington believed it.

Early in May, during a discussion of the ITT case, both Serrano and Franco had hinted that the time was ripe for the United States to give Spain some help. On June 22, however, the very day the French-German armistice agreement was signed, Franco, after Weddell himself had brought up the subject, indicated that Spain needed no aid from the United States. Weddell knew that that was not true. He knew that Spain was in desperate need of aid and he was confident it would accept it from the United States when it dared to, if that time should ever come.

On June 24 the entire embassy staff, including its military members, joined Weddell in reporting that the probability of Spain's entry into the war was increasing, and outweighed, if it did not preclude, the contrary view. Washington itself was deeply skeptical that whatever the United States might do for Spain would redound to anyone's advantage other than Hitler's. But change was in the offing.

On August 8 Stohrer informed Berlin in a strictly secret message that both Foreign Minister Beigbeder and Interior Minister Serrano had repeatedly assured him that Spain, under certain conditions, would enter the war on the side of Germany and Italy. On the same day, however, Beigbeder told Weddell that the telephone matter was settled. A happy Weddell informed an equally ebullient Beigbeder, as he was already authorized to do in that circumstance, that Spain could now obtain all the petroleum that it could transport and that Britain would navicert.

Following up on that encouraging development, Spain's minister of industry and commerce suggested to Weddell that the United States extend a credit of one hundred million dollars to permit Spain to purchase wheat, rubber, cotton, and other materials it was in critical need of. Considering its timing, that was a courageous act on Spain's part, and Weddell, although he held out no hope to the minister, urged Washington to go along. Officers of the State Department's European

Division strongly supported the minister's request, pointing out that it presented only minimum risk since the United States could cut off credit whenever it chose. "But," Herbert Feis, who was the State Department's economic adviser, has told us, "those of us who were concerned with economic matters were doubtful that the idea would work." The idea did not work because the United States would not agree to it.

Britain's attitude was totally different. On October 8 Winston Churchill said in the House of Commons: "There is no country in Europe that has more need of peace and food and the opportunities of prosperous trade than Spain. . . . Far be it from us to lap Spain and her own economic needs in the wide compass of our blockade. All we seek is that Spain will not become a channel of supply to our mortal foes. Subject to this essential condition, there is no problem of blockade that we will not study in the earnest desire to meet Spain's needs and aid her revival."

Churchill's position was secure. He could talk openly and frankly. In the United States, with national elections coming up, the situation was different; at least many persons in political life thought it was. Feis has said, "The whole tenor of the American press showed that if [the United States] granted a loan, and that if later Spain entered the war, those who made the mistake would not long remain in office." That was a powerful deterrent.

Nevertheless the need to do something for Spain persisted and, after some more friendly conversations between Weddell and Beigbeder and much urging by Weddell and the British, President Roosevelt consented to ask the American Red Cross to ship some U.S. government-supplied foodstuffs to Spain and to help distribute them there. In addition, Weddell was authorized to tell Franco that the United States was prepared to discuss credits to Spain if he would confirm his intention to stay out of the war. The way to a closer and more helpful relationship between the two countries seemed to be open.

Beigbeder, in emotion-filled conversations with Weddell, urged that for political as well as humanitarian reasons, the United States should move quickly to supply Spain. "Your president can change the policy of Spain and of Europe by a telegram announcing that wheat will be supplied to Spain," he said on October 2. "I want to tell you that the psychological moment has arrived," he continued.

The psycholgical moment had indeed arrived, but not in the sense Beigbeder had in mind. On October 16 all the forces— political, economic, military, diplomatic, social, and psychological—affecting Spain converged and impelled Franco to carry out a decision he had doubtless made before he sent Interior Minister Serrano, rather than Foreign Minister Beigbeder, to talk to Hitler in September. On October 17 Beigbeder read in the morning newspaper that Franco had dismissed him as foreign minister and had named Serrano in his place. At the same time, also, the State Department learned that Franco himself would shortly meet with Hitler on the French border—an event, it wrongly assumed, which boded ill for the Allied cause. Needless to say preparations for the Red Cross shipment and discussion of credits were suspended. But Weddell still did not despair.

Following Beigbeder's dismissal Ambassador Hoare asked himself whether, given his own intimacy with Beigbeder and Serrano's pro-Axis attitude, there was any justification for his remaining in Madrid. Weddell's reaction to the change was quite different. He had some hope that Serrano, known to be much closer to Franco than Beigbeder, would bring about helpful change. Concerning Demetrio Carceller, who had been brought into the cabinet as minister of industry and commerce, Weddell was frankly pleased. He recommended that preparations for the Red Cross shipments and the study of possible credits be continued.

On October 31, eight days after the Franco-Hitler meeting at Hendaye and twenty days before the Serrano-Hitler meeting at Berchtesgaden, Serrano received Weddell at the Foreign Office. Replying to a question by Weddell, he said, with frankness, or perhaps a bit of bravado, that the change in foreign ministers indicated solidarity with Italy and Germany and a closer rapprochement between Spain and the Axis. With less candor he told Weddell that neither Mussolini nor Hitler had suggested that Spain enter the war. Serrano, when he said those things, may have had in mind that what he told Weddell would reach German ears, a common occurrence in spy-infested Madrid. Indeed he himself may well have informed his friend, Stohrer, of the conversation. The truth is that at Hendaye, Franco, at Hitler's urging, had made a pledge, although only in principle, to end Spain's situation of nonbelligerency and become a belligerent on the side of the Axis.

Serrano also told Weddell that Spain's situation vis-à-vis Germany was very much like the United States' position vis-à-vis Britain, except that Spain had nothing to offer Germany. Spain of course did have things to offer Germany, and had offered and delivered some of them. On the other hand it had never made an active commitment to German victory that corresponded in any degree to the United States' commitment to Germany's defeat. In that sense Serrano was actually exaggerating Spain's attachment to Germany. Here again, he probably had in mind, and even intended, that his statement would come to Germany's attention.

Serrano's words worried Weddell but they did not deter him. "I feel," he telegraphed the State Department, "that every month that Spain remains apart from the conflict is of genuine value and may have results unfavorable to the Axis which cannot now be foreseen." Weddell's words were prophetic but the State Department was understandably alarmed. It feared that Serrano's statement meant that Spain had decided to jump on the Nazi bandwagon. It was equally fearful that the American public would reach that conclusion. It told Weddell that the new situation could be remedied only by a clear-cut public declaration by Spain that it would remain neutral and would not assist Italy or Germany in any way in their struggle with Britain. When Hoare learned from Weddell of Washington's instruction he, as Weddell himself had already done, protested, and London sent out urgent appeals to Washington to modify its position. The Department did modify its position but not greatly; it now instructed Weddell to tell the Spanish government that public opinion in the United States would improve and relief measures would be greatly facilitated if Spain would make a public declaration of its intention to remain neutral. Even in its watered-down form,

the statement, if it had been made, might well have brought
Hitler's wrath down upon Spain and changed the course of
history to the detriment of freedom in the world. (Weddell's
approach to Franco may have been helpful to Spain in a way
that was not foreseen. On December 11 Serrano told Stohrer
that Weddell had wanted to talk to Franco about neutrality
but that Serrano had prevented him "energetically." At the
time Spain was desperately resisting German pressure to force
it into the war.)

Spain, happily, never made such a declaration, and Serrano,
on November 12, assured Weddell officially that Spain would
resist to the last man any effort by German or Italian forces to
cross the Spanish frontier. Feis, on the basis of the information then available to him, suggests that Serrano was lying,
but both Franco and Serrano had in fact warned Hitler, in
diplomatic language it is true, that the Spanish people would
react violently to any effort to force them into the war.

On November 29 Franco received Weddell "with great cor-
diality, almost with warmth." When Weddell brought up the
familiar subject of Washington's problem with public opinion
Franco reminded him, laconically, that through no fault of
Spain, Germany had 250 idle divisions, many of them on
Spain's border. Weddell, after some discussion asked Franco if
he might tell Washington that 1) Spain did not envisage any
departure from its present international attitude, and 2) it did
not contemplate giving aid to the Axis powers. Franco said
yes to the first but quickly added that no one could foresee
what the future might hold. Weddell urged the Department to
accept Franco's statement.

Meanwhile a straitened Britain was supplying what it could
to Spain and urging the United States to quickly send wheat
in order to prevent further famine and the possibility that
Spain, in desperation, would throw itself into Germany's
arms. Secretary of State Hull replied, mournfully, that the
Spanish government seemed to be doing everything it could
to antagonize popular opinion in the United States. He referred to Serrano's "widely advertised trip to Berlin, presumably to bring the two countries closer together." He had no
idea that Hitler, by that time, was referring to Serrano as

"that crafty Jesuit." Britain began to make arrangements for Spain to get wheat from Canada and Argentina.

Weddell and the British continued to press Washington to do something to increase trade with Spain, but Washington was indifferent. On December 10, just three days after Franco had rejected Hitler's plan to move into Spain on January 10, 1941, the Department sent Weddell a long, rambling telegram complaining about anti-American statements of the Spanish press and reported anti-American activities of Spain's representatives in various parts of the world, particularly Latin America. An impatient Weddell dispatched a curt personal telegram to the secretary and undersecretary of state, suggesting in effect that they ignore such reports while Spain's fate depended largely on action the United States might take. He was saying, in so many words, "Let's get on with the job."

Although Washington eventually did provide some flour and milk for the American Red Cross to deliver and help distribute, it still refused to do anything to improve trade. And even the Red Cross aid, which the British had begged us to send, was a trade-off for American aid to Vichy, France, which Washington wished to extend but that the British were loathe to approve. It turned out that Britain had the same kind of public opinion problem with aid to conquered France that the United States had with aid to a still free Spain.

It is amusing, in retrospect, to note how quickly, in the circumstances, the United States acquired at least a verbal enthusiasm for aid to Spain which, up to that point, it had been reluctant to extend. In a message to Churchill, after the latter had agreed to permit American aid to Vichy to pass through the British blockade, President Roosevelt told him, sanctimoniously (at least a sanctimonious telegram bearing the president's name was sent to London): "I feel that it is of the utmost importance to make every practical effort to keep Spain out of the war or from aiding the Axis Powers. If the policy of affording relief is to be undertaken, I am convinced that it should be undertaken now without further delay." That was the kind of exhortatory message that occasionally managed to be cleared in the Department and had little effect other than to annoy. Except for brief periods following

France's surrender and Spain's occupation of the Tangier international zone, the British had been making that very point for months, as had Alexander Weddell, Roosevelt's ambassador in Madrid, with little effect on the president or on most other top officials in Washington.

On April 10, 1941, the State Department dispatched a telegram to its embassies informing them that the Unites States did not intend to stay on the sidelines of the great war that was going on; that it intended to play its part in resisting the forces of aggression; and that it wished its representatives to reflect that in their bearing and in their conversations.

That stirring message undoubtedly reflected President Roosevelt's attitude, if not yet that of the Congress or the American people, but persons in the Madrid embassy could be forgiven for doubting that it offered much hope for improvement in our government's attitude toward Spain. How seriously Weddell took the message, or whether it caused him even slightly to alter his bearing in conversations with Spanish officials, I have no way of knowing. Its sequel, however, was far from encouraging for the United States. For Weddell it was a personal tragedy.

I have already referred to Serrano's action in refusing, over a period of some five months, to permit Weddell to see Franco, a development that brought about a break in Weddell's relations with Serrano and in my being plucked out of Havana and sent to Madrid to conduct relations with the Foreign Office. Weddell and the State Department attributed Serrano's attitude to his pro-Germanism, but it was more complicated than that, and I consider that much of the fault was Weddell's.

On April 19 Weddell called on Serrano and, as instructed, informed him of the United States' determination to resist the forces of aggression. Following that he asked Serrano to arrange an interview for him with Franco. One purpose of the interview, which Weddell did not reveal to Serrano, was to tell Franco that he was now authorized to initiate discussions with a view to broadening and liberalizing the basis of mutual trade between Spain and the United States. That was a message that Weddell had been waiting a long time to be able to give to Franco.

Unfortunately, after making his request to see Franco, Weddell turned to other business. In his later telegram to the State Department he noted that Serrano had just returned from a conference with Franco and seemed depressed and irritable. In retrospect Serrano may have had good reason to be depressed since neither he nor Franco could be certain at the time that Hitler had abandoned or deferred indefinitely his plan to march through Spain and take Gibraltar. Nor of course did Weddell know there was such a plan. If he had known he would not have bothered Serrano with a trivial matter.

Weddell informed the Department that he had remarked, "smilingly," to Serrano that it was inconceivable to him that Spain had renounced its sovereignty, as would seem to be indicated by two airmail envelopes addressed to Americans in Spain which he handed to Serrano. Each of the letters bore a German censor's stamp. Serrano promised to look into the matter. Weddell did not make Serrano any less depressed or irritable than he already was when he then charged, in effect, that the German press attaché was writing stories for Spain's government-controlled newspapers, a charge that must have particularly angered Serrano because it was true.

The episode of the letters (which the State Department had forwarded to the embassy in a routine way) was pointless since it clearly was a case of their having gone astray, as wartime letters often did. Nothing could be gained by showing them to Serrano, or at least by making a point of them, just as little could be gained by talking immediately afterward about the German press attaché's relationship to the Spanish press. It was a relationship that everyone knew about, and everyone knew that everyone else knew about it. It was part of the price Spain was paying to keep out of the war.

Furthermore Weddell's report to the Department does not jibe with the story he told me when I arrived in Madrid on June 25. According to that story he had not handed the letters to Serrano; he had "tossed them" onto Serrano's desk, and that is the version that Serrano gives. Serrano says that Weddell had an attitude of great arrogance, and he must have appeared to Serrano to be arrogant, although Weddell was not that kind of man. He was more kindly than arrogant, more hesitant than resolute, and like all irresolute persons he was capable of gestures that were the opposite of calm and considered.

In his telegram reporting the conversation (Weddell did not appear to realize it was an incident although, given the details he put in his telegram, he must have suspected it was), Weddell tells about all parts of his exchange with Serrano but in talking to me, two months later, he referred only to the episode of the letters, and obviously it was that episode that was on his mind and probably on his conscience.

It took Weddell some time to convince himself that there had been a serious incident between him and Serrano. By mid-May he was a worried man, but when he reported to Washington that he had not yet received a response to his request to see Franco, he still did not associate that with his conversation with Serrano.

By the end of May Weddell had become acutely depressed. In a telegram to the Department he noted that he still had no word from Franco. He then went on to tell of the "gravity of the situation" in Spain, of the effect on Spaniards of Britain's loss of Crete to the Germans, and the general conviction in Madrid that Suez would go next. In addition, he noted, the government-controlled press had renewed its attacks on Britain and the United States. "I cannot but feel," he said, "that the entry of German forces into the Peninsula, an entry which would not and could not be effectively resisted, is ostensibly nearer." It may not have occurred to him that his difference with Serrano might have a tangential relationship to that possibility.

On June 11 a deeply concerned Weddell informed Serrano by note that his purpose in seeking an interview with Franco was to discuss the possibility of increasing trade between Spain and the United States. Serrano replied that it was his duty to prevent persons who used the inadmissable language that Weddell had used in the Foreign Office from speaking to the chief of state. Weddell's language was the only reason for what had occurred, Serrano said, and he wanted the American government to know that. Weddell then sent a note referring to an ambassador's right, "immemorially recognized," to be received by the chief of state, but nothing came of that either.

To add to Weddell's depression, Franco, in a speech on the anniversary of the Nationalist revolution, emphasized his contempt for the "plutocratic democracies." In typical Falange style, in reference to the Anglo-American bases-for-destroyers deal, he said: "It is illusory to believe that the plutocracies will make use of their gold for generous or noble enterprises. The exchange of fifty old destroyers for various remnants of an empire is eloquent testimony in that regard." Then, celebrating Hitler's recent invasion of Russia, he added, "The destruction of Russian communism is now inevitable."

Washington, by that time, was fed up with Franco and Serrano, and with Spain in general. After the Weddell-Serrano estrangement had gone on for five exasperating months Secretary Hull, on September 13, gave the Spanish ambassador, don Francisco de Cárdenas, a dressing down that can be compared only with the one he gave Ambassadors Nomoru and Kurusu an hour after Japanese planes had bombed Pearl Harbor. He told Cárdenas:

"While it's most disagreeable even to recall our experiences in dealing with the Spanish Government, I must state that in all the relations of this Government with the most backward and ignorant Governments in the world, it has not experienced such a lack of ordinary courtesy or consideration customarily prevailing between friendly nations as it has at the hands of the Spanish Government. Your Government's course has been one of aggravated discourtesy and contempt in the very face of our offers to be of aid.

"We could not think of embarrassing, not to say humiliating, ourselves by further approaches of this nature, bearing in mind the coarse and extremely offensive methods and conduct of Serrano Suñer in particular and in some instances of General Franco. When I think about the details of the conduct of the Spanish Government toward this Government, what has happened is really inconceivable."

The secretary went on to say that he had little hope that Ambassador Cárdenas could make the slightest impression on

Franco or Serrano since they were capable of adopting so unworthy and contemptible an attitude toward the United
States.

Even in Spain few persons had ever spoken of Serrano in
such derogatory terms. For Franco it was probably the harsh-
est message since Ribbentrop had reminded him that without
the help of the Fuehrer and the Duce there would not be any
Nationalist Spain or any Caudillo.

Cárdenas, who had served long in the United States and
liked and admired its people, left shortly afterward for Madrid. After talking to Franco and Serrano, he told Weddell that
his remarks to Serrano concerning Spain's sovereignty seemed
to be at the bottom of the controversy, and he asked Weddell
if he would be willing to tell Serrano that he meant no offense
by his remarks. Weddell refused, claiming that he, not Serrano, was the aggrieved person and that it was not up to him
to take the first step. In reporting this conversation to the
Department a hopeful Weddell ended his telegram with,
"Meanwhile rumors persist of an impending change in the
office of Foreign Minister." The rumors turned out to be false.

On September 30, with continued help from Cárdenas, the
Weddell-Serrano quarrel was patched up and Weddell saw Serrano. Later he saw Franco and Serrano together. Conversations with both of them were cordial. Weddell at long last
informed Franco that he was authorized to initiate discussions with a view to broadening and liberalizing the basis of
mutual trade between Spain and the United States.

During all the months Franco and Serrano were shunning
him, Weddell continued doggedly to urge the Department not
to permit Spain's economy to deteriorate to a point where the
Germans would appear as friends and saviors, but Washington
paid little heed. It was quite naturally miffed at Serrano's and
Franco's treatment of Weddell. Furthermore, following Hitler's invasion of Russia it felt that German pressure on Spain
would lessen; that there was little justification now in cod-
dling Franco. By the time Caroll and I arrived in Madrid Spain
was having great difficulty obtaining export permits for petroleum. Its loaded tankers lay in American ports for weeks and
even months while our government offered one or another

excuse for not releasing them. Distribution of Red Cross flour and milk, on the other hand, was well advanced, and rapid trips to various parts of the country convinced us of the excellent effect they were having on the Spanish people if not yet on the Spanish government. Even what we had read in the American press concerning "starving Spain" had not prepared us for the reality of the country's poverty. One small incident I thought worth recording:

"Shortly after our arrival in Madrid, Caroll and I made a trip to Seville with the Red Cross representative. We stopped in a vineyard to have a picnic lunch. A vineyard laborer came along, and we invited him to join us. He accepted in a dignified way, and ate slowly but with intense concentration. He also drank some of our wine. Later he said that it was the first wine he had tasted in three years. He was, I repeat, a laborer in the vineyard. He told us that he worked from dawn to dusk. He and his family lived on bread, olive oil, and occasionally a little meat. His two grown-up sons, Republicans, had crossed the border into France during the civil war. He had never heard from them. He asked us if he might take the empty cans home for his little daughter to play with. We gave them to him and also some extra cans of food we had with us. He thanked us gratefully and went on his way. He had not shown a trace of self-pity."

We learned later that our vineyard laborer was a privileged person compared with many city residents. Happily for him, perhaps, he probably did not know that what he called bread contained little if any wheat flour.

Government officials in Washington, for understandable reasons, could harbor resentment against the Spanish government, but it was impossible for us, in Madrid, to dislike Spaniards, an overwhelming majority of whom, we were convinced, shared our purposes.

It was only after many months of hemming and hawing by Washington's political and economic establishment that Weddell, as we have seen, was instructed to tell Franco that he was authorized to initiate trade discussions with the Spanish government. As we know, also, it was some five months before he could carry out that instruction. In any event the "broadening and liberalizing" process that the United States had in mind was not such as to send Franco into paroxysms of joy.

The United States is "prepared to give immediate and careful consideration to the means by which it may be possible for the Government of Spain to obtain surplus commodities in the United States such as wheat, corn and cotton," Weddell was to tell Franco. As an example he was to say that Spain might sell olive oil (which happened to be an important export to Germany), and acquire American peanut oil and wheat with the proceeds.

Reflecting a fear that even that timid offer might be going too far, the Department said it believed that the United States could assist Spain "without resort to credit transactions." Its telegram was nothing if not cautiously worded. Like most Washington communications on economic matters it had the earmarks of having run the gauntlet not only of several State Department bureaus but also of departments and agencies beyond the State Department. It was the least common denominator of many and frequently conflicting views. What the Department was saying of course was that although the United States, in Washington's own words, was "determined to play its part in resisting the forces of aggression," it was not prepared to go so far as to provide modest credits to Spain, whose attitude might be of incalculable help in resisting those forces.

On March 20, shortly before Weddell's fateful conversation with Serrano, Lord Halifax, Britain's ambassador in Washington, had called on Undersecretary of State Sumner Welles and made several proposals. He had told Welles that Britain was about to conclude a credit agreement with Spain but that Spain needed much more help than Britain could give her. He had then urged that the United States announce publicly that it was making food and materials available to Spain; that it would provide 100,000 tons of wheat and up to 200,000 tons of ammonium sulfate at once; and that U.S. exporters and purchasers would soon visit Spain. He had proposed also that the United States finance Spain's purchases.

The suggestion concerning publicity startled many Wash-

ington officials, but in general Halifax's proposals were emi-
nently sensible. If the United States had accepted them the
course of relations with Spain might have been far different
and, incidentally, Weddell's career might well have had a happier ending. Halifax had gone on to suggest, however, that the
United States should isolate Foreign Minister Serrano in every
possible way; that specifically it should make its offer to finance Spain's imports not to Serrano but, confidentially, to
Carceller, the minister of industry and commerce. That suggestion reflected not Downing Street diplomacy but Sir Samuel Hoare's influence on Downing Street, and his distrust and
hatred of Serrano. If it had been carried out, the effect might
well have been not to isolate Serrano but to destroy Carceller.

Nevertheless, the Department accepted this suggestion although in modified form. When it finally authorized Weddell
to undertake discussions for improving trade between the two
countries it instructed him to indicate to Franco that the minister of industry and commerce should take part in the negotiations. The Department was telling the Spaniards who their
negotiators should be—a splendid example of antidiplomacy.

Weddell offered no objection to this last instruction, but he
quickly expressed dissatisfaction with the United States'
offer. He maintained that to say that we were disposed, for
example, to exchange surplus commodities for Spain's scarce
olive oil was to drastically limit the value of the exchange to
Spain. Spain, he indicated, wanted not only wheat and cotton,
which were in surplus in the United States, but scrap iron,
ammonium sulfate, machinery and parts, electrodes, and
other products it needed to restore its agriculture and rebuild
its industries and in short to survive. The Department replied,
primly, that the things Weddell mentioned were in urgent
demand in other (and presumably more important) countries
and that we were not disposed to supply them to Spain
merely to gain Spaniards' goodwill.

Recognizing that a true emergency existed, Weddell made
an additional suggestion. He asked Washington to weigh carefully what Spain's neutrality was worth to the United States
and to the common cause, and then to make Spain a flat offer
of foodstuffs with the sole condition and understanding that

the spaced deliveries would cease the moment Spain entered the war or Germany invaded the peninsula.

That was a no-lose proposition, and when nothing came of it an angry Weddell charged that the United States was applying its ever-increasing restrictions on exports only to Spain and a few other countries. A stung State Department retorted, "Spain's whole policy has been to exclude in so far as possible American enterprises and investment and to restrict its purchases in this country to an irreducible minimum of necessities not available in any other market or only available at great cost." That was the kind of huckster's argument that drove embassy officials to distraction. Spain's meager purchases were made 1) in Germany, for quite obvious economic-political reasons, and 2) in other countries that were responsive to Spain's needs and that offered goods on the best terms. So far as American enterprise and investment were concerned, ITT's problem was already solved, and no other American company could have been bludgeoned into making sizable investments at the time.

The Department challenged Weddell to state what contributions Spain might be prepared to make toward improving relations with the United States. Staying out of the war when that was difficult, to say the least, apparently did not constitute such a contribution. With greater logic the Department informed Weddell that if the United States was to continue to supply Spain the Spanish government must show a willingness to adopt a more normal attitude toward Weddell himself.

When at last he had the opportunity to tell Franco that the United States was ready to discuss increased trade with Spain, Weddell, reflecting Washington's instructions, suggested that the discussions take place in the Ministry of Industry and Commerce. With Serrano at his side Franco replied that Foreign Office technicians would handle the negotiations for Spain. They did, and they handled them well. Both Spain and the United States gained from them.

Meanwhile Washington was learning. It was getting used to living and acting in a world at war. Officials were gaining in experience; judgments were maturing. Weddell's urgings were having an effect. But the knowledge that German submarines were refueling in Spain was sobering. It was the British who had discovered the refuelings and it was Sir Samuel Hoare who was berating the Spanish government for its acts. But it was also Britain which was begging the United States to improve its trade with Spain—to recognize the opportunities as well as the problems that Spain offered. And Washington responded. It worked up new terms for continued trade with Spain—terms that were more generous to Spain and at the same time provided greater guarantees for the United States (and of course for Britain). They were substantially these:

1. Spain could obtain whatever products were freely purchasable in the United States. That was not new.

2. The United States would try to provide Spain with goods in short supply to the extent they were needed for a low wartime level of economic activity. That was as much as Spain could hope for at the time.

3. In return the United States would expect Spain to assist it in acquiring such Spanish products as wolfram, cork, mercury, zinc, lead, and olive oil. That was a reasonable condition; Germany already was obtaining such products in Spain.

4. Spain would make an effort to transport those products in Spanish ships. That was a shot in the dark. Spain would find it difficult to accept. Spanish ships were generally immune from Axis submarine attacks, but "accidental" attacks could occur. And in any case immunity might not extend to the transport of strategic materials to hostile countries.

5. The United States would supply Spain with enough, and only enough, oil to meet its requirements for transportation and other essentials. If that were carried out it would be a great improvement for Spain.

6. The oil would not be used in any manner helpful to Germany or Italy, directly or indirectly. The United States was justified in proposing that condition even though it might be difficult to carry out.

7. Distribution and use of the oil within Spain and its colonies would be subject to American supervision. This would come to mean that Spanish tankers would be checked and sealed by Americans before departure from a loading port, and unsealed and rechecked by Americans on arrival in Spanish

territory in order to insure that no oil had been disposed of on the way. (Washington also wanted to place an American observer on each tanker to insure that this provision was not violated at sea, but the Spaniards pointed out that the Germans would soon discover the device and would halt tankers and remove the observers. The United States quickly abandoned the idea.) In addition the United States would be permitted to station observers throughout Spain and its colonies who would be free to follow the oil from ship to storage to refinery. Our observers would be, in effect, officially accepted spies, free to look into all aspects of the petroleum trade. If Spain agreed to that and Germany did not retaliate it would go a long way toward demonstrating that Germany, for the time being at least, was not the threat it had been a year earlier.

Rather than have Weddell convey our proposed terms, cold, to a Serrano whom Washington considered unfriendly, the State Department, on November 29, handed them to Ambassador Cárdenas in Washington, and the latter, after some discussion and with considerable misgiving, passed them on to Madrid. Meanwhile Spain was running out of oil.

The British regarded what was going on with fear and disapproval. Shortly after Churchill had visited Washington three Spanish tankers that were waiting in Venezuela were permitted to load cargoes, but the United States continued to insist that its terms be met.

On December 7, 1941, the Japanese bombed Pearl Harbor and the United States was at war. The Spanish press hailed the Japanese victories. Germany promptly declared war against the United States.

On January 8, 1942, Ambassador Weddell left for consultation in Washington, where he applied for and was granted retirement; I became chargé d'affaires ad interim.

On January 23, at a British-American meeting with Spain's Economic Committee which Commercial Attaché Ackerman and I attended, the principle of joint Spanish, American, British cooperation in regulating the distribution of petroleum within Spain was agreed to.

On February 14 Franco, speaking to Spanish Army officers,

said, "If there were a moment of danger, if the road to Berlin were open, it would not be a division of Spanish volunteers who would go there but a million Spaniards who would offer themselves." Franco's speech coincided with Rommel's rapid advance in North Africa, and with the fall of Singapore to the Japanese. It provoked dismay in the State Department and harsh criticism in the American press. But Serrano went out of his way to assure me that Spain's policy was still directed at staying out of the war.

In February, too, Spain's refinery in Tenerife closed down for want of oil.

In March Spain accepted our conditions for future trade.

In April four loaded tankers were licensed to depart from Atlantic ports for Spain. The crisis was over.

For four months Spain's problem with the United States had been extremely difficult; her economy had been on the point of collapse. But her problem with Germany may have been more difficult. The Germans detested and feared the idea of American officials snooping freely around Spain, which only recently had been a German preserve. But they had to recognize that Spain needed oil, and that only the Allies could make it available to her in quantity. Germany herself was short of oil even for military purposes. She must have finally agreed not to retaliate against Spain if the latter gave in to United States demands.

Of course Spain must have made some concessions too. Neither the Allies nor the Axis were accommodating Spain unless they obtained some compensation. Perhaps Carceller promised Germany larger supplies of Spain's products, even of tin and other strategic materials that Spain might acquire in the United States. Smuggling is a highly developed art in Spain; not even the fourteen "petroleum attachés" who were eventually assigned to Spain and her colonies could prevent some of it from going on behind their backs. Assuming that some smuggling occurred, however, the new arrangements still constituted a near-decisive victory for the Allies. While German forces were heavily engaged in distant Russia, a belligerent United States was now imposing conditions on Spain. My Foreign Office colleagues were visibly relieved that German pressure was being openly countered by American pressure, and millions of other Spaniards must soon after have felt the same. Despite official censorship news traveled swiftly in Spain.

While our position in Spain was enormously improved, confusion and, at times, dissension at home made it difficult for us to profit from it. The State Department not only had to conciliate differing opinions among its own offices, it also had to deal with the Board of Economic Warfare and, at times, the Army, the Navy, the Treasury Department, the Reconstruction Finance Corporation, the Petroleum Administrator for War, and the War Production Board, to name only some of the more important agencies involved in relations with Spain. Our success in dealing with the Spaniards was being threatened by difficulties in dealing with one another.

The solution was to name Herbert Feis chairman of a newly formed Iberian Peninsula Operating Committee (IPOC) made up of representatives of various offices of the State Department, of the Board of Economic Warfare, and of the United States Commercial Corporation, a new official organization patterned after the United Kingdom Commercial Corporation that had long existed and had borne a large part of the burden of frustrating German economic designs in Spain. The primary function of the USCC, as it was of the UKCC, would be "preclusive buying," an effort to deprive the Axis of vital war materials with little regard to cost. The cost had become too high for Britain to meet alone, while the need for preclusive buying had increased. When Ambassador Hayes arrived in Madrid on May 19, 1942, both the UKCC and the USCC were functioning, and petroleum attachés had begun to arrive in Spain. The United States, at last, had begun to play its full part in Spain (and in Portugal) in resisting the forces of aggression.

6 JORDANA

In an almost exultant mood Germany's Ambassador Stohrer, on April 14, 1939, reminded Berlin that in recent months the Nationalist government had made extensive and valuable political and economic concessions to Germany in return for the "great and decisive" aid Germany had extended to it during the Civil War that was nearing its end. "In the negotiations carried on with Spain," he boasted, "we have had our way for the most part, even down to details."

Stohrer was not exaggerating. Germany had indeed given great and decisive aid to Spain. Most recently it had furnished the large amounts of military supplies that would make it possible for the Nationalist armies to carry out the Catalonia offensive that was to bring final victory. And Spain had made extensive and valuable concessions in return. What was equally true, however, was that Germany had withheld the aid that was needed for victory until Spain had made the concessions Germany gave most importance to—concessions that, if they should be fully availed of, would deprive Spain of

an important part of her patrimony and go far toward converting her into a German satellite.

General Count Francisco Gómez Jordana y Sousa, as foreign minister, had borne the brunt of resisting, delaying, and
possibly limiting compliance with Germany's demands. But
as Serrano was to say of his own later confrontations with the
Germans, it wasn't easy.

By February, 1939, Nationalist victory seemed assured. On
the fifth of that month Stohrer, accompanied by the Italian
ambassador, handed Jordana a formal invitation to accede to
the Anti-Comintern Pact to which Japan, as well as Germany
and Italy, was a signatory. Jordana, who had been informed by
telephone of the purpose of the meeting, and had already discussed the subject with Franco, told the ambassadors that
both he and Franco had strong objections to joining the pact
at that time. They feared that England, and particularly
France, might suspect that accession to the pact involved
wider commitments and might constitute a threat to them.
They might even attempt to frustrate the victory over the
Republicans that now appeared to be in sight. Furthermore
France had a sizable quantity of Nationalist gold in its possession; it might decide to hold on to it.

When Stohrer returned to the subject some two weeks later
Jordana explained to him that so long as the difficult negotiations on de jure recognition by France and England were going
on, he had strenuous objections to accession. After an impatient Foreign Office had instructed Stohrer to push hard to
bring Spain into the pact, Stohrer, who had decided that Jordana was indeed strongly opposed to accession, cautioned Berlin against excessive efforts to win Spain over. He said that
such efforts, given the Spanish character and Jordana's especially, would have the opposite of the results intended. Nevertheless he made persistent efforts to see Franco in order to
discuss the matter with him, but Franco was "too busy" to
receive him.

Meanwhile, however, the Council of Ministers, with
Franco presiding, had decided to accede to the pact without
further discussion. But now Spain had a demand of its own. It

wanted the accession to be kept secret. In deference to its wish, the pact was signed on March 26 without ceremony and without publicity.

Hitler was not pleased with Spain's position, however. After Stohrer had requested Jordana's agreement to an announcement of Spain's accession, and Jordana had countered with the same objections he had put forth against signature, Berlin directed Stohrer to call on Jordana and demand immediate publication. But Jordana, noting that Franco shared his objections to an immediate announcement, refused to give in.

Berlin was now furious. "The reasons given by you for the delay in announcing Spain's accession to the Anti-Comintern Pact cannot be considered valid," it warned Stohrer, and it instructed him to make further "very energetic" representations. "You should reach an agreement concerning the date on which Spain's accession is to be announced and the manner in which this is to be done—if not tomorrow then at least in the course of the week," it said. Hitler was not asking Franco for his cooperation; he was telling him what he must do.

Stohrer telegraphed Berlin that he had conveyed its message to Jordana in great detail and most emphatically. Nevertheless, he reported, Jordana had persisted in his objections. He had maintained that countries that were friendly to Spain must surely be interested in shielding her from difficulties when she was just beginning to recuperate from her Civil War. Berlin was not impressed.

About that time the non-Spanish press began to report the Nationalist regime's accession to the Anti-Comintern Pact, and the fact that it was being kept secret. On April 5 Franco's Council of Ministers ordered immediate announcement of the regime's adherence to the pact. What else could it do?

Meanwhile, on March 31, the two governments had also signed the German-Spanish Treaty of Friendship even though Jordana had protested that, since there was reason to believe that both Britain and France were interested in a rapprochement with Spain, the timing was unfortunate.

Accession to the Anti-Comintern Pact and signature of the German-Spanish Treaty of Friendship were high on Germany's agenda for Spain, but achieving near-monopoly rights in the mining field had even higher priority; it also provoked deep resentment on the part of Spaniards.

Ambassador Stohrer tried to be moderate in his talks with Spaniards, but Johannes Bernhardt, who was director of HISMA, an official German trading company, had fewer inhibitions. From the beginning of his mission he communicated with Nationalist officials in frank and sometimes offensive language. He did not hesitate to inform them of the facts of life as HISMA and, frequently, the German government saw them. One of the facts was that in return for the support they needed in order to achieve victory in the Civil War the Nationalists must turn over to Germany virtual control over the rich mining industry in Spain and Spanish Morocco.

On July 12, 1937, accepting the fact that the Civil War was going to be long and difficult and that it could not be won without additional German support, the Franco regime subscribed to a secret protocol which provided: "The Spanish Nationalist Government will facilitate as far as possible the establishment of Spanish companies for the opening up and economic utilization of mineral resources and other raw materials and for other economic purposes serving the general welfare, under participation of German citizens or German firms as compatible with the general stipulations of Spanish law." On the strength of that protocol HISMA acquired claims to seventy-three mining concessions and invested an estimated 100 million Reichsmarks in them.

On October 19, 1937, however, a disturbed Nationalist government decreed that all mining rights granted after July 19, 1936, were null and void. When Stohrer told Franco that Germany was concerned over the possible effects of the decree on the rights Germany had acquired and might acquire in the future, an evasive Franco informed him that the decree had been issued because of the danger that the "Red" government might sell out everything. He promised Stohrer that German interests would be protected.

Some nine months later, when nothing had been done to carry out Franco's promise, Bernhardt, in a brutally candid conversation with Undersecretary of Commerce and Industry

Fernandez Cuevas (at a time when the secretary himself was
declining to receive Bernhardt because of "illness"), complained that the close cooperation between military and economic factors that was required in order to assure final Nationalist victory was lacking. He noted, specifically, that
people in Germany did not understand how week after week
could go by without the question of the mines that Germany
wished to acquire being definitely settled. He warned that for
Germany the settlement of the mining question was a measure of Spain's desire for German-Spanish cooperation. As if
he had not already made himself painfully clear, Bernhardt
added that Germany regarded the matter of the mines as the
focal point in German-Spanish cooperation and a scale for
measuring whether and to what extent the cooperation which
Germany had extended freely and openly had found an echo
in Spain. Germany required a clear picture of things so that it
could judge correctly the value or the worthlessness of Spanish friendship, he said.

In an embassy memorandum of November 4, 1937, Bernhardt candidly set forth Germany's primary economic objective in Spain and the means by which it might be achieved.
He said:

"It is clear to us that [mining rights constitute] the whole
aim and purpose of our assistance to Spain in the economic
field. . . .

"The objective of our economic interest in Spain must be
the deep penetration into the main sources of Spanish wealth,
namely, agriculture and mining. Whereas the products of agriculture fall to the share of the German Reich more or less
without effort, since the Spaniards are forced to find a market,
the mining problem is of tremendous importance in every
respect.

"Reduced to a clear formula, it may be said that the success
or failure of our efforts in Spanish mining will determine
whether our assistance to Spain was successful or misplaced.
Clearly recognizing that [mining rights are] the real objective
of our economic effort, we must resolve this problem with all
the means available. It must be stated here that these same
means must be found and applied in all fields and that we

must, therefore, exert diplomatic, military and cultural influence in order to attain this single objective of establishing ourselves economically. . . .

"The solution of the whole problem as it stands now will have to be forced if it cannot be attained by reasonable means. . . ."

Pressure on Spain increased when the much feared Colonel General Hermann Goering, who was in charge of Hitler's Four Year Plan, named Bernhardt his personal representative for economic matters in Spain. Germany, it now became clear, intended to include Spain in the plan. Goering wanted to send the under state secretary in the Economics Ministry to Spain to "hold a pistol to General Franco's breast" and demand Germany's "war booty" that was being withheld from it. He was dissuaded from doing that however. Other German officials wanted to be less obvious if equally determined.

Franco and other Nationalist officials continued to say that the decree of October 9 was aimed at preventing the "Reds" from selling out Spain, but Bernhardt said to Stohrer: "Let's not let them pull the wool over our eyes. The mining decree is aimed at us." He was correct in that.

On January 26, 1938, Jordana told a complaining Stohrer that because of the great number of mining rights that Germany was claiming, and the fact that the protocol of July 16, 1937, stipulated that utilization of Spanish mineral resources by or for Germany should be carried out only as compatible with the general provisions of Spanish law, a detailed legal examination of the claims was necessary. Stohrer retorted that the examination was certainly taking a long time. He insisted on being given a specific date by which the Spanish answer would be ready. Colonel General Goering, he reminded Jordana, attached special importance to the matter. Jordana replied, testily, that Spanish cooperation could be effective only if German participation were less extensive. Like a small boy daring a companion to knock the chip off his shoulder, Stohrer asked Jordana if he would put that in writing. Jordana said he would but that he would have to submit the letter to Franco first. Nothing came of that.

Jordana then reminded Stohrer of a consideration that

might have escaped his (and Colonel General Goering's) attention. He recalled that the Spanish people's mentality was such that they tended, following a change in government, to call the former regime to account for its acts. He, himself, because of his role in the Primo de Rivera dictatorship, had been condemned by the Republic, first to death and then to life imprisonment, and he had spent two years in prison. He therefore had to attach great importance to abiding strictly by Spanish law, "since one could never know what might happen." Stohrer did not report to Berlin what comment, if any, he had made to that.

Stohrer lost no time in continuing his campaign. The next day he called on José Antonio de Sangroniz, *chef de cabinet* at the Foreign Office and a notably outspoken person, to express displeasure at the conversation he had had with Jordana. He told Sangroniz that the treatment Germany was receiving was improper and incorrect in the light of the sacrifices the Germans had made and were still making for the Nationalist State. He suggested that with a stroke of the pen Spain could settle the mining rights affair—in which Colonel General Goering was so much interested—in Germany's favor.

To this Sangroniz, after asking permission to speak frankly, replied that it was not correct for Germany to act as it did. Instead of purchasing a few mining rights and discussing with the Spanish government how it might acquire others, it had aroused wide opposition by buying an incredible number of mines and rights (Stohrer reported to Berlin that Sangroniz actually had used much stronger language), and as a result the Spanish government had had to adhere strictly to law in handling the matter. Sangroniz' argument was quite justified even though it did not fully explain Spain's delays in acceding to German wishes.

On June 5, nearly six months after Stohrer's conversation with Sangroniz, and after Stohrer had made fruitless efforts to discuss mining rights with Franco, the Nationalist government made a concession of sorts, but its nature and the manner in which it was communicated to Germany was a shock to Stohrer who, by this time, was wondering whether his job as ambassador was in jeopardy. Franco sent Jordana to inform

Stohrer that he had signed a new mining law that took into consideration Germany's demands and represented the absolute limit of what the Nationalist government could do to meet them. Jordana said that Franco had feared that if he, himself, received Stohrer during the last few days of the final revision of the law, as Stohrer had requested, the impression might arise that the changes were made in response to German pressure. The changes in the law were: 1) legalization of 40 percent instead of 25 percent foreign capital interest, and 2) greater possibility for the Spanish government to make exceptions in Germany's favor. Jordana explained that the law had already been signed and that therefore no changes could be made in it. As a courtesy to the German government, however, it would not be published for a few days so that Berlin might say that it had been informed in advance.

A distressed Stohrer reminded Jordana that, under instructions from his government, he had made two requests of him: 1) that he might speak to Franco concerning the matter of mining rights, and 2) that Spain do nothing definite until after he had spoken to Franco. Stohrer recalled that neither of those requests had been granted. The way the matter had been handled constituted practically an unfriendly act, he maintained. If he was no longer persona grata he would ask to be recalled at once, he said.

Jordana assured him that both Franco and he esteemed him highly. He reminded him at the same time that enemy propaganda constantly stressed that Spain was dominated by Germany and that she was subjected to, and acted under, German pressure and perhaps, occasionally, under Italian pressure too. If Franco had received Stohrer during the time the law was being discussed, he explained, enemy propaganda would have claimed that Spain had acted under German pressure. An incensed Stohrer, recalling that Jordana had told him in a recent letter that it was not customary for the Spanish government to make a law known before it had been approved, signed, and published, now reminded him that neither was it customary for one government to put at the disposal of another several thousand soldiers and large quantities of war matériel and to permit the soldiers to be killed and the war matériel to be destroyed. Jordana was not moved.

Stohrer made a final effort. He asked Jordana to give him a copy of the law to send to Berlin by courier and to permit about a week to pass before publishing it. Jordana said he would try to arrange that. Franco later agreed to delay publication—for two days. Stohrer, in his report to Berlin, expressed the belief that the new mining law, although it was by no means gratifying, seemed to be acceptable to German interests. Berlin did not agree.

In the spring of 1938, after two years of civil war, the new Daladier government in France opened the frontier with Spain to the passage of military supplies for the Republic. Between April and May some 25,000 tons of war matériel, most of them sent from Russia, crossed the Pyrenees into Catalonia. When Russia sent 300 aircraft Daladier had them transported in huge trucks even though it was necessary to cut down miles of trees along highways of Aquitaine in order to let them pass.

On the night of July 24–25 a well-equipped Republican army, led principally by Communists, crossed the Ebro River in an offensive that threatened to force the Nationalists into agreeing to a negotiated peace. The Nationalist armies finally turned the Republicans back, but the cost in men and munitions was tremendous. During the counteroffensive Nationalist planes dropped 10,000 pounds of bombs every day. Nationalist supplies reached a point where only immediate and massive aid from Germany would make possible a continuation of the war.

The Spaniards talked to the Germans about planes, artillery, and tanks, and munitions for them. The Germans talked about mining rights in Spain. On August 20, Bernhardt, who was now expert in tying military aid to mining rights, told Fernandez Cuevas that people in Germany did not understand how week after week went by without the question of the mines being settled. For Germany, he reminded him, the settlement of the mining question was a measure of Spain's desire for German cooperation. What he was really saying

was, "Unless you let us have the rights we want we shall
withhold the aid you need for military victory." And as Colonel General Goering's personal representative in Spain he had
ample authority to say it.

By October 18 the Nationalists were beginning to yield on
mining rights, but they were being exasperatingly deliberate
about it. In a top-secret memorandum of that date Berlin's
Economic Ministry noted that possible delivery of new and
increased amounts of matériel to Nationalist Spain was being
considered, but that among matters that must be cleared first
was the guaranty of German mining rights. On November 7
Berlin informed Stohrer that the Reich government had decided to fulfill Franco's wishes, but that first of all Spain must
acknowledge in figures the past deliveries of war matériel and
the expenses connected with them (Stohrer was to point out
to the Spaniards how lucky they were that Germany was not
charging the costs of supplying personnel). In addition Spain
must immediately authorize more than 40 percent foreign
capital participation in Spanish mining companies.

Twelve days later Franco agreed to comply with Germany's
demands. Specifically: 1) German capital participation in the
mining companies established by HISMA would be permitted
to the extent the Germans desired, 2) a mining company with
100 percent German capital could be established in Spanish
Morocco, and 3) duty-free import of mining machinery, and so
forth, to the value of 5 million Reischmarks and repayment of
that amount by deliveries from the mines would be permitted.

Stohrer reported that Jordana added to the foregoing a
lengthy statement concerning the firm intention of Nationalist Spain to continue to orient itself toward Germany politically and economically after the end of the war. Nationalist
Spain was obviously prepared to go to the limit to assure the
military aid it required.

Germany was prompt to send the matériel the Nationalists
needed.

By March 31, 1939, Republican resistance had ended.

Among other gains for the Nationalist government was an
insight into some of Germany's real aims in Spain, and some
of the means she was prepared to resort to in order to achieve

them. That insight would serve Jordana well when, following Serrano's dismissal in September, 1942, he became Nationalist Spain's foreign minister the second time.

During the first seven months of our tour in Madrid Caroll and I lived in the Ritz Hotel; later we visited it often. The Ritz was not only Madrid's finest hotel but also the center of its limited social life. But it often gave the impression that Madrid was a German-occupied city. With at least five Germans to every Englishman and American there, most of the Germans wearing military or Nazi-party uniforms, there was much clicking of heels and raising of arms, and much Nazi-style gaiety.

The Germans were not satisfied with enjoying themselves; they wanted others to know they were having fun. Frequently when the day's work was over Caroll and I would sit in the hotel lobby watching the pageant and trying to fit it into the larger picture of the war. With the Wehrmacht advancing swiftly through Russia, and Allied military men hoping against hope that the Russians could hold out a few months longer, with the Falange helping to flood Spain with Axis propaganda, with the Nazis themselves strutting around the lobby with all the ostentation they were capable of, we had little cause to be amused. And yet we were.

The Germans were putting on a show; they had rehearsed it often and they were letter-perfect. But they were heavy players. Englishmen and Americans, Spaniards and Frenchmen, and Italians too, would come to the hotel and relax. But the Germans' good times were always organized. Their parties were too stiff or too loud. They always seemed to be trying to impress others, but they seldom succeeded. There was a self-consciousness about their performances that was actually pleasing to Allied observers. While the Germans were laughing loudly, and working hard, we sat back and enjoyed it all.

Another thing we noticed was that, while Italians who came in for cocktails or dinner were frequently accompanied by Spaniards, and even the Japanese, who were generally held in low esteem, were occasionally seen with Spaniards, Germans nearly always came alone or with other Germans. That led us to believe that German friendship with Spain did not

penetrate much below the official level, and that on that level
it was seldom on a personal basis. Not even Italians asso-
ciated much with the Germans. In Havana the Italian minister had dutifully tagged behind his German colleague, although he never seemed to enjoy it, but in Madrid the two
had little to do with one another. Englishmen and Americans,
in contrast, frequently came to the hotel together, and were
often accompanied by Spaniards. Except for representatives of
the Foreign Office and the Ministry of Industry and Commerce these were not generally government officials, but all
of them knew government officials, and some of them knew
much of what was going on, and they wanted to be helpful.

Some of the hotel employees were German agents or were
under direct or indirect German or Falange control. Our
rooms were systematically searched, and private letters were
sometimes removed. But some employees were friendly and
found ways to demonstrate it. When the Germans dined
sumptuously, for example, we were often served the same
food at no extra cost.

Since the Germans were so ostentatious in their dinners
Americans and Britons sometimes retaliated, with help from
the dining room staff. One evening Caroll and I gave a dinner
at which the pièce de résistance was spaghetti. That doesn't
sound like a very big deal, but as a matter of fact spaghetti
was a rare delicacy in wartime Madrid. The maître d'hôtel,
who some alleged was in the Naxis' employ, gave us a table
right next to the German area of the dining room, and himself
served the spaghetti with great deliberation, lifting it up and
letting it fall back so that the entire dining room could see it.
While we and our guests ate smugly the suddenly quiet Germans drooled.

As time went on the Germans' presence in the Ritz Hotel
became less and less noticeable. Their numbers decreased.
Their parties were fewer and quieter. There was almost no
heel-clicking or arm-lifting. When I left Madrid in May, 1944,
German uniforms had disappeared from the city and German
influence had almost disappeared. Change was especially evident while Count Jordana was serving his second term as
Franco's foreign minister.

When Captain Francisco Franco, age 23, was wounded at the Battle of Biutz, in Spanish Morocco, and cited for bravery, he also was recommended for promotion to major, but his age proved to be a problem. After High Commissioner Jordana had expressed the view that his age was an additional recommendation, however, Franco got his promotion. The association between the two was to be long and increasingly close.

As a very young officer Jordana was seriously wounded in Cuba during the Spanish-American War. Many years later, although he had had no interest in military politics and no role in them, he served in Primo de Rivera's military directorate. When, in mid–Civil War, Franco named him foreign minister, many Nationalists thought him too old for the job, but Franco regarded his age and experience as assets. And when Franco, in September, 1942, named him foreign minister for the second time, succeeding the younger and politically ambitious Serrano Suñer, he considered that Jordana's previous experience as foreign minister was especially important. Again he was right.

It would be hard to find two persons as different as Serrano and Jordana. Small, soft-spoken, unmilitary-looking and limpid in his honesty, Jordana, a dedicated monarchist of liberal principles, was just as anti-Communist as Serrano. But he leaned as much toward the Allies as Serrano did toward the Axis.

Jordana hated the sin but he did not hate the sinner. Nevertheless he despised Hitler as much as he did Stalin, and his admiration for the democracies was as sincere and as evident as his repudiation of both nazism and communism. He undoubtedly wished that Spain could be democratic, but even our Savior might have had trouble accomplishing that during the years Jordana served as foreign minister and for some years later. And of course it will take some support and much tolerance from our Savior for Spain to achieve lasting democracy in the future, in conditions infinitely more favorable than those that existed during Jordana's ministries.

Although he had known Franco for many years, Jordana had had little or nothing to do with the Nationalist movement. With no political ambitions of his own, he sought only to serve Spain. Doussinague, who knew him and Serrano well, told me once that while Serrano, as minister, sometimes spoke for Franco and sometimes for Serrano, Jordana always spoke for Franco, and Allied diplomats sensed that. He was thoroughly acceptable to them and thoroughly cooperative with them in circumstances that seldom gave him or his government much freedom of action and that neither he nor Franco could change except gradually and with great care.

On December 27, 1942, I wrote to Caroll in the United States: "The press was very proud this morning because Jordana's name had been used in a crossword puzzle in the *New York World Telegram*. It is very encouraging. I predict he will become popular in the United States." Jordana never became popular in the United States, but neither was he unpopular, as Serrano had been. And the fact that the Falange-controlled press would celebrate the use of his name in an American newspaper's crossword puzzle was a sign that even Falange hard-liners were softening toward the United States. From such small signals we were often able to gauge changes in both government and popular attitudes.

A much more important signal consisted of the appointments Jordana made in the Foreign Office. In addition to appointing Pan de Soraluce undersecretary of foreign affairs and confirming Doussinague as director general of foreign policy, he named Vicente Taberna, who was a close friend of Commercial Attaché Ralph Ackerman, director general of economic policy; German Baraiba chief of European political affairs; and Tomás Suñer chief of American affairs. All those officers were firm Allied supporters. Jordana also put an end to *Falange Exterior* which, in varying degrees, had tried to serve Axis interests in Latin America. As we shall note in the next chapters Jordana, himself, had excellent relations with both Ambassador Hoare and Ambassador Hayes—at times better relations than the two had with each other.

7 HOARE

An authentic hero of British-American action in Spain was Sir Samuel Hoare, who had served in Neville Chamberlain's war cabinet and whom many Washington officials (and perhaps a majority of British subjects) regarded as an appeaser. As Britain's foreign secretary, Hoare, in December, 1935, agreed to a proposal by Pierre Laval, prime minister of France, that a portion of Abyssinia's territory be ceded to Italy which, under Mussolini, was endeavoring to establish a colonial empire in East Africa. News of the agreement created a furor in Britain where it was considered a betrayal of the League of Nations and an act of appeasement of an aggressive Italy. Hoare resigned and was succeeded by Anthony Eden. Hoare did not act like an appeaser in Spain, however.

When Hoare arrived in Madrid, on June 1, 1940, the German Army had already spread over much of France, and many in the British government considered Spain, and possibly Gibraltar, as good as lost. It was during this early period of his mission, when Britain was on the edge of defeat, that Hoare performed his most useful service. It was then, when Hitler was determined to take Gibraltar and close the Mediterranean before invading Russia, that Germany exerted greatest pressure on Spain to enter the war—pressure that Spain resisted and was able to resist largely because Britain made resistance possible. Hoare was a principal architect and a principal instrument of Britain's policy toward Spain.

It is doubtful that any ambassador had gone to his post under more dramatic or more discouraging circumstances. Neville Chamberlain, already replaced as prime minister by a more aggressive Winston Churchill, told him: "I doubt whether it is worth your accepting this mission. You may never get to Spain, and if you do you may never get away. The French army is in hopeless rout, and our own army is already being evacuated from France and is leaving behind most of its equipment. Go to Spain if you wish, but do not expect that in the midst of those defeats your mission can be successful."

But Hoare's friend, Admiral Tom Phillips, deputy chief of the Naval Staff, urged him to go. He said: "You must go at once. It is essential that the Atlantic ports of the Spanish Peninsula should not fall into enemy hands. With the probable loss of France and the French fleet we are stretched to the utmost in our battle with the U-boats. If the Atlantic ports of the Peninsula and with them the coast of north-west Africa go over to the enemy, I do not know how we shall carry on. It is essential also that the naval base of Gibraltar should remain available for our Mediterranean and eastern communications. If you can do anything in support of these fundamental needs of the war, your mission will be of the highest strategic importance."

Hoare went. He went off in a British government plane to a war in which victory might be vital to his country's survival, and to the survival of freedom in much of the world. In Lisbon he found a telegram ordering him to await further word before going on to Madrid. He was later told to continue on to Madrid but to retain the plane for possible use in returning to England. Hoare, privy to many of Britain's war secrets, carried on his person a revolver he had learned to use. He also had a Scotland Yard bodyguard. He feared assassination or kidnapping and was prepared to defend against either. He flew on to Madrid and sent the plane home.

Meanwhile Britain's world was falling apart. Even before Hoare and Lady Maud, his gallant wife, left London, King Leopold of Belgium had offered to capitulate to the Germans. In Lisbon, Hoare learned that the evacuation at Dunkirk had been completed. On June 9 Norway's resistance ended. The following day, Mussolini declared war. Ten days later German tanks reached the Spanish frontier, and Spain became the apprehensive neighbor of Hitler.

Hoare was convinced that he had undertaken an impossible task. Writing to Lord Beaverbrook five days after his arrival, he said that, if he had known of the difficulties he would face, he would not have gone to Spain. But worse was to follow. When he presented his credentials to Generalissimo Franco the latter failed to give him the usual private interview following the ceremony. Furthermore, when Franco finally received him in a room adorned with signed photographs of Hitler and Mussolini, and Hoare made a cautious reference to Spain's economic needs, Franco retorted that Spain needed nothing from the British Empire. Franco then went on to ask why the British did not end the war now, since they could not win it and since the destruction of European civilization would follow if the war went on. Hoare vigorously asserted Britain's determination to win the war, but Franco was not impressed. Neither was Hoare impressed when Franco said that Spain's policy was abstention from the war. Hoare said that he and Franco parted, with the latter unimpressed with the strength and resolve of the British Empire and with himself surprised at Franco's complacent feeling that it was his destiny to be his nation's savior. The impression of Franco's complacency was strengthened with time. Hoare entitled the English edition of his book *Ambassador on Special Mission*, but he gave the later American edition the title *Complacent Dictator*.

Only a month later, in his annual speech on the anniversary of the Nationalist revolution, Franco publicly laid claim to Gibraltar. "Two million soldiers are ready to revive Spain's glorious past," he announced. On the following day the usual

long parade of military forces and the Falange was held. Since
all the rest of the diplomatic corps were going to view it,
Hoare felt he should not absent himself, but when a well-organized claque began to shout "Gibraltar español," he and his
wife ostentatiously left the viewing stands.

Although Hoare was deeply discouraged, he took the offensive in Madrid and maintained it. He had barely had time to
present his credentials when German troops made their appearance on Spain's northern border. They were plainly visible across the small bridge at Irún, and the Spanish press
reported that they would parade in San Sebastián the following Sunday. Hoare leaped into action. He protested that unneutral act, the parade was canceled, and the Spanish military
officer who had authorized it was suspended. Serrano denied
Hoare's version of the San Sebastián episode; he maintained it
was a routine mix-up with no significance, but Spaniards in
general went along with Hoare's version of it.

Hoare had found in Madrid a rudimentary embassy incredi-
bly unprepared for war or even peace. There was of course no
Allied news in the Falange-controlled press, and for the diplomatic pouch to bring the London *Times* to Madrid would
have been contrary to regulations. Such was the power of
bureaucracy that, while German armies were spreading like a
leaden wave over much of France, Hoare had to go to the
highest authorities of the British government to have the
Times sent to Madrid.

On the face of it this was the time for Hitler to march
through Spain, seize Gibraltar, and close the Mediterranean;
to take advantage of a stunned and weakened Britain that was
fighting alone, and of a near helpless and prostrate Spain
whose very existence depended on German tolerance. But the
Germans had not yet come through Spain, and Hoare thought
they might not come through. He quickly acquired an abiding
hatred for Franco and the Franco regime, but his mind ran this
way: Franco might believe in German victory (like most Europeans he did), but *Franco did not want Germany in Spain*.
That was the important thing, and Hoare thought there was a
chance he could build on it. News—and propaganda—and especially trade, which, despite what Franco said to him, Spain

desperately needed, would be the principal bricks he would build on. Later he would say, with complete accuracy, that trade preceded the flag rather than the other way around, since in 1940 the British flag did not impress many Spaniards. Hoare was not the first to grasp the importance of trade. His predecessor, a distinguished career ambassador, had also emphasized it, as indeed London itself had, and the all-important British-Spanish trade agreements had been concluded several months before Hoare's arrival in Madrid.

After his arrival, Hoare worked night and day to reduce the obvious advantages the Germans enjoyed in Spain, while he struggled to obtain advantages for Britain. His progress was related to the course of the war, but he was never satisfied with it. He appeared to think the Spaniards could walk a tightrope while at the same time leaning toward Britain. Or, perhaps more accurately, he wanted the Spaniards to believe they could. And eventually they began to believe it and act accordingly.

In his early messages to London Hoare continued fearful, but in Madrid he was the unflappable diplomat, all confidence. By no word, no act, no gesture did he give any sign that he thought in terms other than British victory. His manner was untroubled, his assurance complete. He rented one of the finest homes in Madrid as his residence, rivaling in pretentiousness the residence of the German ambassador and, significantly, right next door to the German's residence. He played tennis frequently; he had no idea of letting war interfere with his routine.

Soon after he was installed, while the British were reeling from the blow they had received in France, and Hitler was biding his time to land in Britain and end it all, Hoare gave the biggest cocktail party Madrid had seen since the end of the monarchy, with plenty of Scotch whiskey brought up from Gibraltar. Spaniards thoroughly enjoyed it, and many of them lost their hats or exchanged them for unwanted hats, because Hoare's residence, while it was impressively furnished (he was still, with London's permission, using his predecessor's silver to the annoyance of its owner), never had adequate checkroom facilities. In that field Hoare muddled

through, also in typical British fashion. We in the American
Embassy quickly learned to leave hat and coat at home when
we went to a British Embassy reception, even in midwinter. It
was easier to cure a cold in Madrid than to acquire a new
homburg or topcoat one was willing to wear.

The one thing that bolstered Hoare's courage was his
friendship with Foreign Minister Beigbeder. His admiration
for Beigbeder was limitless. Hoare reported to Lord Halifax,
who was then foreign minister, on August 8 that he had been
meeting with Beigbeder repeatedly. He embarked on a series
of visits to the Foreign Office that became daily events. The
visits also became the talk of the town, but Hoare did not
indicate that; possibly he did not know it at the time, although he should have. He should have known that he was
being followed closely. Soon he and Beigbeder were meeting
for private conversations in out-of-the-way places.

Beigbeder flattered Hoare by filling him in on activities of his
that were not known to other diplomats. Hoare reported
proudly that when Beigbeder was negotiating a Spanish-Portu-
guese agreement he showed him the document in its original
form with the penciled notes and amendments of the negotiators written on the margin. He also told us in his book that he
was actually with Beigbeder when the latter authorized Lequer-
ica, the Spanish ambassador in Paris, to act as intermediary in
transmitting to the Germans Pétain's request for an armistice.

On September 27 Hoare, in some excitement, wrote a long
letter to Halifax describing a meeting he had just had with
Beigbeder at a ruined villa of the royal family a few kilome-
ters outside Madrid. During the meeting Beigbeder had explained his short war–long war theory. He had said that Interior Minister Serrano and the young Falangists had staked
their fortunes upon the war's ending that autumn in a complete German victory. Beigbeder, on his part, had staked his
fortunes on the war's lasting longer and not ending in a complete German victory. Beigbeder believed that there was an
excellent chance that his policy would soon be confirmed and
Serrano's discredited.

At the same time, Beigbeder had said, his victory over Serrano would not be popular in Spain. The prospect of a long

war would be blamed largely on Britain, and Britain would be attacked for needlessly prolonging the war to Spain's detriment. In the circumstances he strongly recommended that Britain immediately carry out an intensive radio campaign to convince Spaniards that she was going to insure that the country's economic needs would be met. He urged Hoare to return to London quickly in order to get the campaign going.

Hoare was favorably impressed by Beigbeder's theory. He told Halifax that he thought his and Beigbeder's fates were joined. Happily for Britain Hoare was wrong. Less than a month later he was addressing a letter to Beigbeder lamenting the latter's dismissal from office. Hoare regarded Beigbeder's dismissal as an act of perfidy on Franco's part, and his later dismissal of Serrano as a blessing. It might more plausibly be argued that Franco's appointments of foreign ministers, and his firings, reflected the changing international situations, that they constituted a pattern which even then was visible to many observers but was not recognized by Hoare. As already noted, the replacement of the pro-Allied Beigbeder by the pro-Axis Serrano was a serious blow to Hoare's hopes, and he asked himself, and Halifax too, whether he should give up and return home. He favored returning home, but Halifax urged him to stay. The decision was that he should stay.

Hoare's description of the new foreign minister could not have been more hostile. He wrote, with considerable exaggeration, that Serrano absented himself from the office for long periods, bringing business to a virtual standstill. He said that Serrano had acquired Franco's passion for "ceremonial" visits; that even as interior minister he had visited Berlin and Rome. As foreign minister, he recalled, Serrano accompanied Franco to the meeting with Hitler at Hendaye, and in mid-November he was with Ciano paying homage to the Fuehrer at Berchtesgaden. Hoare was indignant at those examples of what he considered to be Serrano's egotism and exhibitionism. He would have rejected any suggestion that Serrano's visits might have had results that were favorable to Britain. Hoare and Serrano battled verbally for two years. Neither would give in to the other. Serrano developed a degree of respect for Hoare, but Hoare found no merit in Serrano. Hoare

hated Serrano with a burning hatred. He showed it in his conversations in Madrid. He revealed it in his book. He devoted six
pages to reproducing a letter he wrote to an unnamed person in
London excoriating Serrano. In the letter he said that Serrano,
Ribbentrop, and Ciano had much in common, that they were
vain, perfidious, ostentatious, jealous, cynical, and snobbish.
Hoare might have been surprised to learn that Serrano hated
Ribbentrop almost as much as Hoare hated Serrano, that Ciano
hated Ribbentrop more than Serrano did, and that Ciano portrayed Serrano as a lightweight who was moved more by emotion than by knowledge or good sense.

Later in his book, Hoare said that Beigbeder believed that
the British Empire, supported by the inevitable participation
of the United States in the war, would at least prevent a
German victory and possibly accomplish a German defeat. He
thus wanted to maintain friendly relations with the British to
avoid the chance of a new Peninsular War, while Serrano, on
the other hand, didn't hide his feeling that Ribbentrop, Ciano,
and he would meet in London on September 15, 1940, for
what in Madrid was called Hitler's victory cocktail party.
This was what Hoare maintained, not Serrano. Serrano denied
ever having said any such thing, and I doubt very much that
he did say such. Hoare said, further, that Serrano as foreign
minister wanted to reverse Beigbeder's policy of being favorably inclined toward the British Empire and the United States,
and that he seized every chance to display his loathing.

Hoare did not tell us, of course, that at the time Serrano
became foreign minister Hitler was exerting enormous pressure on Franco to enter the war against Britain, and that Serrano's appointment may have helped Spain to resist that pressure. He could not tell us that because he did not know it at
the time of writing any more than he knew that Beigbeder
arranged for the refueling of German submarines in Spain.
Hoare had had nothing but contempt for Serrano in the latter's earlier role as interior minister, and he took it for granted
that as foreign minister Serrano would be hostile to him,
since he represented an Anglo-Saxon government and had
been a close friend of Beigbeder, his rival and predecessor.

Hostility between Hoare and Serrano reached a peak two

days after Germany had invaded Russia when a mob of young Falangists, who were probably carrying out instructions, assembled in front of Falange headquarters in Madrid to celebrate that portentous event. Serrano said, with doubtful candor, that since the leaders did not know what line to take with the demonstrators, they asked him to come and talk to them, and he did. His speech was violently anti-Soviet. "Russia is responsible for our civil war," he shouted. "History and the future of Europe call for her extermination." He said that after saying that he asked the demonstrators to disperse peaceably. Nevertheless, some of them ended up stoning the British embassy.

Hoare, justly indignant at the demonstration and the attack on the embassy, both of which he assumed had been inspired and orchestrated by the Germans, reacted immediately. Assembling the principal members of his staff, the three military attachés in dress uniform, and some of them, according to Serrano, armed, Hoare confronted Serrano at the latter's home and, standing not sitting, delivered a strong oral protest. Serrano said that after he had replied that the Spanish government deplored the incident and would take steps to prevent its recurrence (he was referring only to the attack on the embassy of course), Hoare, trembling with rage, shouted that this could have happened only in a barbaric nation. Serrano showed the protestors the door.

Hoare believed that the Nazis were delighted with the stoning incident, and he was undoubtedly right. Nevertheless I believe the British came out on top. The story that went around Madrid the next day was that some of the demonstrators had knocked at the embassy door, and that when a staff member had opened it and asked what they wanted, they had shouted "Gibraltar! Gibraltar!" "Well you won't find it here," the Englishman had said, calmly, and had closed the door.

In my opinion that story, which delighted Falange-hating Spaniards (a majority of Spaniards that is), more than compensated for the few broken windows that resulted from the demonstration. I consider further that the attack on the embassy was helpful to Britain because when its echoes reached Berlin they made the Nazis feel better about Spain than they had reason to feel. Hoare, himself, apparently well pleased with his own dashing role, reported to London that the incident might prove to be a blessing in disguise.

Serrano charged Hoare with wanting to intervene in Spain's internal affairs, and Hoare did indeed openly favor a prompt return of the monarchy, which Franco was far from having in mind. Soon after Hoare's arrival in Madrid, the Portuguese ambassador, a strong but discreet Allied supporter, gave Hoare a dinner at which he proceeded to embarrass his host by making a strong pro-monarchy speech. Hoare himself suggested that he may have gone too far in commenting on Spain's politics. He wrote that when Jordana was later named foreign minister to replace Serrano he, Hoare, was glad to be in England. Had he been in Madrid, he said, gossip would have invented stories about his vendetta against Serrano and his part in the final act. Franco alone was responsible, he said in all seriousness, since he, Hoare, was in England at the time. Hoare was defending himself against a charge that was never made, but he wanted people to believe that it might reasonably have been made. The idea that some might consider him powerful enough to bring Serrano down was quite congenial to him.

Hoare contrasted the problems Serrano created for him, or that he thought Serrano created for him, with the cooperation he received from Demetrio Carceller, the engaging minister of industry and commerce. He said that few days passed without visits to and from the British embassy and Carceller's ministry. He added that Carceller did not hesitate to criticize his ministerial colleagues, especially Serrano. Carceller, an astute observer and able negotiator, knew of course that criticism of Serrano was pleasing to Hoare. He had boasted to me that he could fool the Germans any time, and he had told the Germans that he could fool the British and the Americans any time. What Hoare ignored or chose to overlook was that while Carceller was in the business of making agreements with the Allies and the Axis that were helpful to Spain, Serrano (like Franco) was in the business of refusing to make the agreements that Hitler most wanted from Spain, agreements that would have brought Spain into the war on the side of the

Axis. As already suggested, it would be venturesome to suggest that the amiable Carceller was more helpful to the Allies than the abrasive Serrano was, but Hoare suggested that; it was what he believed and wanted to believe at the time.

Serrano had little reason to like Hoare, and he did not like him, but I doubt that he returned Hoare's hatred in kind. In mid-1941, when Serrano was denying Ambassador Weddell access to Franco, I asked Carceller why Serrano took a more offensive attitude toward Americans than he did toward the British. Carceller replied that Weddell, in Serrano's mind, typified the rich American businessman whom he scorned and probably envied, while he admired the "English lord" type that Hoare represented. In fact Serrano would have liked to have been an English lord himself, Carceller said. If Serrano had the impression of Weddell that Carceller suggested, he was wrong, of course, but Carceller might have accurately described Serrano's attitude toward the "English lord" that Hoare was to become following his mission to Spain.

Hoare, Serrano maintained, divided Spaniards into two groups—on the one hand puppets of Germany with Serrano at their head, and on the other friends of England and of Sir Samuel Hoare. "A dangerous classification," he called that. Hoare, he thought, should have known that Spaniards were searching for ways to serve Spain. Serrano said, correctly, that Hoare took personal credit for Spain's switch to neutrality. "Let us be honest," he said, "and not forget that Stalin, following the German-Russian rupture, was the cause of Hitler's no longer giving the same attention to matters in the West. It is that rather than all the intrigues of Sir Samuel Hoare which kept the Wehrmacht from our soil."

All Hoare's activities as ambassador were related, in one way or another, to the war. Like any ambassador he had the responsibility of extending protection to his country's nationals, and the war greatly increased the scope and complexity of that function. Following the fall of France, particularly, many Allied Air Force personnel who had been shot down over Europe crossed the Pyrenees into Spain, while French refugees, mostly military men making their way to Algiers, crossed by the thousands.

Some refugees were able to reach a British consulate or even the embassy in Madrid without being detected by police, but most of them either turned themselves in or were apprehended and placed in a large concentration camp in northern Spain that had been constructed to house Republican prisoners during the Civil War. Hoare tried to obtain decent treatment for all those refugees, but it was extremely difficult, less because the Nazis were monitoring closely what was going on than because Spain's resources were so limited. It was difficult even for Spaniards to obtain sufficient food to maintain health. Hoare's agents purchased food and other supplies in Gibraltar and Lisbon and brought them hundreds of miles to the camp. Following the refugees' release, they transported them to Gibraltar or Portugal for evacuation. Given the sparsity of facilities in Spain that was a very creditable operation. Until the United States set up its own refugee program, and the de Gaulle regime did the same, Hoare continued to assume responsibility for looking after all Allied refugees. He built an annex to his residence where he housed many of them en route. All Hoare's refugees were permitted to depart from Spain, most of them to engage in further military service.

Hoare's role in caring for refugees was impressive, but it was dwarfed by his broader activities in gaining facilities for the Allied side and in limiting and lessening facilities Spain extended to the Axis. At the same time, Hoare was selective in his representations to the Spanish government. In his early messages to London he emphasized that for Spain there was no alternative to a policy of accommodation with Germany and that Britain must recognize that.

In another of his letters to Halifax he warned that Britain was in no position to impose preliminary conditions on the Spaniards; that if she should tell them that they must put an end to German propaganda in the press, for example, she would be imposing a condition that Spaniards could not carry out, and any effort on their part to carry it out might be against Britain's own interest. The Germans, already on the Pyrenees, might well respond by demanding free passage through Spain.

In contrast to his view that London should show tolerance of Spain's overt pro-Germanism which, indeed, he hoped might favor the Allied cause, Hoare was untiring in protesting acts that were of direct military assistance to the Axis. For a number of reasons, including geography, greater familiarity with Spanish affairs, and the circumstance that Britain had already been in the war more than two years before the United States was forced into it, Britain bore most of the burden of detecting and protesting such acts, and Hoare welcomed the burden (which American ambassadors were largely spared) and carried it superbly. In a kind of blanket memorandum to Foreign Minister Jordana simply dated "July, 1943," one of the scores of protests he made, Hoare noted several cases of refueling and resupplying German and Italian submarines in Spanish waters. Among other complaints, he charged that Axis agents had been permitted to build up a vast organization for sabotaging British ships; that facilities had been granted to the Germans to set up night observation stations on both sides of the Straits of Gibraltar; and that the Germans had been allowed to build up an espionage organization on Spanish territory and to install wireless transmitting sets. And, touching on a subject that Hayes also had discussed with Franco, or was about to discuss with him (there is some doubt as to which ambassador discussed it with him first), Hoare said that the Blue Division was still in Russia and, unless quickly repatriated, could well be the last non-German unit fighting for the Germans. Also, he added, events were developing rapidly and Spain was in peril of being overtaken by them. The memorandum, which Hoare referred to as his "Grand Remonstrance," covers seven pages in his book.

Not content with the Grand Remonstrance, Hoare, less than a month later, pursued General Franco to La Coruña, in northern Spain, where the latter was spending the summer, and handed him another list of complaints. Since Hoare's last talk with Franco the Italian king had dismissed Mussolini, and Italy was clearly on the edge of military defeat. Hoare was eager to obtain Franco's reactions to those portentous developments. Nevertheless he made a point of saying that the main subjects he planned to discuss were the Falange, nonbel-

ligerency, and, once more, the Blue Division. To his great annoyance, however, he found Franco little disposed to talk about any of the things he had in mind. He said that Franco was miles away from Madrid in wartime, comfortably ensconced in a smoking room, just as willing to discuss crops, weather, or the shooting season as the great events currently taking place in the world. Hoare added that his powerful words just petered out and did not set off any explosions.

Spain's performance improved, but not enough to satisfy Hoare. On January 27, 1944, after submitting still another list of complaints he warned Franco starkly of the possible results to Spain of continued unneutral acts that favored the Axis. Speaking officially, he suggested that if Spain continued to give unneutral assistance to the enemy long after she could plead force majeure, his government would be unable to maintain its existing policy toward her. He suggested, therefore, that Franco reflect not only on the desirability of dealing with Britain's complaints but also on Spain's future relations with the United Nations as a whole. If the Allies should win a decisive victory in the war, as the British government was convinced they would, Spain's most important political and economic relations, Hoare pointed out, would be conducted with those nations. He suggested that Franco and the Spanish government reflect on whether in those circumstances they should permit acts and incidents that would inevitably alienate the Allied peoples. If Spain wished to be sure that the victorious powers would accept her as a partner in world affairs following the war's end, it should cease all unneutral assistance to Germany, he said.

Pierre Daninos has told us that a correct Englishman would lose all his dignity if he talked about himself, particularly at the beginning of a story. Either Daninos was wrong or Hoare was not a correct Englishman. He began the story of his mission in Spain by informing us that his family was one of the oldest pure English families in England, and the oldest banking family in London. He reminded us that he had served thirty-four years in the House of Commons, and that he also had served as First Lord of the Admiralty and as Secretary of State for India, for Foreign Affairs, and for Home Affairs; four times as Air Minister; and as Lord Privy Seal in the War Cabinet. He told us, too, that he had served in the Army during the "Great War," and carried out missions in Russia, Italy, and the Balkans. It was evident that in most circumstances being ambassador to Spain, even on special mission, constituted a considerable comedown for him.

Hoare's record in Spain, particularly in 1940 and 1941, was impressive, but Hoare was not altogether an impressive person. Serrano has told of having looked forward to meeting him because he was a great figure in Europe's history. He told of his disappointment when Hoare called at the Foreign Office and he had the opportunity to talk to him and observe him. Serrano noted that while Hoare was talking he held a handkerchief tightly pressed in the palm of his left hand. He would stuff the handkerchief into his coat sleeve, but would soon take it out and again press it in his hand. Serrano watched the operation, which I myself do not recall having observed, with interest and possibly with amusement, although he was not a man who was easily amused.

Serrano himself had a nervous cough and a nervous twitch which did not escape Hoare's attention. One can picture those two earnest statesmen, talking to each other about matters of life and death to their nations, cordially disliking each other, and carefully monitoring each other's tics.

A politician, although lacking warmth or humor, Hoare was always on stage. Conscious of his reputation as an appeaser, he was determined not to appease in Spain or, what was more important, give the impression that he was appeasing. He was not an endearing person or, to many, even a likable person, but he was confident and disciplined. I suspected that even his rages were planned. I was often in his company, but I saw him flustered only once, and that was on a social occasion. The Hoares were giving a dinner for the Turkish ambassador and his wife. The wife, an Egyptian princess, was charming, but the ambassador, possibly too fully aware of his country's independent role during the war, was on the gruff side; he catered to no person.

The main course that night was a succulent ham that had been brought out from England. When it was offered to the ambassador's wife she declined it courteously, but the ambassador was less gracious. Of course Hoare should have known the problem would arise. A stickler for protocol himself, he was acutely embarrassed. He apologized profusely to his Moslem guests and asked if bacon and eggs would do. The princess smiled and shook her head. The ambassador mumbled something and applied himself to the vegetables.

Hoare did have one amusing story about himself that he told in Madrid. At one of Franco's annual luncheons for the diplomatic corps he saw a pleasant-looking person who appeared familiar, and shook hands with him. Later he was asked why he had shaken hands with the Italian ambassador. Hoare said that he hadn't realized that it was the Italian ambassador. He would have shaken his hand anyhow, he added, since he didn't look upon the Italians as combatants in the war. The story was well received in Madrid because it reflected the opinion most Spaniards had of the Italians' place in the war.

Hoare was not an easy man to like but in their way Spaniards liked him, even when he was being his most difficult. They liked him because he was very much their kind of person—the kind of person they understood and cherished. Like many Spaniards, he was a monarchist. Like many in government, and many outside government as well, he was a reactionary. Like Spaniards, he had his eyes firmly fixed on the past even when he peered into the future. As the war neared its end, Hoare talked to Ambassador Hayes of dividing North Africa into British and American zones of influence. That was the kind of man and the kind of plan the Spaniards could understand. They were thinking along similar lines except that it was Spain that was to gain territory and influence—if Germany won the war that is, and if they were in it under conditions they themselves prescribed.

Almost to the eve of the Allied landings in North Africa, Hoare was maintaining that more than one influential Spanish general was eagerly looking forward to an African campaign (presumably on the Axis side) in which Spaniards could win the rewards and trophies of an easy victory. The truth is that if an influential Spanish general had suggested such a quixotic venture to Franco at that stage of the war there would have been one influential general less on active service in the Spanish Army. The only way the Spanish Army could win a victory of any kind in Africa at the time was to be actively on the side of the Allies, and not even the most pro-Allied Spaniards were recommending that. Hoare was saying also that the Falange was becoming daily more aggressive. Again, the truth was that the Falange was surviving because Franco found it useful; he would shake it off when the time came.

In any event all thought of Spain's engaging in a new African campaign left Hoare's mind when he learned of the approaching Anglo-American landings in North Africa. He made much of his own role in preparing for the landings. He has informed us that during an early visit to London he urged an African campaign, and that, during a later visit, in August, 1942, he was involved in many meetings about the coming offensive. He said that when he returned to Madrid at the beginning of October he had nearly a month to prepare for the beginning of the offensive. Preparations, it turns out, involved principally continuing to carry out the British end of the Allied economic program (but with somewhat greater publicity), and assuring Jordana at the very hour of the landings that they involved no threat to Spain or Spanish interests. Ambassador Hayes was charged with delivering a similar message to Franco at the time.

After the first few days of the landings, Hoare had time to take stock of the world situation, and he decided to give the Spanish government the benefit of his conclusions. In a long personal memorandum dated February 19, 1943, he gave Jordana three reasons why Allied victory was now assured. They were: 1) the growing superiority over the Axis of Allied armaments in quantity and quality, 2) Germany's failure to reconcile any of its conquests, and 3) the certainty of a two-front war in Europe made possible by Russian successes and pending Anglo-American offensives.

So far Hoare was on firm ground, and Jordana did not dissent from his judgment. Spain had excellent ambassadors in London, Washington, Berlin, and Rome, and Jordana knew pretty well how the war was going. But Hoare then looked into the more distant future, and what he saw there was something quite different from what Jordana saw.

Addressing himself directly to the problem that was giving the Spanish government greatest concern, Hoare said that there was no reason for the fears of some neutral countries that a Soviet victory would mean a Communist-dominated Europe. The victory at the end of the war, he promised, would be an Allied, not a Russian, victory; a victory in which the British Empire and the United States would exercise the greatest possible influence. He added, as a clinching argument, that Stalin himself had declared that it would not be Russia's policy to interfere in the internal affairs of other countries.

Jordana was ready for that. In a response to Hoare he stated that communism was indeed the great danger facing the world, and since it was being propagated by a powerful Russia all nations had reason to be alarmed. He added that Spain's alarm was shared especially by Russia's close neighbors. Predicting that Russia would penetrate deeply into German territory he asked which would be the greater danger—a Germany left with strength enough to hold communism at bay in Europe; or a Germany overrun by Russia, which would permit Russia to have an unprecedented empire from the Atlantic to the Pacific.

Suggesting that Germany was the only existing force in the center of Europe that was capable of containing and possibly destroying communism, Jordana said, interestingly enough, that Germany would have to be invented if it did not exist, and that it would be foolish to think that her place could be taken by an alliance of Lithuanians, Czechs, and Rumanians, which peoples would quickly be converted into so many additions to the Soviet Union. If Jordana had added Latvians, Estonians, Bulgarians, and Hungarians to the list he would have been remarkably close to the truth.

Hoare did not retreat from his thesis, however. In a second memorandum he asked Jordana irrelevantly why Hitler destroyed Poland, a former shield against Russia. Hoare was making debating points and making them poorly. He was talking about what had already happened and could not be changed, rather than what might be made to happen in the future, which was his original theme. Hoare told Jordana that a new era was coming, an era of Anglo-American predominance. He predicted that Great Britain would be the strongest military power in Europe, that its influence would be greater than at any time since the fall of Napoleon, and that the Empire's virtually unlimited strength would help to guarantee Europe's peace. Before there was a real opportunity to test Hoare's theories, however, the British Empire that he knew had ceased to exist.

In his book Hoare assumed, probably incorrectly, that Jordana accepted his thesis, and that despite this, Franco did not really change policy and appeared to rely on General Vigón, who was under the influence of Admiral Canaris. When he wrote that, Hoare did not know that Canaris, in 1940, may well have saved England from defeat by revealing to Vigón that Franco could safely ignore Hitler's demands for free passage through Spain to Gibraltar and for Spain's entry into the war. He seemed to think that aside from the Duke of Alba and a few other known monarchists all persons who had intimate relations with Franco were enemies of Britain.

Late in 1943, with the Axis retreating in every sector, Hoare gave serious consideration to the possibility that the Allies should overthrow the Franco government. In a letter to London dated 11 December 1943, he suggested that the time might have come to destroy Franco's complacency by cutting off imports, thus paralyzing Spain's economy. Hoare recognized that such a step would be dangerous; that it might plunge Spain into anarchy; that it might provoke a massacre of Falange leaders or a black terror against the "Reds." Such possibilities in themselves did not disturb him however; what did give him pause, he explained, was that German saboteurs might exploit what occurred to Britain's detriment. If, however, London considered Britain strong enough to ignore trouble in the Peninsula, Hoare thought it could play the economic card with a fair chance that it would destroy the Franco regime. Hoare clearly relished the idea of destroying the Franco regime since he thought there was no chance of

friendly Allied relations with it—even if such action resulted
in chaos in Spain.

Hoare again turned out to be a poor prophet. Franco eventually developed excellent relations with both Britain and the
United States. And long before Franco and the Falange died
falangismo, as an organized political force, had already died.

Great Britain's stake in Spain was extremely high, and
Hoare must have made a great effort, initially, to cotton up to
Franco, but he was unable to. With Hitler supreme in Western
Europe and possessing the power to deprive Spain of the
means of survival, and with England close to defeat, Franco
had made little effort to help him, but Hoare's own nature
was also a factor. Appeaser or not, Hoare had had an unusu-
ally distinguished career. He had dealt with other greats of the
world on an equal basis, and he considered Franco to be small
potatoes compared to most of them, and indeed compared to
himself. He told us in his book that one of his first requests
was for a private audience "with the great man." Sarcasm did
not raise Hoare in the eyes either of his friends or his opponents, but where Franco was concerned it probably provided
him with needed psychological release. Franco's statement,
during their first private meeting, that Spain needed nothing
from the British Empire rankled him during the remainder of
his mission, even though Franco later changed his tune.
Hoare had probably never heard of the archetypal Spaniard
who, when his larder is empty, stands at his front door after
the dinner hour and ostentatiously picks his teeth. Franco
was a true Spaniard.

In the last two chapters of his book, Hoare summed up his
feelings toward Franco, but his words came less from the diplomat who had succeeded brilliantly in helping to insure Allied victory in World War II than from the politician who was
returning to his Chelsea constituency and had a reputation as
an appeaser to overcome. One by one he listed Franco's sins
and alleged sins, the same sins he had devoted many earlier
pages to: Franco's mistreatment of the "Reds" during the
Civil War, his speeches, his desire for German victory, his
likeness to Hitler and Mussolini, the facilities he had given

the Axis. (I have often wondered whether Hoare ever thought it strange that a man as evil as he said Franco was ever came to select Hoare's idol, Beigbeder, to be foreign minister.)

Hoare asked himself whether it might not be argued that Franco's acts were justified by his desire to keep Spain out of the war; that he had given the Axis words rather than deeds. But he rejected that argument out of hand. He said that Serrano in Berlin, and Franco at Hendaye, had already paid Spain's debt in full. He even penetrated Franco's mind and insisted that Franco had served Hitler willingly. When Hoare wrote those things he was presumably ignorant of what had actually gone on in Berlin, Hendaye, and Berchtesgaden. Even if he had known, however, he probably would have given little credit to either Franco or Serrano. (Hoare told us in the preface of his book that he had not attempted to alter or amplify the impressions he had in Spain by what he learned later.)

Left-leaning *PM* in New York could not have condemned Franco in harsher terms or given less recognition of the help Franco had given the Allies, willingly or unwillingly, gladly or sadly, than Hoare did. Even though Franco did not care for the Allies, his hesitancy about entering the war aided them, Hoare said—and staying out of the war also helped Franco to stay in power, he added. Hoare might have said, with equal justice, that if the Allies had helped to keep Spain out of the war it was not for love of Spain or of Franco, and that Franco's clinging to his post was as helpful to the Allies as it was to Spain. After four pages of summing up, Hoare said that there was no answer to the charges he made. Yet, Hoare went on, there was Franco still—fat, smug, complacent, seemingly unworried and undoubting, convinced of his indispensability and wisdom.

How Hoare had changed! No matter that he, himself, had reminded London many times that Spain's policy was helpful to Britain, and that Franco's fall would not be helpful. No matter that he had warned that if Britain should tell Franco that he must stop the German propaganda in the Spanish press it would be asking Franco to do something that might

bring about a German ultimatum demanding the right of passage through Spain to Gibraltar. No matter that he had cautioned London repeatedly that it must be patient with Spain.

Those earlier warnings were profoundly justified when
Hoare made them. Indeed they expressed the rationale of Allied policy toward Spain, which was his own policy. That
policy assumed that if the Allies made it possible for Spain to
stay out of the war Franco would respond. The Allies had
helped and Franco had responded. Yet in his hatred of Franco,
and doubtless out of a compulsion to demonstrate that he had
not appeased Franco, Hoare came close to denying that Franco
had any role in Allied success in Spain.

Referring to his own embassy, Hoare said that it was the
British who, in the perilous days of 1940 and 1941, helped
encourage popular feeling against the war and Nazism. The
British, through trade agreements and personal contacts,
strengthened goodwill on the part of the Spanish people toward the Allies and England during a period when Spain's
government was enemy-controlled.

Of course the Spanish government was as much a party to
the trade agreements as the British government was, and the
trade agreements were as helpful to Britain as they were to
Spain. Furthermore, if the Spanish government had ever been
in the hands of the Axis, which is very doubtful, it was only
briefly, in 1940, when Axis victory in Europe appeared inevitable and imminent, and even then Franco had been careful to
insist on conditions that Hitler was unwilling to meet. And
nothing the British and American governments could have
done would have kept Spain out of the war if the Spanish
government had not wanted to stay out.

Following the Spanish-American War, Theodore Roosevelt
wrote a book concerning his Rough Riding exploits in Cuba.
"Mr. Dooley" said that the book should have been entitled
Alone in Cuba. As Hoare summed up his accomplishments,
one might be tempted to suggest that *Complacent Dictator*
might better have been entitled *Complacent Ambassador* or
even *Alone in Spain.*

Early in his book, referring to the use of Gibraltar as a
staging area for the Allied landings in North Africa, Hoare had

said that it would be impossible to mislead the enemy, since Gibraltar was watched by a legion of spies and was open daily to thousands of Spanish workers. There would be hundreds of Allied ships and thousands of Allied airplanes at hand; and the Germans would demand of the Spanish government an explanation of what was going on, why the neutral ground between Spain and Gibraltar was being used for a tremendous assembling of aircraft and why extensive numbers of ships were being gathered not only at Gibraltar but also in the Bay of Algeciras. The successful use of Gibraltar, within easy reach of Spanish heavy guns that were already pointed at it, was one of the keys to Allied victory in Europe, but in the summing up, his near-total condemnation of Franco, Hoare did not recall that anything like the deception of Germany by Spain ever happened.

Hoare even used information that clearly indicated that Franco was deceiving the Axis in order to demonstrate that the contrary was true. On December 15, 1943, after Spain had shifted from a nonbelligerency that favored the Axis in the short run (but that worked against it in the longer run) to a neutrality that was helping to insure Allied victory, Hans Diekhoff, Hitler's then-ambassador to Spain, reported a conversation he had had with Franco. Diekhoff said that he had protested to Franco against help that Spain had given the Allies—help that included withdrawal of the Blue Division from the Russian front, passage of French refugees through Spain to North Africa, release of Italian merchant ships to the Badoglio government that had replaced Mussolini's Fascist regime, unjustified internment of German U-boat crews, action against German ships in Vigo and in the Canary Islands, "and so forth" (grounds for protest were evidently too many for the ambassador to list them all). Diekhoff went on to say that Franco had listened seriously and calmly (Franco listened to all ambassadors seriously and calmly) and then had explained to him that his actions and planned actions in all those cases were in Germany's interest.

As though this were not enough, Diekhoff reported that Franco also had taken the opportunity to express the wish that Germany would supply Spain not only with more arms

than it had already sent but with more than it was then con-
templating sending. He had emphasized his hope for German
victory and his friendship for Germany, and had "very
warmly" requested Diekhoff to greet the Fuehrer most cordially on his behalf.

One can imagine the fury with which Hitler must have
read Diekhoff's report if indeed anyone had the courage to
show it to him. Nevertheless Hoare included the report in his
effort to prove that even at that late date Franco was determined to enter the war on the side of the Axis provided he
was not involved in any serious fighting.

The fact that the postwar governments of the United
States, Britain, and France, strongly influenced by the Soviet
Union which was determined to bring the Franco government
down and bar Spain from membership in the United Nations,
also used Diekhoff's report as evidence of Franco's collaboration with the Axis, did not excuse Hoare from doing the same
thing. After all, Hoare knew better from his own direct experience. In an earlier letter to London Hoare had said of the
Spaniards, "When the demands come, it is difficult to see how
they can be resisted. The will to resist is there, but not the
power. All that I can do is to try to strengthen the will and
hope that something will turn up before the demands are
actually made." When he wrote his summing up, the demands had been made and Spain had resisted, but now Hoare
talked as though Franco had not had the will to resist.

The Sir Samuel Hoare who emerged from *Complacent Dictator*, far from being the authentic hero I knew in Spain, was a
carping critic, all too ready to blow his own horn. At the same
time he failed to take credit for one of his principal accomplishments; possibly he was not even aware of it, although in
retrospect it is apparent. By the very number, and in some
cases the vehemence of his protests to Franco and Serrano,
and by his overt criticism of both, he helped to convince the
Germans, at a critical period, that the two were more reliable
friends than they were in reality. The fact that the accomplishment was largely fortuitous does not detract from its
importance.

Serrano said, with some justice, "Hoare . . . might have

given us the impartial, serene, documented book which he owed us, the book that History awaited." Rather than that, he suggested, "Hoare preferred an easy success; in the manner of a toreador who salutes his public, he sought to improve the image he projected to constituents who were calling him to account."

It was nevertheless Serrano who may have best characterized Hoare's role in Spain. Serrano said:

"I may say in justice to [Hoare] that he was an extremely valuable servant of the British Empire, and that no other Allied mission in Spain was as useful, as productive, as his was.

"By his presence and by his influence in Spanish politics he succeeded, to an appreciable degree, in counterbalancing German influence, and even in causing numerous sectors of opinion to abandon their faith in Axis victory and in the advantages such a victory might bring. He conspired successfully; he defended his cause with tenacity; he raised spirits; he was in a real sense a power within Spain."

Coming from Serrano, and in the light of the things that Hoare had already said of Serrano in his book, that was praise indeed. Serrano's assessment of Hoare was much more accurate than Hoare's assessment of Serrano—or of Franco.

Hoare served four and a half years as ambassador to Spain; four and a half of the most perilous years in the history of the British Empire and in the life of Britain itself. He could not prevent or even slow down the dissolution of the empire, as he would have liked, but he helped to save some remnants of the world he best knew—most of them well worth saving. Hoare had annoying characteristics, and he was a fallible person, but those characteristics detracted little from the success of his mission to Spain, for which he was to receive scant credit except in his own (and, briefly, in Serrano's) memoirs, a fate he shared with Serrano and Hayes.

8 HAYES

All the books of the old Spanish hands are, in a sense, apologias. According to the authors none of them ever made a mistake, and that is true of Hayes as well as the others. It is also true of this deponent, of course.

Carlton J. H. Hayes, as most of us know, was one of America's most widely read historians. I had studied his Political and Social History of Modern Europe in college and I expected him to be a doddering old man when he came to Spain, but in fact he turned a young sixty the day he and his family arrived in Madrid.

Hayes knew a great deal about Spain's history, but he had never visited the country and he did not speak Spanish. He was completely surprised when Sumner Welles invited him to Washington in the spring of 1942 and told him that president Roosevelt wanted to name him ambassador to Spain. At first he pleaded inadequacy, but Welles, and later the President himself, reassured him on that score and he agreed to accept the post. It was difficult to turn down the president's urgent request at such a critical time in the life of our nation.

Hayes was an excellent ambassador, better than his volume reveals. *War Time Mission in Spain* was not acclaimed by American liberals, and that hurt Hayes. A convert to Catholicism, and a former cochairman of the National Conference of Christians and Jews, he was proud of his liberal background and firm in his liberal views. Little of that side of him was reflected in his book however. What was reflected was that he had gotten along with Franco and that he had called for cooperative relations with the Franco government. Hayes did himself a disservice, from the short-term point of view that is, by publishing his book early, before public antipathy to Franco in the United States had had time to lessen. When, years later, he asked me, in sorrow, if I could understand how some people could have called him a fascist sympathizer after reading his book I told him that I could, even though I knew that he repudiated everything the fascists stood for.

As an historian Hayes could place the Spanish problem in its historical perspective. He had no aspiration for himself other than to do a good job in Spain and when that was done to return to his beloved campus in Morningside Heights. He was able to do both.

My view may be slightly colored, of course, because Hayes and I saw eye to eye on nearly everything, but it could easily have turned out differently. In Lisbon, where he debarked from the Pan American Clipper that had brought him from New York, he was told by a helpful embassy wife that the embassy in Madrid was buying pesetas in Lisbon and flying them into Spain. The story was true, and Hayes soon started to share in the loot, but only after he had given me a hard time explaining that the operation had the Spanish Foreign Office's blessing and was one of the many things that happened in wartime Europe that could not be judged by ordinary standards. The clinching argument I gave him, however, was that the Papal Nuncio was one of the most enthusiastic participants in the racket. Nevertheless a prudent Ambassador Hayes later insisted that a State Department official fly over from Washington and give written approval on the spot to what the Department already knew we were doing.

Three or four days after he had arrived in Madrid, when his

time was taken up getting settled and preparing to present his credentials, Hayes learned to his consternation that a number of telegrams that he had not seen had gone to Washington over his name. "Look here, I want that stopped," he said to me, fearful that his record as ambassador might already have been tarnished. Later he was to learn that more than an occasional telegram might go out from an embassy without the ambassador's having seen it.

When those little matters were cleared up Hayes and I settled down to a working relationship which was a joy to me, and he was generous enough to say that it was a comfort to him.

In his dealings with the Spaniards, Hayes was forthright but kindly. The only Spaniard he actively disliked was Serrano. In a letter to President Roosevelt he referred to Serrano as a petty, intriguing, and very slippery politician, troubled with stomach ulcers and delusions of grandeur, and militantly pro-Axis. In his book he notes that Serrano's habit of slouching in his chair and letting his eyes roam about the ceiling was disconcerting, as were the fascist-saluting Falangist guards who lined the stairway to Serrano's office. Hayes's opinion of Serrano was the common one, but Hayes never got to know Serrano. He talked to him not more than a half dozen times and I accompanied him each time as interpreter.

Serrano got revenge for the unflattering things Hayes said about him. "Since Hayes did not count for anything politically," he said in his own book later, "the two important ambassadors, from the viewpoint of my ministry, were . . . von Stohrer and Hoare." He said, further, that while Hoare was a personage, and one was therefore obliged to pay attention to everything he said, Hayes never made a single interesting observation to him—doubtless because the two did not talk about history. Oddly, in that connection, one of the few requests that Hayes made of Serrano was for help in arranging for the manuscript of George Santayana's autobiography, *Persons and Places*, to be sent from Rome to Madrid in the Spanish diplomatic pouch. The request was granted, and Hayes forwarded the manuscript to Washington. Serrano's sole request of Hayes, in turn, was for help in arranging for the delivery to the Spanish government of thirty-odd Packard cars that had already been paid for. Hayes complied with the request, and the beautiful Packards were soon being driven through Madrid's streets to the admiration and delight of auto-starved Spaniards. Hayes remarked to his staff that not even the most rabid Falangist could be anti-American while riding in a brand new Packard.

Hayes made one error in Madrid, an error that was to cause the State Department and the embassy (as well as the Iberian Peninsula Operating Committee) a great deal of anguish and was to give Hayes a reputation for appeasement that he did not deserve but could never shed. It happened this way:

Some eight months after he arrived in Madrid Hayes was invited to give a talk to the American Chamber of Commerce in Barcelona. He regarded the invitation as an opportunity to communicate with the Spanish people. Even though the controlled Spanish press should fail to publish the speech Hayes could have our information service distribute copies of it throughout Spain.

Hayes was disturbed at the amount of criticism Spaniards were directing at the United States because of what they thought was the miserly manner in which our government was dealing out export licenses for gasoline. In Hayes' view, and in my view too, they were not justified in their criticism. The criticism was getting on Hayes' nerves and he decided to make a frontal attack on it—to remind the Spaniards that according to his method of calculating they were getting a higher ration of gasoline than people along the Atlantic coast of the United States were getting.

I told Hayes that this was dynamite; that the news agencies would excerpt it from his speech and it would make headlines in the United States. But he made the speech, the headlines appeared in the American press, and a storm of editorial protest was directed at the State Department and at Hayes for giving "pro-Axis" Spaniards better treatment than patriotic Americans were receiving.

In his book Hayes told us that the barrage of criticism in the United States struck him as both humorous and pitiful. My own impression is that he was deeply chagrined by it. The speech and the hostile reception it received plagued Hayes during the remainder of his life. It was even mentioned in his long and generally very laudatory obituary in the *New York Herald Tribune.* Hayes was an excellent lecturer, and it is ironic that lecturing turned out to be a weakness rather than a strength in his conduct of the embassy in Madrid. One or two of his lectures were aimed at his colleague, Sir Samuel Hoare, as much as at the Spaniards, but they missed their mark. If it is a truism that a nation cannot expect to gain at the conference table what it has been unable to gain on the battlefield it also is true that Carlton Hayes was unable to gain in the lecture hall anything that he had been unable to gain in direct communication with Sir Samuel.

Hayes had an important role in helping to dissuade the Allies from seizing Spain's Canary Islands as a part of the North African landings, which Washington told him was a possibility. Following Hayes' reasoned protest he was authorized to convey to Jordana, who had replaced Serrano as foreign minister, President Roosevelt's assurance that the United States had no intention of infringing upon the sovereignty of Spain or of any Spanish colonial possessions or islands or protectorates. He was able to tell Jordana, further, that the United States had perceived with great satisfaction the improvement of relations between the two countries that had taken place in recent months. That was by far the most friendly (and most helpful) statement that Washington had ever made to Franco Spain, and it may well have contributed to the success of the landings. And Hayes had many other accomplishments to his credit.

Hayes got off to a good start with Franco. The presentation of credentials is usually a routine affair, more ceremony than substance, but in his case it was both. Looking back, I can see that it was an historic event. Hayes had given much thought to what he would say in the formal address he was required to make, an address which Franco would have to reply to, and he had asked me to draw up a draft for his consideration. I worked on the draft off and on for several days but when I handed it to him I said that I had not come up with anything new or brilliant; that I had kept coming back to the matter of trade, which of course was not new—it was the basis of our Spanish policy. But Hayes was way ahead of me. What was new, he grasped immediately, was that since the speech would be published in the press he would be "going public"; he would be expressing our Spanish policy in an ambience that insured the greatest possible publicity for it. And Franco would have an opportunity to identify himself with that policy. If he did, he would have taken a significant step in the direction of fuller cooperation with the Allies.

On June 9, 1942, at ten o'clock in the morning, Hayes' official staff, "twelve strong" he recalled in his book, and all in full dress, assembled with him at the embassy residence, while a hundred Moorish guards, in native costume and mounted on richly caparisoned stallions, filled the courtyard and the adjacent street. At a quarter to eleven the chief of protocol arrived with five automobiles. In these, and flanked by the Moroccan guards on their prancing steeds, we made our way through Madrid's streets to the applause of a multitude of citizens who had come out to offer encouragement to the new American ambassador, and also to see the show.

At the royal palace we were escorted up the grand staircase, through several large rooms, past a score of soldiers at present-arms, into the long throne-room where Franco, with the entire cabinet on his right and high dignitaries of state, church, and university at his left, stood waiting. Halting some twelve feet away, Hayes, with his staff in a semicircle behind him, read his speech in English (Franco had already read it in a Spanish translation). After praising Spain's history, her culture, and her civilization, and expressing gratitude for the aid she had given the United States in establishing her freedom as a nation, Hayes said:

"My country is devoted ... to the principle that international trade should be freed to the greatest possible extent from the restrictions which have barred the nations of the world from free access to raw materials which should in justice be made available to all peoples on an equal basis. No country is self-sufficient or is capable of becoming self-sufficient without disastrously lowering the living standards of its people. Therefore, within the limitations naturally imposed by the troubled circumstances in which we all live today, my country is prepared to engage in honorable trade with all countries which are in a position to trade with us, exchanging those commodities which we are free to export for those products which friendly nations can send to us without depriving their own people."

Three years earlier, when Ambassador Weddell suggested that trade with the United States would bring benefits to Spain, Franco had shown no interest. Now, replying to Hayes, he said:

"I believe . . . in the good of the economic interchange to which Your Excellency refers in the words you have just spoken, thanks to which the friendly spiritual relations will have the solid support of a correlation of interests between the two countries, based on the principle that no people on earth can live normally by its own economy and that all need one another for the attainment of human ends."

Following the exchanges of speeches Franco led Hayes into an adjacent room for the traditional few minutes of private conversation. But the few minutes grew to fifty. Nor were the two engaged in chit-chat. When Franco expressed the conventional view that Hitler, to all intents and purposes, had already won the war, Hayes spoke of the enormous resources of the Allies and their determination to prevail. He asked Franco if he could contemplate with equanimity the lasting preponderance in Europe of Nazi Germany with its fanatical racism and its anti-Christian paganism. Franco admitted that that was not a pleasant prospect, but he professed to believe that Germany would make concessions if the Allies would. He said that Spain did not wish an Axis victory but that it ardently wished a Soviet defeat.

Little notice was taken in the United States of the subtle shift in Spain's public attitude toward the Allies that Hayes' speech and Franco's response represented; of the common acknowledgment of interdependence; of Spain's implied denunciation of Hitler's vaunted "autarchy," which even then threatened to make Spain an economic vassal of Germany. For another year Franco would continue to make ritualistic and dreary speeches in praise of the Axis, and ample publicity

would be given to them. The United States would vacillate
from time to time in carrying out its commitments under the
policy Franco and Hayes had announced. But for Spain the die
was cast. There would be no turning back.

Hayes has told us that he always got along with Hoare,
that he found him very interesting. And he did. Nevertheless
the two never liked each other. Hayes did not fail to remind
us that Hoare won "fame or its reverse" by the "ill-fated"
Hoare-Laval Agreement. He recognized that Hoare "performed signal service" during the difficult days of 1940 and
1941, but he suggested that Hoare didn't like Americans or
seriously try to understand them; that he still regarded
Americans as rebellious subjects of George III. He told us
that Hoare "doubtless felt, correctly enough, that he had
borne the heat and burden of the 'Peninsular Campaign' for a
year and a half while the United States had held aloof from
the struggle and that the leadership he had then assumed
and had since so ably exercised should be unquestioningly
accepted and obeyed by a colleague from a country which
had just begun to fight Germans."

Later Hayes said: "The trouble was that Sir Samuel Hoare
was intent upon playing a lone hand and was seldom frank
with us about his dealings with London or with the Spanish
Foreign Office. His usual practice was to obtain information
we had while withholding his from us, on the assumption
apparently that it is more blessed to receive than to give, and
then to make independent démarches at the Foreign Office
and afterwards ask us to rubber stamp them."

There was never any quarrel between Hayes and Hoare but
their dislike for each other was well known in Madrid. Hoare
regarded Hayes as an inexperienced and bookish person with a
tendency to lecture his equals, while Hayes regarded Hoare as
a sly politician, always on the lookout for ways of advancing
his own interest and reputation, even at the expense of the
interest and reputation of a friend and ally.

Differences between the two arose almost immediately
after Hayes' arrival when Hoare urged Hayes not to attend a
speech Franco was about to make before the Falange council.
Hayes attended the speech and it turned out to be mild. Later

Hoare sought to persuade Hayes to join him in encouraging a restoration of the monarchy in Spain. Hayes explained that the United States would recognize any government, whether it was monarchist or republican, that the Spaniards themselves might elect and that could demonstrate its capacity to maintain order at home and fulfill its obligations abroad.

It was of course a case of Hoare, the politician, expressing what he thought was politically desirable, and Hayes, the professor, reminding the former secretary of state for foreign affairs of what they both knew was officially correct. Hayes, as well as Hoare, felt in his heart, as most moderate Spaniards whom we knew also felt, that restoration of the monarchy offered the best hope for establishing a lasting peace in Spain, and of course the monarchy was reestablished following Franco's death, which was doubtless the right time to reestablish it, although Hoare did not want to wait that long. And Hayes, when he maintained that the United States would not intervene in Spain's political affairs, was accurately expressing current policy, although as we shall note later both the United States and Britain intervened in Spain's internal affairs without cause or helpful effect after the war was won and appeasement of Soviet Russia had become an important objective of our Spanish policy.

Hoare and Hayes were a study in contrasts. Hoare was a smallish man, hardly taller than Franco whom he called "the little Generalissimo." Prim, precise, almost expressionless, he was solemn and determined. Hayes, fully as determined as Hoare, was a large man with large features, solemn looking but prepared at any moment to explode into hearty laughter. Hoare saw little that might be amusing in serious subjects. Hayes found something amusing in almost everything and everyone including Hoare (although not always) and himself. Hoare was the official, the establishmentarian. Hayes was not taken in by official pomp or station; he knew of too many fools in high places. Hoare, without being particularly religious, was certain that God was on the side of the British Empire. Hayes was deeply religious but skeptical of some of the religious people he knew. Hoare was a monarchist in Spain as well as in Britain. Hayes was a fervent democrat, but he was by no means certain that democracy would survive in the world. Hoare, the politician, had an image to foster. Hayes, the historian, searched beneath the image for truth. Hoare might deceive in order to attain an objective. Hayes was capable of being truthful when caution counseled silence.

In wartime Spain there was a great deal of speculation, especially among diplomats, concerning the kind of Europe that would emerge from the war, and it was natural that Hayes, a world-famous historian, should be asked for his opinions. Sometimes, unfortunately perhaps, he gave them. From comments some of his listeners later made it was evident that far from sharing Hoare's view that Britain (and even the United States) would have an important role in determining the fate of existing colonies, Hayes believed that Britain's postwar role would be greatly diminished, even in Europe itself. Reports of Hayes' statements, some of them doubtless exaggerated, reached Hoare, who did not like them. Hayes clearly had made his statements privately and in reply to questions. Whether he should have made them, even though his questioners might themselves have been saying things that he considered preposterous, as sometimes occurred, is another thing of course.

Hoare complained to some of his close friends that Hayes was inclined to steal marches on him. There was some justification to that charge, but of course Hayes himself had the habit of stealing marches on his American colleagues, although he would not have used that term in his own case. As already noted, long before Hayes arrived in Madrid, Ambassador Weddell had complained to Washington that Hoare, briefed by London and the British ambassador in Washington, had the habit of informing Spain's foreign minister of State Department views before the Department (or Hoare) had communicated those views to Weddell.

At times the lack of coordination between Hayes and Hoare reached unbelievable levels. In the autumn of 1942 Spain was sure that the presence of an enormous Allied fleet off Gibraltar, a part of it in Spanish waters, meant that the Allies were about to land somewhere not far away. On November 6, 1942, only two days before the landings in North Africa, Foreign Minister

Jordana warned Hayes that if the Allies should land anywhere in Morocco, in either French or Spanish Morocco, that is, Spain would be obliged to take military precautions, and might not be in a position to decline German assistance. Hayes correctly interpreted that as a bluff, probably intended for the record, but one could not be sure that it was a bluff, and Spain, with 150,000 troops in Spanish Morocco, was certainly in a position to place great obstacles in the way of the landings if it chose to. Nevertheless what bothered Hayes most was not Jordana's statement but the fact that Jordana had gone on to tell him that he had made the same statement to Hoare a day earlier, and that Hoare had not mentioned it to Hayes. Furthermore when Hayes tried to discuss that highly important matter with Hoare the latter declined to see him on the ground of several previous engagements.

At the same time the Hayes-Hoare relationship had its lighter side, and many amusing stories, some of them well founded, circulated in Madrid. One of the annual reports of the Anglo-American hospital noted that Lady Maud and the American ambassador would share a bed during the coming year, meaning of course that they would share the cost of maintaining a bed in the hospital. Since Lady Maud was not exactly a pin-up girl or Hayes a Lothario this bed-sharing caused a good deal of merriment in the British-American community. Hayes grinned every time it was mentioned to him. Sir Samuel's reaction did not become known to us.

Leaving other characteristics of the two ambassadors aside, Hoare's thin sense of humor made it unlikely that he and Hayes could ever become really close. Furthermore, Arthur Yencken, Hoare's dedicated counselor of embassy, whom we saw often, had little more sense of humor. The two were models of literal-mindedness. Madrid was a hotbed of rumors, and all kinds of stories of Allied activities in the area, most of them false and many of them silly, were circulated there. Hoare, while he was on the subject of rumors, related solemnly that the American ambassador had asked Yencken, late in 1943, if it was true that the British had landed troops in Portugal's Tagus River. I can picture Hayes asking the question and waiting to join Yencken in a good laugh until he realizes that Yencken has taken his question seriously. Being humorous or facetious in the presence of either Hoare or Yencken carried its own perils.

Like Serrano, Hoare wrote his book after he had read Hayes', and like Serrano he didn't like what Hayes had said about him. He retaliated by virtually ignoring Hayes in his own book. Aside from the silly reference to Hayes' question concerning the alleged British landing in the Tagus River, in the English edition of his book Hoare mentioned Hayes by title only once; he never mentioned him by name. In the later American edition he mentioned his name once. That, Serrano commented in his book, was an example of Hoare's "imperiousness." It was, and it also reflected his love of gestures. It was Hoare, standing, flanked by his staff, some in dress uniform, making a formal protest to Serrano. Hayes had little liking for gestures; he was too ready to laugh at himself. Of course, as between the two, Hayes, who arrived in Spain in 1942, was playing from comparative strength while Hoare, in 1940 and 1941, was playing from weakness and playing very well, gestures and all.

Hoare left Spain, scene of one of the notable victories of his long public career, filled with bitterness toward Spaniards. Hayes, who had had outstanding success in his first diplomatic venture, left with a warm feeling for Spain and Spaniards. Hoare refused, politely he said, a high Spanish decoration. Hayes accepted, as a gift of the Spanish government, a portrait of himself by Zuloaga, one of the last works of that eminent artist.

In today's interdependent world the affairs of all nations are related in some way or ways to the affairs of all other nations. Among a diplomat's common sources of information, and among persons he may wish to influence, are other diplomats. Diplomacy is a social as well as a political activity. Dinners and cocktail parties, luncheons and receptions, are given in order to afford diplomats opportunities to know and talk to one another and to persons of the country. In those circumstances wives can do much to promote helpful friendships, and both Lady Maud and Evelyn Hayes tried hard to be friends, but they had little in common.

Lady Maud, like Sir Samuel, came from a distinguished banking family, and as was inevitable, some members of the British community termed the marriage a merger. Lady Maud was a large person, larger than Sir Samuel. Amiable and probably shy, she talked little, and when she did she tended to deliver herself of ponderous nothings. Her favorite expression was "R-a-a-ally?" accompanied by a great show of surprise and interest after one had made a thoroughly commonplace remark.

Evelyn Hayes was a different sort. A devout Catholic of Irish ancestry, she was an articulate and committed activist. She wanted to get to the bottom of things. The priests in Afton, New York, where Carlton Hayes' family had lived for generations, had affectionately dubbed her "the Bishop." Hayes is credited with having arranged for the small Catholic church in Afton to be built in Protestant colonial style, but I learned that Evelyn shared responsibility for that, as she shared responsibility for the church's being built at all.

Evelyn, "the Bishop," could be pontifical at time. "Make no mistake about that!" she would often say after reciting a list of facts and explaining their meaning. Carlton had great confidence in her and told her many things, but by no means everything. And what he didn't tell her she would sometimes try, discreetly, to get from me.

When there was no social chore to perform that evening, as often as not the Hayeses and the Beaulacs would gather in the Hayeses' library to relax and talk, over a couple of martinis that the ambassador prepared by shaking, not stirring. (More than thirty years later the Hayeses' lovely daughter, Mary Elizabeth, would express wonder that the ambassador and I would always shake hands before those convivial meetings even though we might have spent a good part of the day together in the embassy offices, which were housed in the residence building only a few doors down from where we were meeting.) It was clear from some of the conversations that the ambassador was not keeping Evelyn informed of all that was happening in United States–Spanish relations, and that she regarded our meetings as golden opportunities to pick up a few tidbits that the ambassador had neglected to offer her. But I was as careful as the ambassador himself not to reveal state secrets, and the ambassador, enjoying his cocktail, would watch these contests with enormous amusement while Caroll, my wife, sometimes struggled to divine their meaning.

Evelyn was as intuitive as she was intelligent. One day we were sitting in the library when the ambassador was informed that Sir Samuel Hoare would not be able to call that evening as he had planned. No one paid any particular attention to that matter-of-fact announcement except Mrs. Hayes. Suddenly she said, "Sir Samuel has gone to Seville."

"Why do you say that?" the ambassador asked a little impatiently, "As far as you know he hasn't even left town."

"Didn't Archbishop Spellman go to Seville?" asked Mrs. Hayes.

"Yes, of course. You know very well that Archbishop Spellman went to Seville, but what does that have to do with Sir Samuel?" Hayes responded. "Sir Samuel has gone to Seville to talk with Archbishop Spellman," Evelyn said with conviction.

The background of that unusual conversation is as follows: Archbishop Spellman, who was military vicar for Roman Catholic chaplains in our armed services, made several trips to the Vatican during the war. There was always speculation concerning those trips. Among the rumors they gave rise to was one that Spellman was helping to negotiate a separate peace with Italy. The archbishop was an old acquaintance of the Hayeses, who would put him up at the embassy residence when he stopped over at Madrid. On this particular occasion he had spent the night at the residence and on the day we had our conversation he had left for Seville to take an Italian plane to Rome. It was perhaps natural that Sir Samuel should have pondered all the rumors about Spellman's trips and should try to find out whether there was any basis for them by talking to Spellman himself. All this occurred to Evelyn Hayes although it did not occur to the rest of us.

The sequel to the story is that Sir Samuel had in fact suddenly flown to Seville. When the archbishop returned to Madrid he recalled that he had spent the night in Seville at the home of the American consul. He told us, innocently, that on

the afternoon of his arrival at Seville he had left the consular
residence to take a walk around town. To his surprise Sir
Samuel just happened to be strolling past the residence when
the archbishop emerged, and he had joined him in his walk.
The two talked about the archbishop's mission in Rome.

The presence of the pro-Allied Jordana in the Foreign Office
greatly facilitated Hayes' mission to Spain, sometimes in
ways that were far from conventional. Late in 1942, at my
request to Pan de Soraluce, Jordana gave informal recognition
to Colonel Pierre Malaise, a former Vichy military attaché in
Madrid who had joined the new French forces in Algiers, as an
attaché of the American embassy. The arrangement was new
in my experience and doubtless rare in diplomatic annals, if
indeed it had existed before at all. When Malaise was later
joined by two career French diplomats and by Monsignor
Boyer-Mas, a remarkable priest who also was a former member of the Vichy embassy, the four set up their own office and
Hayes obtained recognition of it as the de facto mission of the
Algiers regime. That was a devastating blow to German-Vichy
influence in Spain.

The Hayes-Jordana relationship became particularly important following the Allied landings in North Africa. An immediate result of the landings was that German troops occupied
the large portion of France that, under the Vichy government,
had remained relatively free. A result of that, in turn, was a
new influx of Frenchmen across the Pyrenees into Spain. By
February, 1943, some 12,000 had entered Spain on their way
to North Africa where most of them joined the new French
Army.

The sudden influx of Frenchmen and other refugees from
France was of course too much for Sir Samuel Hoare to
handle, so Hayes, with help from the new Algiers mission,
took care of most of them. He set up a refugee and relief
section in the embassy and placed Niles Bond, an up-and-
coming young Foreign Service officer, at its head. Hayes obtained money and food from the American Red Cross, and
when the problem continued to grow, other private agencies
including the Quakers and the Jewish Joint Distribution
Committee interested themselves in it. Bond helped to orga-

nize the combined Representation in Spain of American Relief Organizations, which was headed by David Blickenstaff, an experienced relief worker, who worked hand-in-hand with Bond.

Blickenstaff's group concentrated on "stateless" refugees, principally Jews, who lacked documentation. By November, 1942, some 2,000 refugees were being cared for. Furthermore the Spanish government itself, by permitting Sephardic Jews living in German-occupied territories to assert Spanish nationality, made it possible for a much larger number of Jews who remained in their countries of residence to avoid being sent to concentration camps and probable death.

By that time Spain was making concessions to the United States in many areas, but Hayes was not satisfied with the progress being made. Like Hoare he wanted the Spanish government also to improve its attitude toward Soviet Russia. And like Hoare he failed to convince it that it should. Neither Hayes nor Hoare foresaw the cold war, and their predictions concerning Russia's place in the brave new postwar world sound naïve today. The Spaniards were much closer to a correct appraisal of Russia's intentions and capabilities than the Allied representatives (or the Allied governments) were.

Jordana unknowingly opened the door for Hayes to discuss Spain's relations with Russia. There was a kind of perverse innocence in authoritarian Spain that frequently, as Emmet Hughes had discovered, failed to understand that the United States government, even when the country was at war, could not prevent the American media from saying things that were displeasing to foreign governments, or to the United States government itself for that matter. "We don't slander you" (although they often did), Spanish officials would remark piously, "so why do you slander us?"

On June 14, 1943, Jordana handed Hayes a *note verbale* protesting the content of an American motion picture, *Inside Fascist Spain*, which was attracting a great deal of comment in the United States. In his note he expressed surprise that Spain was being portrayed as "fascist" when that was "notoriously untrue." The Spanish government, he stated, had repeatedly explained that the regime was "exclusively Spanish."

Hayes welcomed Jordana's communication. It provided an opportunity to let the Foreign Office (and, he hoped, the Falange) know how others saw Spain. In a long letter to Jordana he explained why Spain was generally viewed in the democracies as "fascist." He pointed out that:

"Spain has a single political party created and imposed upon the country by executive decree. No other political party is permitted to exist and all open opposition to this single party is suppressed.

"The members of this party wear uniforms and are organized on a semi-military basis, as in the case of the Nazi and Fascist parties.

"A form of salute made popular by the Fascists and Nazis has been adopted by this party and is made compulsory for all inhabitants of Spain, whether or not they are members of the party.

"The party possesses an armed militia, as do the Nazi and Fascist parties.

"The party has a totalitarian doctrine, as do the Nazi and Fascist parties.

"The Spanish press is strictly controlled by a censorship under party direction. The press openly attacks all enemies of the party and of the regime, while giving no opportunity for reply, or for criticism of the party or regime.

"There is no freedom of public assembly in Spain except for members of the party. . . .

"The German Gestapo has been allowed unusual facilities in Spain and has intimate relations with the Spanish police. The so-called Himmler agreement has permitted the Gestapo to obtain custody of and to return to Germany persons whom the Gestapo has wished to take into custody, and such persons have been deprived of the elementary right of self-defense and appeal to Spanish courts."

Hayes went on and on, and the final paragraph was the most devastating of all. He said:

"Inasmuch as the Ministry of Foreign Affairs has reiterated . . . the opinion that the Spanish system is not a Fascist system, the Embassy would be interested to receive and to communicate to its Government the Ministry's opinion as to the precise ways in which the Spanish system can be differentiated from the Fascist system."

And Hayes went further. On June 29 he called the Foreign Office's attention to an article in the Falangist newspaper, *Arriba*, reporting a speech made in Vienna by Dr. Suendermann, subdirector of the press of the German Reich, in which, in opposition to the Allies' "Four Freedoms," he set forth four "Liberties":

"1. To free nations from Jewish influence;

"2. To free the world from the nightmare of the bloody bolshevik regime;

"3. To free intellectual and manual workers from capitalist exploitation for the benefit of free creative expansion of all abilities; and

"4. To free the world from Anglo–North American imperialism."

Hayes expressed "profound surprise and regret that the article had been permitted to be published in the Government-directed Spanish press in Spain." He went on to say, "I would like to inquire frankly whether the reader of such an article in the Government-directed Spanish press would not be justified in believing that Spain is a Fascist country."

Seldom if ever had an American diplomat officially so criticized the government of a country with which the United States had cooperative relations. And seldom if ever had a government accepted such criticism without retaliation of some kind.

In replying to Jordana's *note verbale* Hayes had been speaking officially. Now, taking advantage of the excellent relations he still had with Jordana he sent him a "personal" letter in which he attacked the problem of Spain's attitude toward Soviet Russia. Among other things he said:

"At the same time, I am seriously troubled by the continuing attacks on Russia by Spanish leaders and by the Spanish press. I do not refer to Spain's general opposition to communism, but rather to specific statements and actions which confuse communism with Russia, one of the principal allies of the United States in the war. . . .

"Russia is an important member of the United Nations.

Any attack on Russia, therefore, is an attack on an important ally of the United States. Complacency toward Nazi Germany, on the other hand, is complacency toward an enemy of the United States. By systematically attacking Russia, while showing excessive complacency toward Nazi Germany, Spain is evidencing partiality toward Germany, and unfriendliness toward one of the United Nations.

"There is no country in the world, with the exception of Russia, which welcomes *communism* within its borders. Spain's attitude in this respect does not differ from the attitude of most other countries. However, all free countries in the world are also opposed to *Naziism,* and I believe it is fair to estimate that a majority of Germans now are opposed to it. In failing to take an official stand against Naziism, Spain is practically alone among the free countries of the world. . . .

"The United States and Great Britain, by maintaining trade with Spain, are co-operating effectively in helping to overcome conditions in Spain which might encourage the growth of communism, and my Government is not content that Spain, on its part, should reciprocate by systematically attacking Russia, an important ally of the United States and Great Britain, while making it appear that it is attacking communism. . . .

"My Government does not subscribe to the theory, frequently expressed by Spanish officials, that the present war must end in a war against communism. My Government looks forward to continued cooperation by the other United Nations with Russia during and after the war, and it is doing everything possible to help lay the basis for such co-operation. It considers that Spain, in its own interest, and in the interest of its relations with the rest of the world, should also be helping to lay the basis for peaceful co-operation with the United Nations, including Russia, in the future."

Jordana's *note verbale* of June 15 protesting American press criticism of fascist Spain had undoubtedly been written by the secretary of popular education or some other high Falangist official. His reply to Hayes' letter criticizing Spain's attitude toward Soviet Russia, in contrast, was drafted in the Foreign Office.

Addressing Hayes as "My dear Ambassador and Friend,"

Jordana said, "With reference to relations with Moscow there are two points of view: yours and mine." He suggested that Hayes' view derived largely from the war psychosis which was natural in a belligerent country. War, however, was a transient phenomenon; the basic problem, he maintained, was bolshevism. Nor was bolshevism a purely internal problem, he said. The Communist movement in Spain had been organized by agents sent out from Russia. While Spain had nothing against Russia as a nation, it noted with great concern that Russia had assumed the mission of organizing revolution in the world. . . . He went on for five pages.

On December 2 Hayes replied to Jordana. In a second personal letter he said, among other things:

"I venture to suggest . . . that, in so far as a war psychosis exists among the belligerents in the present international struggle, a similar psychosis, resulting from the recent domestic struggle within Spain, continues to affect a large part of the population of this country, inspiring them with an exaggerated fear of Russian communism and, at the same time, with an unreasoning reliance on Nazi Germany as the bulwark against communism. . . .

"I maintain that at the present time and in the future critical postwar period, Russia presents—and will present—no such menace to Europe and to the world at large as that presented by the unholy alliance of Nazi Germany and pagan Japan. . . . It is clear to me that the Russia of the present and the future, responding to the resurgence of national and religious feeling which the terrific contemporary ordeal is producing among the masses of the Russian people, can be depended upon to give more than lip service to the basic principle of international comity and co-operation."

What Hayes said was 25 percent British-American conventional wisdom and 75 percent British-American hope. While he was preparing that communication our Army attaché, Colonel William Hohenthal, who had served as Army attaché in Berlin and had witnessed the evacuation of Allied forces from Dunkirk in May and June, 1940, was already trying to figure out in his own mind how an expansionist Russia could be kept from permanently dominating the countries it would soon be occupying on its way to Berlin. At the same time an increasingly critical American press was accusing Hayes of "appeasing" Franco.

In July, 1943, Allied forces invaded Sicily. That was a sensational event that we in Spain had to take advantage of. The small but modern plant that the embassy had acquired to print its weekly Information Bulletin quickly turned out a broadsheet announcing in large letters, and perhaps with some exaggeration, that the Allies had invaded the Continent. Caroll and I, as it happened, were about to drive to Valencia on the Mediterranean coast. Taking copies of the broadsheet with us, we tossed them into the streets of towns we drove through. They were eagerly snatched up by the townspeople.

In Valencia we chose a modest restaurant to have dinner in. Besides the broadsheets we had with us samples of a propaganda device that Washington had sent us for distribution. We called it a fire bomb. It was a map of Germany with the principal cities marked in large letters. The fire bomb was impregnated with powder that one could ignite with a cigarette. The game was to bet on which German cities the lighted powder would spread to—which cities were going to be bombed, that is. After we had ignited one or two fire bombs, Spaniards began to gather around our table. More and more came over to see which German cities were going to be bombed that night, and they cheered with every bombing. Looking back it was a macabre kind of enjoyment but it left no doubt in our minds concerning the attitude of *Valencianos* toward the United States and the war, and their readiness to demonstrate that attitude.

Fourth of July that year marked another "high" in United States–Spanish relations. Two years earlier, when Weddell was being "shunned," the only Spanish official who attended the embassy's July 4 reception had been the Foreign Office's chief of protocol. All others had been ordered to stay away. But in 1943 a thousand Spaniards showed up. They included not only the Jordanas and nearly the entire Foreign Office staff but also a good number of Falangists. Spaniards were seeking to show friendship for the United States. All of them also were happy to enjoy the excellent food and drinks the embassy provided. Food was still not plentiful in Madrid, and whiskey and martinis that one could drink without seriously endangering one's health did not exist outside diplomatic (and a few official) circles. Carlton Hayes decided it was time to capitalize on that good feeling—in Spain's interest as well as that of the Allied countries.

On July 29 Hayes called on Franco on his own initiative, without instructions from Washington, that is (and without notifying Hoare in advance), and after noting that the United Nations were now sure to win the war, and that any government that had not been sympathetic toward them would find itself in an intolerable position at the war's end, he made three suggestions to him. The first was that Spain should abandon its ambiguous nonbelligerency and in unequivocal terms declare its neutrality. The second was that the Falange should stop attacking the Allies and in other ways serving the interests of the Axis. The third was that Spain should withdraw its Blue Division from Russia and refrain from further intervention in Russia's affairs. "What would happen if Russia declared war on Spain?" Hayes asked, "Russia is an ally of the United States and Great Britain."

(In his book Hayes makes a point of saying that this was the first time, so far as he knows, that any Allied protest against the Blue Division was made to General Franco, but it may not have been the first time. Hoare, it will be recalled, included withdrawal of the Blue Division among the numerous suggestions he made in his Grand Remonstrance of "July, 1943," but since, for reasons of his own, he fails to give us the exact date he made the remonstrance, we are left in the dark as to which ambassador made the first move to get the Blue Division withdrawn from Russia. This is one of a number of questions arising from the sometimes bizarre British-American diplomacy in Spain during World War II.)

The conversation lasted an hour and forty minutes, and to Hayes' surprise Franco reacted to his suggestions calmly. A year earlier he had talked to Hayes about "two wars," the one between Germany and Russia in which Spain ardently wished for Russian defeat, and the one between the Allied powers and the Axis in which Spain took no part. Now he talked of "three wars." One was between the English-speaking countries on the one hand and Germany and Italy on the other; in that war Spain was neutral. The second was the war against Japan, and Spain would gladly cooperate in winning that war. The third was the war against communism. As a result of a kind of breakdown of traditional civilization, Europe was honeycombed with Communist cells, he said, and Russia would stir up and utilize those cells in its own interest.

When Hayes reminded him that the United States and Britain as well as Russia would be winners in the war, Franco agreed that they would, but he added, interestingly enough, that after winning they would withdraw from the Continent and leave it to Russia. Hayes took exception to that view. He said that the United States and Britain would continue to act jointly with Russia after the war was over; that Europe would not have to choose between communism and fascism. He was confident that democracy would be the choice of the masses everywhere.

Franco did not agree with him on that point. Nevertheless he promised to give earnest attention to all the matters that had been discussed, and Hayes left with a feeling that he "had cast a good deal of bread upon the water," as indeed he had.

Results were prompt. Anti–United Nations discrimination in the media was sharply reduced. Three American newsmen were soon broadcasting from Madrid. And on October 1 Franco, at his annual reception for the diplomatic corps, formally declared Spain's neutrality. As for the Blue Division, Jordana told Hayes that the decision to withdraw it had been reached but that it would involve some delicate and painful negotiation with the Germans, which would take time. As it turned out it took longer than Jordana anticipated.

As might have been expected Hayes dutifully and confidentially informed Sir Samuel Hoare of his conversation with Franco. What could not have been expected was what followed. After hearing Hayes' report Hoare hurriedly alerted British and American correspondents that he was about to discuss important matters with General Franco. Following that he made his celebrated flight to La Coruña and said substantially the same things to Franco that the latter had already heard from Hayes. Soon after that he flew to London. From there the BBC broadcast to the world that Hoare had *demanded* that Franco withdraw the Blue Division.

Franco had some of the characteristics of Lyndon Johnson. When he was going to do something he wanted to be the first to announce it. And he didn't want to do it under pressure. Following Hoare's gratuitous publicity he toyed with the idea of leaving the Blue Division in Russia a while longer, and the Nazis must have toyed with the same idea. Negotiations were difficult and prolonged. And when the division was finally withdrawn Hoare took most of the credit.

During 1943 Hayes had more problems with Washington than with Spain, and most of them had to do with petroleum. The Western Hemisphere was Spain's only source of petroleum, and since the United States controlled that source it was Washington's handiest instrument for exerting pressure on Spain. Hayes sometimes thought it was too handy; that the United States resorted to it too readily.

Early in March, while Spaniards were reacting favorably to such requests as noninternment of Allied airmen, the return, uncompromised, of secret equipment in forced-down Allied planes, informal recognition of the Algiers regime, and free passage through Spain of thousands of French military men who would swell de Gaulle's forces in North Africa, Jordana informed Hayes that unless the United States could make available a small quantity of 87-octane gasoline, Spain's commercial airlines would have to close down. But Washington demurred. Hayes, and Hoare too, protested that the airlines were important to Allied communications with North Africa, but Washington still did not respond. It did, however, ask Hayes to try to induce Spain to purchase a number of American military planes that had landed in Spanish Morocco in error during the North African invasion. Hayes understandably declined to make such a request; it was a clear case of Washington's right hand not knowing what its left hand was doing. Meanwhile the Spanish airlines had ceased to operate.

Despite urgent requests by Hayes and by British authorities it was four months before a small quantity of aviation gasoline was supplied. Spain's airlines were able to resume opera-

tions, but at reduced capacity. All that was as nothing, however, compared with Washington's decision to reduce Spain's
supply of petroleum for general use.

In April, 1943, the embassy learned that the Iberian Peninsula Operating Committee (IPOC), in Washington, was planning to reduce Spain's 1943 petroleum allotment from
500,000 tons a year to 400,000 tons; it feared that from the
military viewpoint Spain was dangerously overstocked. In a
personal telegram to Secretary Hull a highly disturbed Ambassador Hayes asked how, in the light of Spain's steadily
improving attitude toward the Allies, such a reduction could
be justified under either the Atlantic Charter or the secretary's own policies.

In his response Secretary Hull gave what he himself obviously considered to be the principal reason for cutting the
petroleum program. "To leave the program as it has been," he
said in a personal message, "would not be viewed favorably by
public opinion in the United States; criticism of the oil program for Spain is greater than criticism of any other foreign
policy matter."

Hayes did not accept that. "The weight and importance of
public opinion in a democratic country like ours," he replied,
"is quite well known to me." And he continued, "When
much of that opinion, however, is so badly misinformed as it
is about contemporary Spain, I doubt whether it should be the
determinant of our Government's foreign policy in critical
war times. . . . Nor can I believe that such a reduction would
at all satisfy the noisiest and most irresponsible makers of
this misinformed public opinion; these aim at depriving Spain
of any and all petroleum. On the other hand, I cannot bring
myself to believe that the more enlightened and thoughtful
segments of American public opinion, regardless of their attitude toward the present Spanish Government, wish to deny
the people of Spain ready access to foodstuffs and other necessities of life that must be produced and transported with the
aid of petroleum products."

Washington stuck to its decision and there followed a confrontation between Hayes on the one hand and the State Department and IPOC on the other that remains unique in my

experience. For weeks the Department "advised" or "suggested" to Hayes that he halt departures of Spanish tankers for the United States (authorizing a departure committed the United States to make petroleum available to the tanker), and Hayes, using his own discretion, kept authorizing the tankers' departures and justifying his decisions in long telegrams to the Department.

The Department, and especially IPOC, which still resented Hayes' Barcelona speech and the political pressures it had aroused in the United States, were distraught. Officials began to speak darkly of Hayes' "revolt." At the same time, when Secretary Hull hesitated to take firm action against Hayes, reminding his subordinates that Hayes was the president's selection and that he had been sent to Spain to win, the subordinates themselves were close to revolt, and Hull finally gave in. He flatly ordered Hayes to stop authorizing tanker departures for the United States.

At that point, toward the end of May, Prime Minister Churchill was visiting President Roosevelt in Washington, and an unabashed Hayes suggested to the Department that the president discuss the matter with Churchill before the latter departed. He sent a similar telegram directly to the president. The Department changed its tune abruptly. It called Smith, our petroleum attaché, to Washington. Smith's visit ended in what Hayes called a "love feast"; the old schedule was restored. Feis, who was IPOC's head, denies that the visit was a love feast, but he agrees as to what the results were. And he also makes clear that Washington officials deeply resented what they considered to be Hayes' assumption that he, not they, was the true custodian of Spanish policy and programs. Hayes made no such assumption. He undoubtedly stretched to an extreme his authority as the president's representative in Madrid, but his subordinates, career officers and wartime appointees as well, backed him to the hilt. Ralph Ackerman and I drafted nearly all the messages that so infuriated some people in Washington, and we initiated many of them. But Hayes was responsible for them and Washington never forgave him for them. Its resentment did not help matters when the wolfram crisis arose.

The highlight of Carlton Hayes' mission was doubtless

Spain's decision not to oppose the 1942 Allied landings in
North Africa, and the subsequent announcement by the Spanish government that it would resist invasion from any side—
which meant from the Germans. His most difficult and oner-
ous service, however, had to do with the United States decision, in 1943, to put pressure on Spain to place an embargo on
wolfram exports to all countries. An understanding of that decision and its sequel requires a little background.

The British-American preemptive purchasing program, it
will be recalled, was aimed at depriving Germany of commodities that might be helpful to her in her war effort. Of
those, wolfram, used in the hardening of steel, was by far the
most important. As the war went on, Spain and Portugal,
practically contiguous with Germany following the latter's
occupation of France, had become that country's principal,
and almost sole, suppliers.

It will be recalled, too, that the Allies' device for depriving
the Germans of Spanish (and Portuguese) wolfram, or at least
for limiting the amounts they could acquire, was to outbid
them. The result was a boom that was unlike anything Spain
had experienced since the discovery of gold in the Americas.
Hundreds of poor farmers discovered wolfram in their fields,
and new mines were opened overnight while the price of the
mineral rose form $200 to $20,000 a ton. In addition the government imposed a tax on exports that reached $10,000 a ton.
For Spain it was a gold rush; the Germans needed wolfram so
badly that they would pay almost anything for it, and the
Allies were always prepared to offer a little more than the
Germans were paying. Following the penury and the misery
of the Civil War years, and the comparable hardships of the
years that immediately followed, this new affluence was like
a dream that wolfram producers and many persons in the
government hoped might never end.

In the autumn of 1943, when it appeared that the Allies at
last had priced Germany out of the market, the latter found
herself once more rich in pesetas. She had obtained them
principally in two ways: by collecting from Spain the cost of
the "voluntary" aid she had given the Franco forces during
the Civil War, and by substantially increasing her exports to

Spain of war materials, industrial machinery, and other products. To offset Germany's charges Franco had submitted his own bill for the "voluntary" services of the Blue Division, which he was now trying to bring back to Spain. As was inevitable, however, Germany's charges greatly exceeded Spain's, and the difference plus returns from increased German exports went to pay for renewed imports of wolfram. The boom was on again.

The arrangement was tolerable to the Germans because it gave them renewed access to Spain's precious wolfram, while for Spaniards, who were now reasonably safe from direct involvement in the war, it meant that they could continue, for a time at least, to live in the best of all worlds. Americans saw things quite differently however. The Axis had been expelled from Africa, Italy had surrendered, and both the Germans and Japanese were in full retreat. In those circumstances, American and British officials in Madrid talked of possible ways of depriving Germany of wolfram without the expenditure of additional large sums of money. The word "embargo" was spoken more than once, and it reached the ear of Ambassador Hoare, who did not like it (for Britain Spain was a convenient source of iron, potash, and citrus fruits among other products). A cautious British government notified Washington in September that it was reluctant to pursue a more severe economic policy toward Spain. A month later it reiterated its satisfaction with the economic status quo in Spain.

Both the State Department and the American embassy, on their part, believed that the time was coming for Spain to impose an embargo on the export of wolfram to all countries (as already noted, the Allies themselves were not dependent upon the Iberian Peninsula's wolfram); that the military situation made that feasible and Spain's long-term interest made it desirable. And of course it would signal a dramatic improvement in the Allied position in Europe. On October 22, in the middle of his lively discussion with Jordana concerning Spain's attitude toward Soviet Russia, Hayes, once more on his own initiative and without consultation with Hoare, called on Jordana and handed him a "personal memorandum" pointing out that complete victory for the Allies was now in sight, that the United States would do everything within its power to shorten the war, and would do nothing that might lengthen it. The memorandum stated further that when the bulk of Allied armies went into action the expenditure of materials would increase correspondingly and all such materials would be needed for the purpose of ending the war in the shortest possible time. "This rule applies to petroleum products as well as to all other products," it added.

What Hayes was saying was that the United States would use its economic strength, including its control over Western Hemisphere petroleum supplies, to insure, to the extent possible, that Spain did not supply Germany with products that might help the Axis to prolong the war. What he had principally in mind, and what Jordana knew he had in mind, was wolfram. Jordana expressed no surprise at the memorandum. He promised to give it "sympathetic consideration."

By this time Spain had already moved substantially in the Allied direction. Besides abandoning nonbelligerency for neutrality and withdrawing most of the Blue Division from Russia, she had supported Portugal's concession to the Allies of military bases in the Azores. Hayes had even induced her to give the Allies direct control over travel of Axis nationals between Spain and Spanish Morocco. At the very time he was preparing a friendly and cooperative Jordana for a specific request that Spain put an end to wolfram exports, however, the Foreign Office made an error of protocol which, in Washington's eyes, gave us an instrument with which to bludgeon Spain into meeting our wishes.

At the outset of the Far Eastern war, the Japanese, catching General Douglas MacArthur's planes lined up neatly on the ground, had quickly gained control of most of the Philippine Islands, and late in October, 1943, the new Philippine regime sent the Spanish government a telegram informing it of José Laurel's "accession to power." The Philippines, for some three centuries, had been an important part of Spain's great empire, and Spaniards continued to have strong cultural and emotional (and some economic) ties to the Islands. A routine acknowledgment of the telegram went out over Jordana's signature.

(A declassified United States government intercept now reveals that at the time the acknowledgment was sent Jordana was making strong protests through the Japanese Legation in Madrid against alleged maltreatment of Spanish clergymen and destruction of Catholic churches in the Philippines, difficulties in the way of sending assistance to needy Spaniards in the Philippines, and the abolition of Spanish as an official language in that country [National Archives, RG 457, Records of the National Security Agency, SRS 977, "Magic," Summary No. 426, May 26, 1943]. I consider it likely that Jordana and Franco, without counting the possible cost, hoped that a response to the Laurel telegram would help in the solution of those problems.]

Tokyo and Berlin lost no time in announcing Spain's "recognition" of the Laurel government and, for Spain, the fat was in the fire. Not only the British and American press, but the official BBC and the Voice of America undertook a strident campaign of vilification of Spain for having given aid and comfort to the country that, in President Roosevelt's words, had bombed Pearl Harbor on "a date that will live in infamy." It soon became evident that Spain, from being a country that was prepared and even eager to cooperate with the Allies but that still had the problem of German forces concentrated on its northern border and German submarines that could sink Spanish vessels with relative impunity, had become a country that was to be forced by public invective and other means to bow to our will.

Under Ambassador Hayes' instructions I went to the Foreign Office to ascertain what the Laurel fuss was really about. To my surprise an embarrassed Pan de Soraluce told me that the Foreign Office had indeed acknowledged the telegram from the Laurel regime but that there was no intention on its part to recognize the regime. I told Pan that in all my experience I knew of no precedent for a government's sending such a message to a government it did not recognize or plan to recognize. Returning to the embassy I drafted a strongly worded note to the Foreign Office protesting its reply to the Laurel telegram, but the State Department instructed the embassy to withhold it while it consulted with other government departments.

Time went on. Spain made it clear to the world, repeatedly, that it had not recognized the Laurel regime, and did not intend to recognize it, but Washington was not appeased. On November 6, without consulting the embassy or obtaining British cooperation, the State Department instructed Hayes to request of the Spanish government (a) a complete and immediate embargo on wolfram exports to all destinations without any quid pro quo and (b), in conjunction with the British ambassador, to request the removal of German agents from Tangier. Four days later the Department told us that a high Department official had informed Spanish Ambassador Cárdenas that, *to clear up the Laurel incident,* Spain should forthwith place an embargo on the export of wolfram, release Italian warships and merchant vessels that had taken refuge in Spanish harbors following Italy's surrender, expel German agents from Tangier, and, of all things, grant landing rights for American commercial planes in Spain—all matters that were being discussed by the embassy in Madrid.

We in the embassy were appalled at this turn of events. We could picture our bold economic warriors in Washington licking their chops and saying to one another, "Now we've got them where we want them." All the frustrations officials had suffered from Spain's double-talk, its equivocations, its praise of Hitler's Germany, and its collaboration with Germany were being compensated for without consideration of whether Spain's actions might have served American as well as Spanish interest. We in Madrid had wanted to try, initially at least, to induce a friendly government to go along with us in a move that we considered was in the interest of both Spain and the Allies. Now Washington, instead of persuading a friend, seemed intent on producing an enemy or, at the best, a resentful and recalcitrant co-actor.

Sir Samuel Hoare, who had finally joined Hayes in requesting an embargo on wolfram exports, shared the embassy's dismay at the new turn of events. He was afraid that Franco, though nearly ready on his own to accept Allied demands and impose such an embargo, would inevitably be forced to reject such demands if they were publicly forced upon him. The British government supported Hoare in that view.

On January 18, 1944, nevertheless, after matters had passed

the point of no return, Hayes recommended to the State Department that petroleum shipments be quietly suspended without previous explanation. That was done. But at that point a new complication arose. A maverick BBC, in London, broadcast to the world that the Allies had shut off petroleum supplies to Spain because the Franco regime was pro-Axis; the Voice of America picked up the same line. Hayes and Hoare implored their governments to put a stop to such official criticism, and it promptly ceased, but by that time much of the free media had taken up the cry.

Foreign Minister Jordana responded to the suspension of petroleum shipments with mingled sorrow and anger. Other Spaniards in and out of government responded as they might have been expected to. They hunkered down for a long siege. Trucks disappeared from the highways and private cars from the city streets. Fishing vessels remained in port. More and more factories were shut down. But at Hayes' insistence Spain decreed a temporary embargo on the export of wolfram, which remained in effect until the crisis was over.

When Jordana told Hayes that by cutting off petroleum supplies the United States was delivering an ultimatum to Spain, Washington maintained that it was not. But it was. When Jordana said that United States action was a repudiation of the guarantee that President Roosevelt had given at the time of the North African landings that Spain had nothing to fear from the United Nations, a guarantee that had been emblazoned on the front pages of Spain's newspapers, Washington said that it was not a repudiation of that guarantee. But Jordana still thought it was.

To make matters worse, when the Department, after the fact, asked the British to go along with its request for a total embargo they refused. Henceforth while Hayes was insisting on a total embargo Hoare was telling Jordana that Britain would settle for less. He was also telling him that if the United States refused to supply the petroleum Spain needed British companies would supply it from Middle Eastern sources. In addition, while the Department was exerting pressure on Spain it was exerting no similar pressure on Portugal, which was exporting more wolfram to Germany than Spain had been exporting. Washington had what it considered good

military reasons for that distinction, but one could not blame
the Spaniards for thinking it constituted rank discrimination
against them.

Meanwhile Demetrio Carceller, the peripatetic minister of
industry and commerce, was assuring the Germans that their
wolfram needs could be met clandestinely, and there is no
doubt that they were able to smuggle some wolfram out of
Spain, although hardly in the quantities they desired.

Back in the United States the *New York Times* published a
series of articles by its veteran correspondent Harold Denny
that tried to present the Spanish situation in objective terms.
But the author was roundly denounced as an appeaser and a
Fascist, and media attacks against Spain increased rather than
diminished. Ambassador Hayes, concerned at the torrent of
criticism, submitted his resignation, saying that his continuation in office might be embarrassing to the president during
the forthcoming national elections. The president lauded
Hayes' accomplishments and urged him to stay on. He agreed.

Jordana continued to plead for a resumption of petroleum
shipments while Spain was trying to reach a peaceable adjust-
ment with Germany, but Washington refused. A Madrid movie
theater showed a newly imported American film entitled
Boom Town. It was a drama built around gushing oil wells.
The Spaniards, long inured to hardship, laughed heartily, some
might say hysterically. But Jordana was not laughing. In a personal letter to Hayes he said that if an understanding were not
reached soon Spain would be forced to enter into an agreement
with Germany. Hayes told him that such a step might compel
the United States to cut off all exports to Spain.

In Washington a tired Secretary Hull finally lost patience
with what was going on and in a moment of pique he suggested to Halifax that Britain might want to make a separate
agreement with Spain, in which event it should also take over
the responsibility of supplying Spain with petroleum. When
Mr. Churchill indicated to President Roosevelt that he was
ready to do just that, Hull capitulated. On April 20 Hayes told
Jordana that he was authorized to agree to Spain's limiting its
wolfram exports to Germany to 20 tons for May, 20 tons for
June, and 40 tons a month thereafter. The following morning

Jordana informed him that he could go along with that. The wolfram crisis had lasted three months but it was now over. American-controlled oil once more flowed to Spain. In June, following British and American pressure, Portugal imposed a total embargo on wolfram exports.

Britain and the United States had won an important battle, and Britain took full credit for its role. Immediately after the agreement was signed Hoare flew to London and Winston Churchill indulged in paeans of praise for Spain and for Generalissimo Franco, while the BBC added to the atmosphere of generous approval. In contrast Washington, instead of taking credit for victory, blamed the British because victory was less than complete. When Jordana suggested that the three countries issue a joint communiqué on the agreement that had been reached, Hull informed the embassy that "because of the situation here" he must include in any press release a statement to the effect that he had "arrived at the settlement at the request of the British Government whose supply situation was different from that of the United States." Hayes begged him to change his mind but he refused. He told Hayes, "A compromise with Spain will not be popular, and the fact that it is favorable to us will not allay all criticism. Without detracting from what you have accomplished I feel I must inform our people that it was at British insistence that we accepted a settlement on a basis short of what we wanted."

Our gains had transcended wolfram of course. Other objectives we and the British had worked so hard to attain also had been achieved, again in varying degrees. The German consulate in Tangier had been closed, German agents had been expelled from Spain and Morocco, and the last straggling remnants of the Blue Division had been withdrawn from Russia, Italian warships and merchant vessels had been released. Spain, in balance, was now on the Allied side. Germany still had large stocks of wolfram stored in the country but most of it was still there when, later in 1944, the route through France to Germany was cut following the Allied landings in Normandy.

In mid-1943 Ambassador Hayes and I had driven up to the

International Bridge at Irún and gazed at the detachments of German soldiers and the menacing armament on the French side of the bridge. When a Spanish guard asked if we wished to cross over I had replied, "Not now, thanks, but next year we shall."

I never crossed that bridge, but on Sunday afternoon, August 27, 1944, Hayes, Hoare, and Monsieur Truelle, the French minister in Madrid, crossed the bridge together with their aides, drove through Hendaye, where Franco had had his memorable meeting with Hitler, and on to St. Jean de Luz and Biarritz to the wild plaudits of the French people. Hayes would stay on as ambassador another five months, but his wartime mission to Spain was already accomplished.

On May 7, with the wolfram crisis over, I departed for Washington on my way to Paraguay where I had been named ambassador. In the State Department I had a long conversation with Cordell Hull who was gracious enough to say that he would not have changed a single thing the embassy, under Ambassador Hayes, had done. He went on to complain that the British were taking credit for many gains in Spain that the United States had contributed to, and he asked me to give him a report on our accomplishments in Spain, which I did. I said, among other things, that if we had received little credit for our accomplishments it was partly Washington's fault; that it frequently acted as though it were ashamed of them; that it often appeared to give more importance to uninformed public opinion at home than to our interests in Spain. But Mr. Hull already knew that.

In his *Memoirs* Hull said, "We were never friends of the Franco regime, and I felt that that regime was bad for Spain and the world." The truth is that Secretary Hull, under whom I served in the Department of State and for whom I had not only respect but affection, had little idea of how Spain, in the 1930s and the 1940s could be most helpful to itself and the rest of the world. But the fact that he thought that Franco was bad for Spain and the world illustrates the problem that we in Madrid, and like-minded persons in Washington, had in obtaining support for a program that in retrospect was of enormous importance to Spain, to the Allies, and to freedom in the world.

9 INSTRUMENTS AND OBSTACLES

What kinds of tools does an ambassador have to work with in wartime? In Spain they were a variegated lot.

The Foreign Service officer component was small, experienced, and effective. More than half became ambassadors. The Auxiliary officers, temporary appointees with legal or economic training, in some cases both, also were effective. One of them, Covey Oliver, became an ambassador and, later, an assistant secretary of state.

One of my first acts, after arriving in Madrid, was to examine the embassy files back to the First World War. Our ambassador at the time the monarchy fell was Erwin B. Laughlin, a career diplomat who, judging by what I read in the files, spent his summers quite properly in San Sebastián while the Foreign Office was installed there, his winters in Marrakesh where the climate is infinitely superior to Madrid's, and the rest of his time mostly with monarchists in Madrid, when he was not in the United States or traveling in Europe that is. Even after the king's prime minister had declared, following the municipal elections of April 12, 1931, that the monarchy was doomed, the ambassador continued to assure Washington that it would survive.

Our ambassador to the Republic that followed was Claude Bowers, an historian-politician, a close friend of President Roosevelt, and a fervent Democrat. In late June or early July, 1936, Bowers wrote an interesting letter to his sister in Indiana. The sister revealed its contents to the local newspaper, and shortly thereafter the world press was quoting Bowers as saying that the Republic was as strong as Gibraltar. The Republic, in fact, was on its last legs. Very shortly afterward the Civil War broke out.

Each of our ambassadors had been ideologically and emotionally committed to the government to which he was accredited. The lesson was clear; in our dealings with the Franco government, and in acts that might affect that government and its attitude toward us and toward the war that was going on in Europe, we should not be swayed by sympathy or ideology. That was the embassy's attitude during the war years. Neither Ambassador Weddell nor Ambassador Hayes would have permitted any deviation from that road.

Another thing that impressed me in reading the files was the little communication there was between the embassy and the monarchical government. Still another was that communication, when it did take place, was principally in writing. There seemed to be more formal notes than memoranda of conversations. Carefully prepared notes, many of them drafted by technicians in Washington, were replied to in equally formal notes from the Foreign Office. The Civil War years were special of course. Bowers, while continuing to be ambassador to Spain, spent the entire period in southern France while one or another Foreign Service officer represented the United States in beleaguered Madrid and in other cities where the Republican government might be temporarily functioning or trying to function. A different kind of diplomacy was clearly required in the Spain of the 1940s.

When I told Undersecretary of State Sumner Welles, before

leaving for Madrid, that I was surprised that I, who had never served outside Latin America, was being assigned as deputy chief of mission in strategically important Spain, he told me that I would find my Latin American experience at least as helpful as experience in Europe would be. And he was right.

During my tour in Madrid nearly all the embassy's senior officers below the rank of ambassador were Latin American-ists. Most diplomatic communication in Latin America was oral. Few problems that could not be solved, or at least greatly reduced orally, were solved through a medium of notes. A note was almost an admission that negotiation had failed.

In Latin America, where interests were common and rela-tions close, American diplomats were accustomed to discuss-ing matters that were of the highest importance to the Latin Americans, and we discussed them without equivocation. Now, in Spain, we were engaged in a process that would help to determine not only Spain's future but the outcome of the greatest war in history and the shape of the world to come, and we spoke and acted without equivocation.

The British embassy, like the American, was manned by highly experienced, competent officers; its military attachés (and of course its economic officers) were especially effective. Brigadier Torr, its Army attaché, and Captain Hillgarth, its naval attaché, had served in Spain earlier, were fluent in Span-ish, and had close friends among civilians as well as military men. Ambassador Hoare, as we have seen, was relentless in protesting clandestine activities of the Axis countries, and acts of the Spanish government that might favor the Axis, and his military attachés (as well as Britain's secret agents) were expert in searching them out and helping to limit them. Americans contributed little in that field. Hayes wrote: "Many rumors reached us, especially from opponents of the existing Spanish Government, that Spain was supplying petroleum to German submarines. Such rumors were always investigated but were invariably found to be baseless." As we have seen, however, there were numerous refuelings of Axis submarines in Spain. Two of them, unknown to the embassy of course, took place almost immediately after Hayes' arrival in Madrid, before our petroleum attachés had learned their jobs.

Nevertheless one of our Army attachés, Colonel William Hohenthal, was outstanding. It was he who had served in Berlin and had accompanied the German forces to Dunkirk where he watched the Allied flight from the Continent in 1940. Dignified, genial, competent, Colonel Hohenthal earned the respect and affection of the Spanish military. He became one of the embassy's most valuable officers. His predecessor, in contrast, was an aging colonel who did not understand Spanish and was of no use to the embassy or probably to the War Department.

The Office of Strategic Services (OSS) sent over a group of young and middle-aged men who spoke Spanish—at least enough Spanish to get them into trouble. The first ones to arrive refused to be identified with the embassy; they wanted to be independent. But when the Spanish police caught two of them in their very first illegal currency transaction they promptly claimed diplomatic immunity. The embassy "adopted" them and with Pan de Soraluce's help I had the two released from jail and we spirited them out of the country. When I left Spain a German vice consul, arrested for the same offense as our OSS agents, was still languishing in a Spanish prison. But that was not the sort of thing that could be spread over the front pages of the American press.

One "secret" operator, an internationally known expert in European wines, who was well known in Spain, was picked up by the police and had his head shaved in a local prison. I "sprang" him, too, and we hid him in the attic of the embassy residence until we could get him, also, south to the border. Years later I read a highly romanticized press version of that person's wartime exploits in Spain. The truth is that his service was very brief and quite inglorious.

The OSS in North Africa trained Spanish refugees in communications and demolition work (the Foreign Office said they were Communists, and some doubtless were), and introduced them clandestinely into Spain. The demolitionists were to derail and blow up trains, destroy bridges, and commit other acts of sabotage when the Germans came through on their way to Gibraltar. Some of them were caught, and the embassy had some explaining to do, as did the wretched Spaniards whose fate I never learned but I can readily imagine since the OSS promptly disowned them. One day I was called to the Foreign Office and shown a large crate that had arrived at a Spanish port addressed to "Office of Strategic Services, c/o American Embassy, Madrid, Spain." It had come from the United States. The crate was opened in my presence; it contained carefully itemized demolition gear. I explained that the crate must have been misdirected; that it clearly was meant to go to our forces in Algiers. Pan de Soraluce accepted my explanation.

OSS agents learned a lot in Spain. They settled down, and after we had weeded some of them out, joined the team. When they did, embassy officers placed them in contact with the Spanish military who had been monitoring their activities in a bemused sort of way. The Spaniards, in turn, introduced them to some anti-Nazi and enterprising Spanish smugglers who knew every path and almost every accessible rock and cranny in the Pyrenees. It was not long before our agents, under the protection of the Spanish military, were receiving abundant and reliable information through that and of course through other and more rapid routes. When I visited General Eisenhower's headquarters in Algiers, early in 1944, I was told that the best intelligence on German troop concentrations in France was being received through Spain.

Among our intelligence agents were the petroleum attachés who, like the Spanish smugglers, became familiar with many little-known spots in Spain and Spanish Morocco. Their job was to see that the petroleum Spain was permitted to import was not used in ways that might further Axis interests, and since they saw persons and places that other agents could not reach they sometimes saw things that were new to us.

It was the embassy's good fortune not to have the kinds of problems with the petroleum attachés that it had with the OSS agents, but it might have had problems if it had not been for the quality of their leadership. When Walter Smith, an experienced petroleum man who spoke excellent Spanish and liked Spaniards, arrived to organize and head the petroleum attachés he was, like the OSS agents before him, without instructions from Washington concerning the kind of relations he would have with the embassy. He assumed, in the absence of any other indication, that he would be quite independent of embassy control. Happily for us, Smith was a highly intelligent, reasonable, and cooperative person, quite experienced in team play. I was chargé d'affaires at the time, and I explained to him the necessity of submitting to the ambassador's leadership and of cooperating closely with other members of the embassy staff. Smith said he was relieved at being a part of what he considered a logical and necessary arrangement.

Of course Foreign Service officers also contributed to intelligence of the OSS variety. From time to time I had contacts with persons who claimed to have information concerning activities of Germans in Spain, and sometimes in Germany itself. My contact who became best known was a German lawyer, Otto John.

A personable man who appeared to be in his middle thirties, John, in his role of representative of the German airline, Lufthansa, visited Madrid with some frequency. I first met him early in 1942, at the home of a Spanish diplomat, where he identified himself as a member of an anti-Hitler conspiracy. John visited me at my home several times and Caroll and I found him a very likable person. I eventually introduced him to Colonel Hohenthal, and the two continued the conversations.

John told me, among many other things, that Germany was constructing, at Peenemünde, on the Baltic coast, a rocket (the V-2) that would be capable of reaching London and possibly of forcing the evacuation of that city. We know now that the British knew about Peenemünde then or soon afterward and were taking preliminary steps to meet the threat. On August 17, 1943, 571 British planes bombed Peenemünde, with the result that development of the rocket, as well as of a pilotless plane that also was being developed, was delayed and their effectiveness greatly limited.

How accurate or helpful most of the reports John gave me I had no way of knowing; Washington never commented on them. It did, however, convey to me a warning from British intelligence to be wary of John. Nevertheless the same British later took him to London where he advised the BBC on broad-casts to German troops and helped to interview high-ranking German prisoners. After the war had ended he participated in the prosecution of Field Marshal von Manstein.

Later, in November, 1950, John was made head of West German Counter-Intelligence, an office that he held until July 15, 1954, when, according to his statement, he was drugged, kidnapped, and turned over to Russia's KGB in East Berlin. From there, for tactical reasons he later maintained, he made a long series of radio broadcasts that were not unpleasing to the KGB. The KGB took him for a protracted and unwanted tour of Russia's principal cities and summer resorts. During much of this time it was placing pressure on him to testify that the German resistance had made a secret agreement with the Allied powers to continue the war against Russia in the event of a successful coup against Hitler. John refused to say that or anything like it.

After seventeen months John escaped from the Russians and returned to Bonn where he was charged and convicted of treason and sentenced to four years of hard labor. He served thirty-two months. Following his release from prison John wrote a book, *Twice Through the Lines*, which had worldwide distribution. In it he denied the charge of treason. He attri-buted his kidnapping and arrest largely to intrigues of the famous English defector, Kim Philby, and of former Nazi sup-porters in the German military. He maintained that under today's German law he could not have been indicted for trea-son. The noted English historian, H. R. Trevor-Roper, who worked with Philby during the war and wrote the introduc-tion to John's book, was convinced of John's innocence. He praised him highly.

In his book John quoted me as saying, in October, 1942, that there was no prospect of an early end to the war by invasion from the Atlantic coast or of the formation of a sec-ond front on the Continent. Later he noted that I was recalled from Madrid because of my cautious handling of the Span-iards. He said that my departure meant for him the loss of a valuable contact.

John's reports on me do not enhance his reputation as an

intelligence officer. In reality I was recalled because I had completed my mission in Spain and had been named ambassador to Paraguay. Nor can I believe that I ever commented on the possibility of the Allies' invading Europe from the Atlantic or any other coast. In any case any opinion I might have expressed on that subject would have been worthless.

Having said that, I wish to add that my impression of John is that he was an earnest and courageous worker for freedom and justice not only in Germany but throughout the world. I feel privileged to have had a brief association with him, and I know that Colonel Hohenthal, himself an earnest and courageous worker for freedom and justice who is no longer with us, also cherished his association with John.

Given the times we were living in, my association with John was more or less conventional. Late in August, 1942, however, I had an experience of quite a different kind. Under secret orders from the State Department I drove through unoccupied France to Vichy in order to obtain from our embassy there information and impressions that the Department did not want transmitted through normal channels. Caroll accompanied me on the trip, which required us to carry with us not only the gasoline we needed to reach Vichy but enough also to bring us back to Spain. Most of our baggage, in the circumstances, consisted of containers of gasoline packed in the car's trunk as well as on the rear seat and floor.

My conversations with selected persons in the embassy had to do principally with the possibility that the United States might "be forced to break relations with Vichy." Embassy leaders exhibited no enthusiasm for such a step.

The conversations ended, Caroll and I left Vichy early one morning, our only additional baggage being two bottles of perfume Caroll had purchased at scandalously low prices. Not far from the city we came to a bridge over a small stream. To the right of the bridge, and this side of it, was an automobile occupied by four men, two on the front seat and two behind. They wore identical suits. The car doors on the left were open and the men, leaning in our direction, watched us intently as we passed. We had no doubt that they were Gestapo agents.

As we drove along I watched the car and its occupants in our rear-view mirror, and surely enough they began to follow us. I increased our speed to sixty, to seventy, to eighty, and beyond. Our "super-deluxe" Ford sedan would leave the agents behind in the countryside but they would catch up with us in the cities where we had to feel our way. They could have captured us, or even killed us, by shooting out our tires, but they never tried to do that. Late in the afternoon we escaped from them in a small Basses-Pyrénées town when I turned, almost literally on two wheels, into the patio of a hotel as the owner was about to close the large door that covered the entrance. Without being asked to the hotel owner placed the car, with its tiny American flag, in concealment.

Inside the patio we heard the agent's car swish by, and an hour or two later, through a slightly opened door, I saw the agents return and occupy the room next to ours, which the hotel owner had told us was permanently reserved for the Gestapo. The following day, after the agents had departed, presumably on their return trip north, we continued our journey to Madrid. All our wartime synthetic rubber tires were blistered, but they carried us home safely.

Had the Gestapo agents really been trying to catch us, or were they merely following us on their way to their night's lodging and giving us a scare at the same time? We never knew. So much for my incursions into the worlds of James Bond and the Nazi Gestapo.

Our information program, although not as effective as the older British program, proved to be very useful. Its first director was Earl T. (Tom) Crain, a Foreign Service officer who had no background in journalism but a great deal of experience in communicating with Spanish-speaking people and a keen understanding of the power of the truth. With few facilities beyond a mimeograph machine, the Voice of America broadcasts, and brief cables on world developments that the embassy had induced the State Department to furnish, Tom turned out bulletins that became so popular that long lines of Spaniards formed outside the embassy information office and consular offices throughout Spain despite the fact that police frequently harassed them, wrote down names, and arrested some.

Popular interest in the bulletin, and Falangist concern over it, inspired Ambassador Hayes to enlarge the information operation. He persuaded Washington to send Spanish-speaking Emmet Hughes, a budding historian who had been one of the ambassador's star pupils at Columbia University (and whom we have already quoted), to help out. Hughes took over the information project and quickly gave it a professional touch.

Once the Office of War Information (OWI) was in high gear in Washington, its director, Elmer Davis, wanted to send his own man over to head the program, but Hayes insisted that Hughes remain in charge. After a sharp cable exchange between those two strong-willed men Davis asked Hayes, in exasperation, "Is Hughes the only man who can do that job?" Hayes replied with a single word, "Yes." Hughes remained.

Following the war's end Hughes had a distinguished career as chief of the *Time-Life* Bureau in Rome, as a *Time-Life* editor, as an assistant to President Eisenhower, as an author, as a public relations advisor to Nelson Rockefeller, and as a professor at Rutgers University. He was the author of candidate Eisenhower's statement (made during the Korean War), "I shall go to Korea," which helped greatly to elect Eisenhower president.

Although OWI was unable to replace Hughes it nevertheless sent over a plethora of men, almost none of whom Hayes had asked for or wanted. Some of them were helpful; others may have done us harm. Few knew much about Spain, but all of them had impressions concerning Spain, largely unfavorable. Some had experience in communicating but a number of those wanted to communicate the wrong things. In any event the need for an information program lessened rapidly as the local press published more and more news of Allied military successes. Spanish readers, reacting to the censorship they had been subjected to for many years, magnified even the most sensational Allied victories. They were our best propagandists.

True to his academic background Hayes also inaugurated an ambitious cultural program. At his request the State Department sent him a cultural attaché. In addition he induced the Department to purchase a beautiful Madrid home that was filled with exquisite antiques. He called it the *Casa Americana* and it served to house our information and cultural activities. It became the scene of many lectures and discussions concerning Spain and the United States. Spaniards and Americans mingled freely in the *Casa Americana* and friendships were formed there.

Hayes' most popular cultural contribution, however, may have been the showing of the motion picture *Gone with the Wind.* Limousines that had been stored in garages for years, and smaller cars, many of them fueled with coal gas, formed lines that led to Madrid's largest theater while hundreds approached the theater on foot. Many of the country's highest officials attended the showing. The members of the nation's Catholic hierarchy were among its most appreciative viewers. Enemies of art and the United States scattered nails in the street, and some tires were punctured, but that added to the emotion of the event. Persons may differ as to whether *Gone with the Wind* is great art, but what cannot be doubted is that *madrileños* were crazy about it. Scarlett O'Hara became a real person to them, and they fell in love with Melanie Wilkes. Watching Yankee troops overrun Atlanta was a kind of catharsis after their own Civil War.

While some of the people Washington sent us were unsatisfactory, a majority were eager to help and did. A greater problem for us was the attitude of certain high officials in Washington who openly opposed our Spanish policy. One of those was Henry Morgenthau, Jr., secretary of the treasury and President Roosevelt's neighbor on the Hudson River whom Roosevelt frequently indulged. Morgenthau detested not only Hitler and his followers but Germans in general (the "Morgenthau Plan" he devised would have destroyed Germany as a viable political and economic unit), and he had no regard for Germany's friends or for those who appeared to be her friends. Spain was a prominent member of the latter group. The Treasury Department had the power to hold up tankers that were to carry urgently needed petroleum to Spain, and sometimes it exerted that power in ways that were not helpful to our objectives in that country.

Another who opposed our Spanish program was Henry Wallace, who in addition to being vice president of the United States headed the powerful Board of Economic Warfare (BEW) which had an important voice in formulating and carrying out the program. In his *Memoirs* Secretary Hull, after noting that Morgenthau often interfered in foreign affairs, said, "In that practice he ran a close race with Vice President Wallace" whom Hull described as "in many ways an extreme leftist." Wallace was a friend and admirer of Ralph Ingersoll, *PM*'s publisher, and he shared many of *PM*'s views. He thought it was a mistake to work with Franco in Spain and Salazar in Portugal, and BEW often reflected his attitude.

In 1942, while Secretary Hull was absent in Moscow, Wallace induced the president to issue an executive order giving BEW sweeping authority to deal directly with foreign governments and to send representatives abroad for that purpose. Hull said later that the order would have virtually created a second State Department. My own view is that it might well have brought Spain into the war on the side of the Axis.

When, following Hull's return from Moscow, the president learned that Wallace had not consulted the State Department in the matter, he angrily reversed his decision and created a new agency, the Foreign Economic Administration (FEA) to take over BEW's functions. In mid-1944, when I left for Paraguay, the Washington-Madrid diplomatic machine, the Spanish portion as well as the American, was working smoothly.

10 EPILOGUE

Following the end of World War II Spain's international position underwent kaleidoscopic change that was brought about less by events within the country than by attitudes and purposes in the Allied world. On May 25, 1944, Winston Churchill, then at the height of his fame and glory, had opened a debate in the House of Commons with a ringing eulogy of the Franco regime's contribution to the Allied cause. "There is no doubt that if Spain had yielded to German blandishments and pressure . . . our burden would have been much heavier," he said, and he added, "In the dark days of the war the attitude of the Spanish Government in not giving our enemies passage through Spain was extremely helpful to us. It was especially so at the time of the North African liberation. . . . I must say that I shall always consider a service was rendered . . . by Spain, not only to the United Kingdom and to the British Empire and Commonwealth, but to the cause of the United Nations."

But only a little more than a year after Churchill had said that he and Harry Truman, who had succeeded Roosevelt in the American presidency, joined the Soviet Union's Joseph Stalin in closing the door to Franco Spain's membership in the shiny new United Nations Organization which was to guarantee peace and promote freedom in the world. The declaration they signed in Potsdam, Germany, said: "The three governments . . . feel bound to make it clear that they, for their part, would not favor any application for membership [in the United Nations] put forward by the present Spanish Government, which, having been founded with support of the Axis powers, does not, in view of its origins, its nature, its record, and its close association with the aggressor states, possess the qualifications necessary to justify such membership."

Spain was barred from membership in the United Nations Organization in order to appease the Soviet regime that itself had been expelled from the League of Nations for its unprovoked aggression against Finland, the same Soviet regime that had concluded a non-aggression pact with Hitler's Germany, and Stalin the head. Franco was condemned as a totalitarian and aggressor by Stalin, the number-one totalitarian in the world, and the assassin of millions of his own people. And the same United States press that had condemned the United States' realpolitik in Spain while Franco was frustrating Hitler's plan to close the Mediterranean and preempt North Africa, was now enthusiastic when its awkward effort at realpolitik favored Soviet Russia's purposes.

Following his exclusion from the United Nations, Franco moved rapidly to prove Spain's eligibility to membership. He gave the Spanish people a *Fuero de los Españoles*, a bill of rights that rivaled the Potsdam Declaration in hypocrisy, listing as it did in impressive detail all the rights of Spaniards that the regime was trampling on and would continue to trample on. But Salvador de Madariaga, who rarely found it possible to speak a good word of Franco, asked, "If Stalin was declared peace-loving in San Francisco and Potsdam, why shouldn't Franco be declared liberty-loving in Madrid?"

Nevertheless Ernest Bevin, who became foreign secretary in Clement Attlee's Labor government in England, and whom Madariaga described as one of the few earnest enemies of the Franco regime, declared, "We detest the [Franco] regime." As for the United States, when Norman Armour, our ambassador in Madrid, returned to Washington in November, 1948, he was not replaced. The French closed their border with Spain to keep Spaniards out.

But the Allies had barely begun. On March 4, 1946, the American, British, and French governments declared jointly "that 'so long as General Franco continues in control of Spain, the Spanish people cannot anticipate full and cordial association' with the victors over Hitler. [They] expressed the hope that 'leading patriotic and liberal-minded Spaniards [might] soon find the means to bring about a peaceful withdrawal of Franco.' "

In March, too, the State Department published the texts of fifteen documents taken from German official files, which it clearly hoped would give the impression that the Franco government had wished for German victory and had cooperated with Germany to that end. One was the document that Ambassador Hoare later included in his book as evidence of Franco's guilt.

In an accompanying statement the Department said, "There is no intention of interfering in the internal affairs of Spain." But then it proceeded to interfere. It said, "It is hoped that leading patriotic and liberal-minded Spaniards may soon find the means to bring about a peaceful withdrawal of Franco, the abolition of the Falange, and the establishment of an interim or a caretaker government under which the Spanish people may have an opportunity freely to determine the type of government they wish to have and to choose their leaders."

Spain replied to the Department in a brief paper of its own. The Spanish paper stated that "the reiterated and urgent requests of the Axis that Spain enter the war were met, first by repeated and skillful delays and later by a categorical refusal"; that "during the entire war Spain maintained its independence of decision"; and that all of that had been accomplished "notwithstanding the pressure and the threat represented by the presence, on its border, of the most powerful armies in the world."

We know now, as we knew in large measure then, that

what the Spanish government alleged was correct, but the documents the State Department chose to publish were intended to give the opposite impression. Nor was the ritual over. On April 6, 1946, the United Nations Security Council, not to be left behind, indicted Spain because "the present regime is endangering international peace," a ridiculous charge if there ever was one. The accuser was Poland, a Soviet-occupied country. Neither was the United Nations General Assembly about to be left out of the act. A resolution it adopted on December 12 provided that Spain was to be debarred from representation in United Nations agencies and conferences, and also that in the event the internal situation in Spain had not improved within a reasonable time the Security Council should consider "adequate measures." Meanwhile it called on all members of the United Nations to withdraw their heads of mission from Madrid.

The United States ostentatiously debarred Spain from receiving Marshall Plan aid and shut off public loans to the country.

Franklin D. Roosevelt, at the time of the Allied landings in North Africa, had given his word to General Franco that Spain had nothing to fear from the United Nations, but Roosevelt now was dead and, besides, the great powers distinguished between Spain and its government. They knew they were intervening in Spain's internal affairs but they were convinced that they were doing it in Spain's interest. At least that is what they maintained.

Franco reacted to his critics with the equanimity he had always shown. How could he be accused of being a dictator, he asked his hand-picked Cortes, when the Cortes had approved so many important laws he had submitted to it? He clearly saw no inconsistency in his having recently dismissed six members of the Cortes, one of them the Duke of Alba, his former ambassador to Great Britain, for having signed a message of greeting to the pretender to the throne. Madariaga said, "This pretender was in fact the only man who was not pretending. The Soviet group and the Government of France, then under Soviet influence, were pretending to be indignant at Franco, the two Anglo-Saxon powers were pretending to hope that liberal incantations would suffice to remove him; and General Franco was pretending to be the scion of the political marriage of Gladstone with Isabel the Catholic." Madariaga hit the nail on the head. For every hypocrisy that Soviet Russia and the democracies accused Franco of engaging in, Madariaga gave us a matching hypocrisy of Soviet Russia and the democracies.

On March 31, 1947, Franco, pursuing his own deliberate way, announced that a law soon to be enacted would declare Spain a monarchy once more, but that there would be no king while he, Franco, lived. At his death a Council of the Realm to be created would propose to the Cortes the name of a prince of the blood to be king. On June 8 an obedient Cortes enacted the law by a unanimous vote, and the same day Franco called for a referendum on it. The government later declared, with due solemnity, that the results were 12,628,983 for, 643,501 against, and 320,877 invalid. In hypocrisy Franco could keep up with Soviet Russia and the democracies any day, and so far as results in Spain were concerned he could plainly surpass them.

And now a new element entered the picture. The American Congress had rediscovered romantic, enchanting Spain, and the hordes of senators and congressmen who invaded the country were eager to meet Franco and talk to him. He was a celebrity whom they all wished to know. And besides, many of them were having second thoughts about Spain as well as about the Soviet Union.

On December 10, 1948, Churchill, no longer prime minister but still a member of the House of Commons, said in a House debate. "No Britons or Americans have been killed in [Franco] Spain. . . . The way in which Hitler and Mussolini were treated by General Franco is a monumental example of ingratitude." He confessed that at Potsdam he had agreed to exclude Spain from entry into the United Nations as part of an effort to induce Stalin to support the Charter. But now it had become evident that Stalin had not the slightest intention of supporting the Charter except in ways that might further his plans for world domination.

Tolerance of the Franco regime continued to increase. On December 20, 1948, *Time* conceded that the regime "clings to old institutions and traditions, notably the church, instead of trying to replace them. It is not strongly ideological. It does not propagandize itself as the utopian answer to everything, or as an irresistible urge of historical force. Franco himself calls his government 'provisional' and speaks of a future return to 'normalization.' " Coming from *Time* that was extravagant praise.

When a group of Latin American countries called on the General Assembly to revoke its resolution advocating the withdrawal of ambassadors from Madrid, a repentant United States supported it. Although President Truman swore that it would be a "very, very long time" before he sent an ambassador to Madrid, he sent one seven months later. The world's war to defeat Franco had lasted nearly twice as long as Spain's Civil War. Again Soviet Russia had had a leading role, and again Franco had won.

Meanwhile Franco, the first among Spain's "Africans," had given up Spanish Morocco, although not willingly. After France had announced a policy of working for the development of Morocco, "as a modern, free and sovereign state," Franco, in an interview with American journalists, said that it would be a serious error to introduce democracy into Morocco, as France was doing; that it would be better to follow Spain's policy of waiting until the Moroccans were prepared for self-government. Madariaga noted that this, coming from the man who did not allow the Spaniards to govern themselves, was a "gem." It was a gem, of course; it also was pure Franco. Hoare would have called it an example of Franco's complacency, and it was that too. One reason for complacency may have been that by that time Spain had gained, as friend and ally, the most democratic and most powerful nation in the world.

On July 16, 1951, Admiral Forrest Sherman, chief of naval operations and member of the United States Joint Chiefs of Staff, arrived in Madrid and called on Franco. The two got along fine. On September 26, 1952, the United States and Spain concluded three agreements, two on mutual defense and another on economic aid. Military and economic cooperation between the two countries has continued.

Franco is no longer with us nor is the Falange. Today's Spain, with its monarchical-democratic government, is a member of the United Nations Organization and of NATO as well. It is at peace with its neighbors and, generally, with itself. How long internal peace will last no one knows. History tempers optimism. Nevertheless the opportunity to institutionalize today's freedom is there. British-American relations with the Franco regime during World War II helped to create that opportunity, as they helped to insure Allied victory in the war.

SELECTED
BIBLIOGRAPHY

INDEX

SELECTED
BIBLIOGRAPHY

Books

Beaulac, Willard L. *Career Ambassador.* New York: Macmillan, 1951.

Burdick, Charles B. *Germany's Military Strategy and Spain in World War II.* Syracuse, N.Y.: Syracuse Univ. Press, 1968.

Churchill, Winston S. *The Second World War,* vol. 5, *Closing the Ring.* Boston: Houghton Mifflin, 1951.

Ciano, Galeazzo (Count). *Ciano's Diary, 1939–1943.* Edited, with an introduction, by Malcolm Muggeridge. Foreword by Sumner Welles. London: Heinemann, 1947.

Crozier, Brian. *Franco.* Boston: Little, Brown, 1967.

Davies, Joseph E. *Mission to Moscow.* New York: Simon & Schuster, 1941.

Doussinague, José M. *España tenía razón (1939–1945).* Madrid: Espasa-Calpe, 1950.

Eby, Cecil. *Between the Bullet and the Lie: American Volunteers in the Civil War.* New York: Holt, Rinehart & Winston, 1969.

Feis, Herbert. *The Spanish Story: Franco and the Nations at War.* New York: Knopf, 1948.

Goebbels, Joseph. *The Goebbels Diaries, 1942–1943.* Edited, translated, and with an introduction by Louis P. Lochner. Garden City, N.Y.: Doubleday, 1948.

Hayes, Carleton J. H. *The United States and Spain: An Interpretation.* New York: Sheed & Ward, 1951.

————. *Wartime Mission in Spain, 1942–1945.* New York: Macmillan, 1945.

Hoare, The Rt. Hon. Sir Samuel (Viscount Templewood). *Complacent Dictator.* New York: Knopf, 1947.

Hughes, Emmet John. *Report from Spain.* New York: Holt, 1947.

Hull, Cordell. *The Memoirs of Cordell Hull.* 2 vols. New York: Macmillan, 1948.

John, Otto. *Twice Through the Lines: The Autobiography of Otto John.* New York: Harper & Row, 1972.

Kleinfeld, Gerald R., and Tambs, Lewis A. *Hitler's Spanish Legion: The Blue Division in Russia.* Carbondale: Southern Illinois Univ. Press, 1979.

Madariaga, Salvador de. *Spain: A Modern History.* New York: Praeger, 1958.

Matthews, Herbert L. *The Yoke and the Arrows: A Report on Spain.* New York: Braziller, 1957.

Payne, Stanley G. *Falange: A History of Spanish Fascism.* Stanford, Calif.: Stanford Univ. Press, 1961.

Saña, Heleno. *El Franquismo sin mitos: Conversaciones con Serrano Suñer.* Barcelona: Ediciones Grijalbo, 1982.

Serrano Suñer, Ramón. *Entre el silencio y la propaganda: La historia como fué. Memorias.* Barcelona: Ediciones Planeta, 1977.

————. *Entre Hendaya y Gibraltar.* Rev. ed. Barcelona: Ediciones Nauta, 1973.

Thomas, Hugh. *The Spanish Civil War.* Revised and enlarged edition. New York: Harper & Row, 1977.

Articles

Burdick, Charles B. " 'Moro': The Resupply of German Submarines in Spain, 1939–1942." *Central European History* 3, no. 3 (Sept. 1970), 256–84.

Detwiler, Donald S. "Spain and the Axis during World War II." *Review of Politics* 33, no. 1 (Jan. 1971), 36–53.

Halstead, Charles R. "A 'Somewhat Machiavellian' Face: Colonel Juan Beigbeder as High Commissioner in Spanish Morocco, 1937–1939." *Historian* 37, no. 1 (Nov. 1974), 46–66.

Lindley, Ernest K., and Weintal, Edward. "How We Dealt with Spain: American Diplomacy at Madrid, 1940–1944." *Harper's Magazine* (Dec. 1944), 23–33.

United States Department of State Sources

Documents on German Foreign Policy, 1918–1945. Series D. Vol. III, Nos. 2, 464, 591, 655, 664, 689, 699, 740, 782, 784, 786. Vol. X, No. 87. Vol. XI, Nos. 70, 124, 497, 682. Vol. XII, Nos. 73, 375. Vol. XIII, No. 314.

Foreign Relations of the United States 1941. Vol. II. *Europe.*

The Spanish Government and the Axis: Official German Documents. Nos. 1, 11.

INDEX

Abraham Lincoln Battalion, of the International Brigades, 40

Abyssinia, portion ceded to Italy, 135

Ackerman, Ralph, 99, 118, 134, 185

Alba, Duke of, 98, 153, 210

Albania, Italian expulsion from, 13

Algeciras, Bay of: military activity in, 29, 30, 50

Algiers, French regime in, 174

Allied powers: invasion of North Africa by, 19–20, 48, 51, 151, 169–70, 174, 185–86, 207, 210; invasion of Sicily by, 180; opposition to Franco among, 51; refugees from, 145–46, 174; shipping sabotaged by Italy, 29; Spain's appeasement of, 2–3, 5, 19, 20, 21, 24. *See also* Great Britain; United States

Ambassador on Special Mission (Hoare), 137

American Red Cross: and refugees, 174; in Spain, 22, 103, 104, 107, 113

Anarchists, in Spanish Civil War, 33

Anti-Comintern Pact, 5, 122–24

Arias Salgado, Gabriel, 55

Armour, Norman, 209

Arriba newspaper, 177

Asturias, province of: in Spanish Civil War, 33–34

Atlantic Charter, 184

Axis powers; Falange appeasement of, 55; Spain's appeasement of, 1–2, 3, 4, 5, 6, 29, 46, 79. *See also* Franco, pro-German speech of; Serrano Suñer, Ramón, pro-German views of; Spain, assistance to Axis (German) submarines by

Azores: Allied military bases in, 188; rumored American attack on, 88

Baraiba, German, 134

Barcelona, in Spanish Civil War, 33

Beaulac, Caroll: in conversation with Franco, 42

Beaulac, Willard L.: as ambassador to Paraguay, 194, 202, 206; arrival in Spain in 1941; 108, 109, 195–96; article on American policy in Spain for

221

Willard L. Beaulac served in Spain during the Second World War as United States Counselor of Embassy and, from time to time, Chargé d'Affaires, from June 1941 to May 1944. Prior to that he had served in various consular and diplomatic capacities in Latin America as well as in the State Department in Washington, D.C. Following his service in Spain he was United States Ambassador to Paraguay, Colombia, Cuba, Chile, and Argentina, and subsequently Deputy Commandant for Foreign Affairs of the National War College. Articles by Beaulac have appeared in *U.S. Naval Institute. Proceedings*, and the *National Review*. His earlier books are *Career Ambassador; Career Diplomat; A Diplomat Looks at Aid to Latin America;* and *The Fractured Continent: Latin America in Close-Up*.